The British tradition of federalism

Studies in Federalism
edited by Murray Forsyth
Centre for Federal Studies
University of Leicester

The British Tradition of Federalism

Michael Burgess

Fairleigh Dickinson University Press
Madison • Teaneck

Leicester University Press
London

LEICESTER UNIVERSITY PRESS
A Cassell imprint
Wellington House, 125 Strand, London WC2R 0BB, England
and **Associated University Presses**
440 Forsgate Drive, Cranbury, NJ 08512, USA

First published in 1995

British Library Cataloguing in Publication Data

A CIP catalogue record for this book is available from the British Library

ISBN   0 7185 1495 5 (Pinter)
       0 8386 3618 7 (Associated University Presses)

Library of Congress Cataloging-in-Publication Data

Burgess, Michael, 1949–
    The British tradition of federalism / Michael Burgess.
      p.   cm.
    Includes index.
    ISBN 0-8386-3618-7 (alk. paper)
      1. Federal government—Great Britain. 2. Great Britain—Politics and government—19th century. 3. Great Britain—Politics and government—20th century. 4. European federation. I. Title.
JN297.F43B86   1995
320.441—dc20
                                                                    95-2304
                                                                    CIP

Set in Monotype Baskerville by Ewan Smith
48 Shacklewell Lane, London E8 2EY

Printed and bound in Great Britain by
Biddles Ltd, Guildford and King's Lynn

For Adam and Marie-Louise and in memory of Pam

Contents

Series editor's preface

The previous volume in this series has focused mainly on the practice of federalism outside Britain – notably in Canada, Germany, the former Soviet Union and the United States of America. Michael Burgess's book turns the spotlight round and looks at federalism in relation to the United Kingdom itself. As might be expected, he is concerned not primarily with the practice of federalism – though he makes some interesting preliminary observations about the balance between central and local government in the United Kingdom – but with federalism as a doctrine, an idea, a political programme.

Dr Burgess seeks to show that there has been a long, indigenous tradition, within the United Kingdom, of advocating federal remedies for political and constitutional problems. Starting with the debate over the future of the British Empire in the second half of the nineteenth century, he moves to a consideration of the proposals advanced for a solution to the Irish question both before and after the establishment of the Irish Free State in 1922. He then turns to the desperate search for a solution to the problem of European security on the eve of the Second World War, and examines the British attitude to European unification after the war. Throughout this exegesis Dr Burgess traces and rekindles the federal ideas of a succession of British writers and statesmen – some unfamiliar, like William Edward Foster, others of recognised stature, like Joseph Chamberlain, and others, like Lionel Curtis, whose names are known but whose place in history remains blurred.

Dr Burgess emphasises particularly the continuity of the British federalist tendency, the way federal ideas were carried forward from one generation to another. He tells in conclusion the curious story of how the advocacy of federalism by a particular British publicist and statesman – Philip Kerr, Lord Lothian – influenced the ideas of one of the most zealous advocates of European federalism after 1945, the Italiam Altiero Spinelli.

Dr Burgess's endeavour to rehabilitate the federal tradition in British political debate will, I hope, do something to reduce the extreme suspicion of federalism that has been so marked a feature of the British attitude to European integration since the war. The book must also be see in a wider context. Over the past 150 years the predominant trend in the teaching and interpretation of the political history not only of Britain but also of all the major countries of Europe has been to emphasise the progressive formation of a single political unity – a single 'nation' and a single 'state' – out of disparate territorial and ethnic elements. The stress has been on the transmutation of distinct parts into an organic whole.

The ending of the European empires, the relative diminution of the importance of the European 'nation-states' on the world stage, and the growth of European integration as a transmutation of these states themselves, have encouraged a rather different interpretation, which had never, in the past been completely displaced. This alternative interpretation stresses precisely the enduring importance of the parts out of which the 'whole' of the nation-state has been created, the associative character of these states, and the wider civilisation to which they all belong. The present book can be seen as contributing in an original way to this shift of interpretation.

Murray Forsyth
Hong Kong, February 1995

Acknowledgements

This study has been a long time in the making. Its origins date back to the research for my doctoral thesis at Leicester University during the years between 1973 and 1976. At that time I could not see the wood for the trees. I did not realise that my historical study of the Imperial Federation League in the late nineteenth century was actually a connecting link to the British tradition of federalism. This became obvious to me only after many subsequent years of research. During the 1980s, however, I gradually became aware that I was not alone in my continuing interest in British federalism. Others were also working in the area. Initially, the historical evidence was fragmentary. British federal ideas seemed episodic. There appeared to be no palpable connection between the political movements, separated in time and circumstance, which championed the federal cause. But slowly and surely the pieces, rather like a jigsaw puzzle, were added to the British tradition of federalism. The book should be seen in this context. It is my own attempt to present the British tradition of federalism as a composite whole.

During the last twenty years, while the idea for this book was simmering, I have learned much from my colleagues and friends about both British and European political development. It would be impossible to acknowledge every intellectual debt that I owe – there are far too many – but I would like to mention John Pinder and Roy Pryce, both of the Federal Trust for Education and Research in London, who have always been a reliable source of encouragement and advice to me over the years. The intellectual benefits which I derived from the 'Federalism study groups' of the mid-1980s, organised by them under the auspices of the Trust, were invaluable. The Federal Trust of course continues to fulfil its active educational role in the promotion of federal studies and in particular in the field of European integration. I would also like to thank Dr Colin Eldridge at St David's University College, Lampeter for his patient advice and support during the years immediately after my doctoral baptism. Finally I must acknowledge Professor Murray Forsyth, who was my politics tutor and supervisor during my postgraduate years at Leicester. His intellectual influence upon me was considerable, although I do not wish to burden him with any responsibility for what I have written here or elsewhere. Working broadly in the same area, we have maintained regular contact during the last twenty years. His intellectual interest in federalism acquired an organisational shape in 1988 when the Centre for Federal Studies was created at Leicester University with him as its Director. Since then the study of federalism and federation has flourished at Leicester, providing those of us who maintain a keen interest in the subject with a convenient intellectual meeting place. In 1994 Professor Forsyth took early retirement, and it is to be hoped that his successor will maintain the high standard of scholarship in this subject according to the Centre's founding principles.

Michael Burgess

Introduction: confronting the past

In this book I intend to demonstrate the existence of a distinct British tradition of federalism. For a country which is generally held to be the archetype of unitary government, this intention may initially seem futile. After all, there does not appear to be sufficient evidence to justify such a purpose. The claim that federalism is an integral, if neglected, part of the larger British political tradition does seem far-fetched. Indeed, some defenders of the British constitution might regard it as subversive. The very attempt to expose and underline this particular dimension of British constitutional and political development serves to call into question the most basic and cherished assumptions upon which the United Kingdom has been governed.

Up until quite recently the old conceptual lenses of a dominant unitary tradition had effectively guaranteed a unitary interpretation of our constitutional and political past. They had preserved a view of the United Kingdom which confirmed the fundamental principles of the British constitutional system. It is this historical orthodoxy which the book is intended to challenge. If we disregard the conventional wisdom of many British historians and political scientists, it is possible to rediscover a part of our constitutional and political heritage which has been consistently overlooked. And if we can successfully reinstate this important dimension of our overall political tradition, it will enable us to reappraise both the present and the future. The door to rival images and perceptions of the British state can be unlocked and we will be able to look at the United Kingdom in a new light. The consideration of different and competing perspectives of the British state would no longer appear subversive. On the contrary, it would be deemed perfectly legitimate. Alternative reform proposals would then have to be taken seriously.

What I propose here, then, is a revisionist history. It is an attempt to restore the importance of federal ideas to the British political tradition. It is intended to challenge the unthinking assumption that these political ideas are alien to the mainstream of the British political tradition. It is also my purpose to show precisely how federal ideas have been regularly used by British political elites as the basis for practical political responses and solutions to the various problems of the British state during the last century. One paradox which emerges from this study is the glaring gap which has opened up between legal and constitutional theory and the practice of British government. The divergence is particularly evident when we consider the venerable notion of sovereignty, but the main contention here is that such constitutional propositions were never fully attainable, even in their heyday when most vociferously proclaimed.

In its approach the book is unusual. It does not attempt to chronicle the sequence of historical events and circumstances which together have sustained the British federal tradition. Rather it is organised around three central themes which are, respectively, 'Empire, Ireland and Europe'. I have referred to these three central themes as 'issue arenas' which build upon the framework of analysis outlined in Chapter 1. They are, as it were, the empirical focus of the book. Their main purpose is to furnish the historical evidence for my central thesis. They provide the developmental perspectives which interact to reveal a fundamental continuity of British federal ideas: a single intellectual tradition which spans the last century.

The structure of the book is designed to underline the basic continuity of the British federal tradition. This decision was guided mainly by my determination to destroy the conventional illusion that British federal ideas have been merely episodic. This old orthodox opinion is not only erroneous, it is also plainly misleading. It suggests that federal ideas have played merely a minor role in British political development during the last century; it relegates them to the sidelines of British political history. However, if we are led through the past via a different route, the underlying continuity of federal ideas is confirmed. The origins of the United Kingdom are both complex and deep-rooted. They can be located and properly understood only by reference to a multi-national history. Most historians and political scientists would begin their investigation by focusing first upon the expansion of the English kingdom from about the tenth to the fifteenth centuries on the assumption that this was the core area of early state-building. This is defensible provided that we bear in mind the separate, distinct histories of the constituent units that eventually formed the United Kingdom. To do otherwise would be to distort history by imposing a deterministic framework upon the past.

Wales was the first territory to be formally attached to England by the Act of Union of 1536. In practice it was assimilated into the English legal, economic and political system, but its own distinctive identity was protected and preserved by geographical remoteness and by a complex combination of religious, linguistic and social class cleavages. The origins of an independent Scottish state stretch back at least to the fourteenth century, but the first step on the road to union with England occurred in 1603 when the Union of the Crowns voluntarily tied Scottish fortunes to those of England. In that year James VI of Scotland became James I of England as well and introduced the first 'national' flag. The separate Scottish and English parliaments survived until 1707 when they were finally united to form Great Britain – the Union of England, Wales and Scotland – with a single parliament. Ireland's route into the United Kingdom was similar to that of Wales in the sense that it too had been subject to military conquest by England, but it differed in significant ways from the experience of Scotland. In contrast to Scotland there had been no successful attempt to create an independent Irish state although a separate Irish Parliament had evolved since the middle ages. It was not until the late sixteenth century that the Tudors established effective political control over the whole of Ireland. A combination of strong rule by the Tudors and the impact of the Reformation served to confirm English hegemony and reduced Ireland to the status of a colony. The Irish Parliament was abolished following the military defeat of the first Irish nationalist uprising in 1798. This defeat led to a policy of increased integration so that the United Kingdom of Great Britain and Ireland became a reality only in 1801.

This brief sketch outline of the critical junctures in the making of the United Kingdom reminds us that, as a state, it is only about two hundred years old. Indeed, it is slightly younger than the United States of America. But the making and remaking of the United Kingdom did not end in 1801. In 1921 the first rupture in the state structure occurred when Ireland was partitioned with the effect that six counties were truncated to form Northern Ireland. Since then, what we might call the reorganisation of the United Kingdom has determined its current constitutional status as the United Kingdom of Great Britain and Northern Ireland. Whether or not the United Kingdom as it is presently constituted will remain intact is a question which has been repeatedly posed since the 1960s. This growing sense of doubt about the Union has usually taken the form of modest proposals for some kind of devolution, but the shadow of federalism has also fallen across the constitutional debate among British political elites. Changes in the postwar British political economy, the resurgence of sub-state nationalisms in Wales and Scotland, and British membership of the European Union have each spurred a deep-seated reappraisal of the state.

Today there are important reasons for believing that a new and difficult crossroads has been reached in the history of the United Kingdom. New pressures for constitutional change are building up in the polity. They spring from a variety of sources, but recent changes in the structure of the British economy, the governmental hegemony of the British Conservative party, the intensification of widespread political discontent in Scotland and increasing economic and political integration in Europe are undoubtedly the most significant of these. Alongside these imperatives for change must be placed the unresolved problem of Northern Ireland and a veritable host of competing difficulties which include, *inter alia*, immigration, race relations, citizens' rights, welfare issues, the reorganisation of local government and even the future of the monarchy.

Although it is yet only dimly perceived, each of these difficult problems has important constitutional implications. The genius of the British constitutional system has been to disguise constitutional questions as mere political issues. They have usually been sufficiently defused to be rendered relatively harmless. But this proven formula for political stability has now outlived its usefulness. It is threadbare. Existing constitutional assumptions and the structures and practices which reflect them are no longer able to contain the new forces which have emerged in the 1980s and 1990s to challenge what seems like a complacent inertia. Their capacity successfully to canalise, contain and ultimately defuse serious threats to the Union has been severely attenuated.

The book seeks to make a modest contribution to the current debate about the nature, meaning and future of the United Kingdom. If it assists in some small way in opening up the debate to a wider range of constitutional reform proposals than exists at present then it will have been worthwhile. No prescriptions for constitutional reform are proffered here; it is sufficient for us to deconstruct the unitary myth and to call attention to a neglected tradition of federalism in the body politic. We will turn now to the conceptual framework which underpins the subsequent empirical focus upon 'Empire, Ireland and Europe'. This framework of analysis is the starting-point for a re-examination of state-building and national integration in the United Kingdom.

CHAPTER I

The British tradition of federalism: framework of analysis

In order to establish an analytical framework within which to locate the origins and subsequent development of the federal idea in the United Kingdom it is necessary to identify three separate dimensions to our subject. First, we must recognise the significance of the distant past, stretching back at least to the Middle Ages, which helped to shape and mould the early political attitudes, expectations and activities of the emergent English public. We will be looking, in effect, at the early growth and development of England and the English state. This legacy, after all, determined what today are called customs, conventions, habits and popular traditions. Secondly, it is essential that we situate the federal idea in the context of the making of the United Kingdom. Recent research on how and why England's constitutional and political authority was gradually extended formally to incorporate Wales, Scotland and Ireland in the United Kingdom is vital to this study. Indeed, I shall argue that the continuity of federal ideas in modern British politics and government during the last century derives directly from the early processes of state-building and national integration which were peculiar to the United Kingdom. Finally, I wish to incorporate in this framework the published research of those historians and political scientists who have made important recent contributions to our understanding of our own past. In particular, the recent research on national identity and the peculiarities of the multi-national state are central to the sources of the British federal tradition. And they are especially important for the way in which they have shed new light upon the contingent nature of the United Kingdom.

Together these three dimensions to the British tradition of federalism provide us with an alternative perspective of the past which rivals the unitary orthodoxy. In combination they also enable us to challenge what I shall call the 'unitary myth' which continues today to exert a dominant, if unjustified, stranglehold upon the politics of constitutional reform. Once we strip away the elements of the unitary myth, which continue to represent a powerful symbolism in British constitutional politics, it is possible to conceive of federal ideas as perfectly rational, legitimate responses to a wide variety of practical constitutional and political problems which have confronted successive British statesmen during the last century. Here it is appropriate to connect the analytical framework outlined above to three separate but intimately linked pathways into British constitutional and political evolution. These three distinct routes into the past are, respectively, 'Empire, Ireland and Europe'. In this way the analytical framework used in our study serves to explain precisely why Empire, Ireland and Europe together have been the continuous source of British federal ideas since at least the 1870s. In short, it explains why there have been persistent attempts to reconstruct the Union along federal, or federal-type, lines. The bulk of the book, then, is devoted to an analysis of these three discrete issue arenas, but its overall purpose is to produce a coherent developmental perspective of the British federal tradition. It is of course important not to make exaggerated claims for this strand of the larger British political tradition, but it is equally important that we do not completely ignore it. To do so would blind us to a significant and continuous source of constitutional reform proposals, and it would lead us ultimately to misunderstand the very nature and meaning of the United Kingdom itself. We will begin our study of the British federal tradition by sketching the broad outlines of our analytical framework which is divided into three parts.

The framework of analysis

(i) The continuity of history

In his classic work entitled *The Problem of Federalism: A Study in the History of Political Theory*, which was first published in 1931, Sobei Mogi remarked 'we cannot fail to realise that the political organisation of Great Britain has taken the form of a self-governing community from the time of the early settlers'. 'Experience in local self-government', he added, 'and the training given by parliamentary institutions, enlightened by the tolerant teaching of Protestantism and the growth of political philosophy, determined the essential features of federalism as developed by the people of Great Britain'.[1] What did he mean by this observation? Twenty-five years later, William Livingston claimed that the 'many elements of federalism in the British society, and the diversities that constitute this federal quality', were the direct consequence of 'tradition' which 'binds so much of practice'. And like Mogi, he underlined the significance of 'the spirit of representative government' which had 'for so long prevailed'.[2]

In 1982 Richard Rose noted in his *Understanding The United Kingdom* that 'Parliament, with origins in the thirteenth century' was 'a particularly important example of continuity'. Although it had changed only slowly from an aristocratic to a modern democratic assembly, it had 'always been a representative body'. And 'politicians have maintained continuity of political institutions'.[3] These three assertions reflect a body of scholarly opinion which underlines the importance of a long representative tradition in British politics and government. Indeed, elements of significant public participation in the early polity can be detected at least as far back as the Middle Ages. Keith Thomas acknowledged this fact in an influential study of 'crises of political development' published in 1978:

> Since the middle ages England has possessed a bewildering mass of local institutions – parish vestries, courts baron, courts leet, village communities – each accustomed to making bylaws, appointing officers, and levying rates. They dealt with a variety of matters of local concern, and they were composed in many different ways. But they frequently afforded even the humblest members of the community some experience in self- government and the opportunity to participate in matters closest to their own interests.[4]

A peculiar inherited social structure and distinctive economic, social and political institutions help to explain the early evolution and progress of the English polity. But other, additional factors need to be taken into account if we are fully to appreciate the significance of the continuity of history to our study. Thomas, for example, called attention to the inadequacies of English bureaucracy. 'England', he argued, 'was early in developing a central administration, but slow in producing a corps of administrators'. By the sixteenth century, this meant that:

> Ordinary law enforcement and local administration were carried out by that uniquely English functionary, the justice of the peace, typically a country gentleman, firmly rooted in his community, unpaid, conscientious, but prepared to enforce only those aspects of royal policy of which he approved. ... The Crown, in other words, accepted the basic pattern of local authority rather than attempting to penetrate it with its own bureaucracy.[5]

Clearly the making of England itself and the particular structure of authority which evolved from the earliest times combined to determine the background of limited centralisation and a flourishing local participation in public affairs. Important philosophical developments should also be mentioned in this context. In the British philosophical tradition we must look to the gradual appearance in the seventeenth and eighteenth centuries of what is generally known as 'social contract' theory. In the great pantheon of British political thinkers who helped to shape the new philosophical climate in which old, encrusted ideas of authority and obligation were quickly discredited, the names of Algernon Sydney, John Locke and David Hume (some would include Edmund Burke) loom large. Political theorists trace a fairly consistent line of thought, grounded in social contract, natural rights, popular consent, the legitimate resistance to authority and utilitarianism, which calls into question the very essence of sovereign power. Indeed, the whole philosophical debate referred to here could be compressed and simplified as one dealing with the nature and meaning of sovereignty.

These subversive philosophical ideas had their most visibly devastating impact upon the early British imperial experience. The American Revolution of the late eighteenth century served notice that the traditional nature of authority and power had been successfully challenged. In 1776, the year that the leading colonial revolutionaries drafted and issued the Declaration of Independence, it is clear that the underlying political theory in colonial America was largely identical with that of seventeenth-century England. The belief in the state of nature, the conception of natural rights, the idea of consent and the notion of government on the firm basis of contract each infused the Declaration and legitimised the twin ideas of limited government and the guaranteed right of resistance against arbitrary power. The philosophical environment was therefore conducive to political speculation and constitutional experimentation. It is important to note that none of the political thinkers mentioned above contributed anything directly to the modern federal idea, but they did help to lay the philosophical foundations so vital to its later emergence.

Let us summarise the significance of the 'continuity of history' to the British federal tradition. The mainstream scholarly literature on the making of England furnishes evidence to suggest that there are important continuities in English political development which resulted in a certain form of limited central authority. From the earliest times an English political tradition had developed in which local institutions flourished, various forms of participation in public affairs had evolved and citizens claimed inviolable rights. From the perspective of monarchy, central power had waxed and waned throughout English history, but it had never succeeded in imposing complete authority. The penetration of central power left plenty of room for local self-determination. In his magisterial work entitled *Kings or People*, Reinhard Bendix has confirmed this interpretation:

> By the time of the Norman conquest, more than a thousand years of Roman rule and Anglo-Saxon kingdoms had given great impetus to a structure of local rule which provided continuity despite much internal political strife and centuries of struggle against foreign invasions. ... From the Norman conquest until the seventeenth century, English history moved back and forth between strong assertions of royal authority and strong countervailing tendencies of local autonomy and political representation. From the perspective of kingship, English medieval history since the Roman occupation is a record of discontinuity. ... From the perspective of local institutions, however, the same history shows much continuity.[6]

The discontinuities of history cannot of course be ignored, but the practice of a loose, limited authority which allowed for considerable regional and local autonomy is one of the most compelling themes of early English political and constitutional history. If we add to this the challenge of religious dissent so vividly manifested in the Reformation of the sixteenth century, and perpetuated into the seventeenth century, it becomes clear why Sobei Mogi should have referred to the 'tolerant teaching of Protestantism' at the beginning of this section. In many ways it was a significant discontinuity of English history, but its importance for our purposes here lies in the fact that it represented yet another example of the opposition to different forms of centralism. Protestantism not only rejected the legitimacy of the Roman Catholic church, but it also embraced important political principles which challenged traditional authority. In simple terms these principles threatened established hierarchy by championing consent, spiritual equality, public participation and nonconformity. To this extent, Mogi's 'tolerant Protestantism' conforms to the continuity of history in the sense that it reinforces the idea of limits to established central authority and extends the notion of public participation.[7]

In summary, then, the 'continuity of history' suggested here constitutes an integral part of the early British political tradition out of which later, more modern, ideas and concepts like federalism would emerge. Even allowing for the growth of the Tudor state and the undoubted strengthening of government and the monarchy during the late fifteenth and sixteenth centuries, 'English society developed a balance between strong central and strong local rule'.[8] This formative British political culture was one which did not lend itself to easy definition, but it was certainly characterised *inter alia* by political participation, limited central authority, a coexistence of central and nonconformist social and political values, and a philosophical environment conducive to flexible forms of institutional and constitutional authority. Small wonder that William Livingston should have reminded us not to 'ignore the presence of certain federal elements in the British society' and later 'in the processes of British government'.[9] Let us look now at the second part of our analytical framework which shifts the focus of our study to territorial concerns.

(ii) The making of the United Kingdom

During the last decade a burgeoning academic literature has sought to illuminate and underline the complex and subtle processes by which England's constitutional and political authority was gradually extended formally to incorporate Wales, Scotland and Ireland in the United Kingdom.[10] This literature has clarified several previously obscure issues surrounding the evolution of the United Kingdom and confirmed, via the re-examination of old received assumptions, its accidental and contingent character. Indeed, Richard Rose counselled strongly against the unthinking presumption inherent in the very notion of 'the making of the United Kingdom':

> The United Kingdom is initially best approached as the product of a multiplicity of historical events. It is certainly not the product of a logical plan, nor is it the product of a particular ideology. To refer to the making of the United Kingdom is to oversimplify. It treats the Union in its present form as if it were consciously made – and as if it had a purposeful maker. It did not; the United Kingdom today is the resultant of very disparate events and processes during more than four centuries.[11]

One important consequence of this general conclusion has been the necessary and penetrating reappraisal of traditional political concepts and
terminology applicable to the United Kingdom of Great Britain and Northern Ireland. Many myths have been dispelled about its presumed political
homogeneity and the nature of its political integration, and it is now openly
acknowledged that the question of the state is neither as simple nor as straightforward as we might previously have been led to expect. The English national
characteristic of skirting around awkward subjects rather than confronting
them is well displayed by the studied avoidance of the question of the state.[12]
Rose has commented on this intellectual puzzle that constitutes the United
Kingdom:

> In international law the United Kingdom is a state, that is, a Kingdom that claims
> sovereign authority within given territorial boundaries. ... But the state is rarely
> used to describe the contemporary United Kingdom. ... To describe the United
> Kingdom as a state is to import a continental European term to political discourse
> in Britain. The idea of the state as a thing in itself ... is alien to British political
> thinking.[13]

The conundrum is only partly resolved by Rose when he describes the United
Kingdom as a 'problematic state'. The unusual case of the United Kingdom
has been tackled, as regards Northern Ireland, by denying the integrity of
the United Kingdom rather than by its firm assertion, as would be anticipated
in most contemporary states. Instead, distance has been imposed by Westminster to deflect the awkward challenge of Northern Ireland.[14]

But it is also important to note that this underlying notion of 'statelessness'
– of being without an idea of the state – to which Rose refers, actually
antedates the Anglo-Irish Treaty of 1921. Indeed, it precedes the formal
creation of the United Kingdom itself in 1801. As I shall shortly demonstrate,
this received sense of being unaware of the state is also indissolubly linked to
the peculiar push and pull of incomplete political integration in Great Britain
spanning several centuries before the modern partition of Ireland. If the
United Kingdom was not inevitable, if it was not the product of a logical
plan, what does this suggest about the lack of a public perception of the
United Kingdom state? Indeed, what does it tell us about the nature of the
United Kingdom state itself?

If Rodney Barker is correct, as I think he is, to argue that a description of
the state is primarily about its 'historical capacity', then consideration of
England's agonising journey along the road towards Union furnishes revealing
evidence of the reluctance (some might say failure) of the state to fulfil its basic
objectives of peace, order and security via formal constitutional mechanisms.[15]
We are therefore left with something of an historical paradox: it was precisely
the 'historical incapacity' of the English state to achieve its fundamental aims
by 'informal' means which compelled it to implement 'formal' Union. Formal
Union was actually a symptom of weakness rather than strength. And

recognition of this paradox suggests either that we should question the historical capacity of the English state, its assertive strength, or that we should seriously reconsider and reappraise its historical political strategy. Rose observed that each territorial part of the United Kingdom came under the Crown 'by a separate act, specific to particular historical circumstances and reflecting local conditions'.[16] This observation reveals an important characteristic of the English state, namely, its diplomatic passivity. The historically passive role of the English state has been part of a deliberate accommodationist political strategy designed to achieve voluntary compliance. Willing complicity, after all, is usually cheaper and often more effective than force.

Given the dangers outlined above of making oversimplified and superficial assumptions about the making of the United Kingdom, what does the recent literature which deals with it tell us about the federal idea? How does it help to explain the emergence of the British federal tradition? Here I shall utilise the work of Jim Bulpitt, whose *Territory and Power in the United Kingdom* first ~Bulpitt appeared in 1983.[17] In terms of the twin processes of state-building and national integration, it is an important contribution to our understanding of the United Kingdom. However, it is also invaluable to this study for the way in which it both explains the existence of early federal-type relationships and supports the legitimacy of British federal ideas.

Bulpitt's work also offers an implicit explanation for the English obliviousness to the nature of the state which Rose had already claimed. His thesis posits an elite operational code of territorial management designed to secure the goals of the authorities in London by a tacit system of indirect rule offering considerable autonomy to local elites. It buttresses the view outlined above that the English state deliberately chose a backseat when and where possible. Put simply, it preferred a maximum of advantage with a minimum of commitment. The framework of a set of imperial-type relations between England and the periphery which Bulpitt utilised serves to pose the key question: when should the state resort to outright annexation or incorporation? And the answer is: only reluctantly and as a last resort. Informal control was a symbol of strength and inner confidence; formal control was indicative of a perceived decline arising out of a growing inability to resolve difficulties both at home and abroad.[18]

If this summary of territorial management and modernisation is correct, it helps us to understand not only that peculiar sense of being without an idea of the state, but also the essentially contingent nature of the Union. In other words, it underlines another important feature of the 'unplanned' Union, namely, the variety of possible outcomes. If the idea of an intrusive, meddlesome and ubiquitous state was never purposely entertained, a number of alternative state scenarios merit legitimate consideration. Bulpitt's thesis serves to emphasise the flexible, accommodative nature of the state which adjusted the practice of territorial politics to achieve political settlements sufficiently attractive to rival protagonists to be lasting. Without wishing to enter the main debate about the nature of territorial politics in the overall evolution of the United Kingdom, there are two observations to be made regarding the implications for the British federal tradition. First, the bargaining character of the state implicitly accepted 'an operational federalism' between centre and periphery 'supposedly absent from English constitutional development'.[19] Territorial practice outstripped constitutional theory. Secondly, the acceptance of rival models of territorial development in Britain, if not Ireland, suggests that indigenous federal ideas and proposals for constitutional change were neither as radical nor as utopian as their critics would have us believe.

The federal idea, broadly conceived, was simply one among many possible outcomes in response to perceived challenges to the state. The notion of a fully-fledged federal political system or, at least, federal instalments like colonial representation in the British Parliament, was, moreover, a perfectly legitimate alternative perspective of the reformed state. All that was required to trigger it into life as an active force in British politics was a unique conjunction of internal and external circumstances sufficient to threaten the existing conditions of peace, order and stability. During the last century there have been several such conjunctions of circumstances which have prompted a variety of state reform proposals. Indeed, in the period surveyed in this study it is clear that there have been several critical junctures in British political and constitutional development which have produced uncertainties serious enough to encourage elite reform responses. Different combinations of uncertainties engendered by domestic, imperial and foreign events and circumstances have acted as a powerful spur to the public visibility of the federal idea in the United Kingdom. And it is important to note that the periodic resurgence of the idea springs from an underlying, continuous tradition of British federalism.

We can already see that parts (i) and (ii) of our analytical framework obviously interact and overlap with each other to sustain the thesis that British federal ideas are a legitimate, if neglected, dimension of the overall British political tradition. They combine to present a formidable body of evidence which testifies to the indigenous nature of federal ideas. They are, in short, British federal ideas for the British. This brings us finally to the third part of our analytical framework and it is one which takes us into the cloudy and imprecise world of national identities.

(iii) The multinational state

The United Kingdom, as Rose reminded us, 'is not a natural entity'; it 'was not created as the reflection of a single national identity'. Whatever it is, then, the United Kingdom 'cannot be considered a conventional nation-state'.[20] We can take these useful observations as a warning against the attempt to fit our subject into a conceptual framework which is too narrow and constricting. This means that we must be careful how we use particular terms to describe the component parts of the United Kingdom. Recent research has demonstrated the complexity of identity in the United Kingdom and its implications for the future of the state. Here I shall utilise the recent work of two British historians who have made significant intellectual contributions to the continuing debate about nations, nationalisms and national identities in the United Kingdom. I will also look briefly at the published papers of a symposium on 'national identities' in the United Kingdom and Ireland held in Wales in 1990.

The first of these historical contributions, by Hugh Kearney, alerts us to the pitfalls of interpreting our past solely through English eyes. In his *The British Isles: A History of Four Nations*,[21] Kearney underlines the dangers of dominant and dominating concepts of political and social science discourse which serve only to simplify and distort the complexity of our own history. He compels us to reconsider whether or not we have a single national history. British history is not English history, but 'the notion that we have several national pasts has been obscured by the understandable dominance of England, particularly since the industrial revolution'.[22] We have, then, a multi-national history. Scotland, Wales and Ireland – and now also Northern Ireland – each have their own respective national histories, cultures and identities which have grown and been nurtured both before and after the creation of the United Kingdom. But this does not tell the whole story. Kearney's view is that the concept of the multi-national state makes a good deal of sense both of past and present but it ignores 'the unifying factor of "Britishness"'.[23] He claims that all but a small proportion of the inhabitants of the United Kingdom accept the term 'British' when applied to them even if they do not apply it to themselves without some thought. Today 'British' is actually a convenient shorthand for the people of Great Britain and Northern Ireland.

Kearney reaches one particular conclusion which is important for our study of the British federal tradition: 'there has been a "British" history over and above our "multi-national" history'. This leads him to answer the question 'four nations or one?' with the appropriate reply 'four nations and one'.[24] But of the nations surveyed in his work it is the 'British nation' which is 'most problematic' precisely because 'it seems to be made up of four other nations'.[25] What, then, is this 'unifying factor of Britishness' to which Kearney alludes and what are its origins? Let us briefly explore these questions by turning to the second historical contribution to the current literature about national identities in the United Kingdom which we mentioned above. In her *Britons: Forging the Nation, 1707–1837*, Linda Colley has ably demonstrated how in a 130-year long historical period a distinct sense of British national identity was forged.[26] But it was a particular kind of national identity. Great Britain was 'an invented nation superimposed, if only for a while, onto much older alignments and loyalties'.[27] Here Colley is implicitly in agreement with Kearney: 'Britishness was superimposed over an array of internal differences'. Utilising Benedict Anderson's helpful definition of a nation as 'an imagined political community', she claims that it is plausible in this period to refer to 'Great Britain as a nation' and to an emergent 'British nationalism'.[28] The sense of being 'British' is complex precisely because the combination of forces which both created and sustained it was itself complicated. Colley has summarised these binding elements in simple terms: a common investment in Protestantism (which naturally excluded Ireland); the threat and tonic of recurrent war, especially with Catholic France; and the overall impact of a huge overseas empire with its attendant triumphs, threats, profits and unfamiliarity. Other agencies which also played a part in fusing the English, the Welsh and the Scots together were: Great Britain's geographical position as a compact island; the relatively advanced network of transport and communications; the early development of free trade within its boundaries; the swift pace of urbanisation in England and Scotland; and the precocious and ubiquitous nature of its newspaper and periodical press. Above all, however, Colley insists that 'Protestantism lay at the core of British national identity'.[29] Religion and war combined to forge a nation of Britons.

A knowledge of the past helps us to understand the present, but it is also 'necessary to understand the present meaning of past history'.[30] What does the recent literature concerning nations, nationalisms and national identities in the United Kingdom, as it has been briefly sketched above, tell us about the British federal tradition? How far does it help us to confirm the existence of such a tradition? Part of the answer is obvious: between 1801 and 1921 the United Kingdom comprised four separate, distinct and territorially concentrated sub-state national identities which, at least theoretically, lent themselves to various forms of institutional autonomy, one of which was conceivably federal. Bulpitt's thesis has already supported this view. But the discussion above has also shown that, in Rose's words, 'at least six different national identities can be found within the United Kingdom: English, Scottish, Welsh, Ulster, Irish and British'.[31] Kearney, preferring the concept of 'culture' to that of 'nation', alludes to 'at least eight cultures' in the British Isles.[32] How can we resolve this apparent conundrum? Let us probe a little further into the United Kingdom as a multi-national state.

In a recent collection of essays edited by Bernard Crick and entitled *National Identities: The Constitution of the United Kingdom*, the coexistence of a multi-national and an overarching British past is a theme shared by many of the contributors.[33] However, it is in Crick's own essay entitled 'The English and the British' that support for a tradition of federal political ideas can be found. His main argument is rooted in a distinct English tolerance of diversity. Recognition of diversity, the practice of cultural tolerance and the nature of indirect rule each reflected the main English priority, namely, holding the United Kingdom together. This had important strategic implications for English identity. 'Englishness' was elusive, and necessarily so, precisely because its passivity paid dividends. Crick points out that since the main business of politics for the old English governing class was holding the United Kingdom together, any deliberate cultivation by the English of a 'cult of nationalism' would be disruptive.[34] In other words, English political elites had a vested interest in maintaining a low profile especially in matters which impinged directly upon national cultural identities. Selective self-restraint maintained their political dominance of the United Kingdom.

We can see mirrored in Crick's main argument the central tenet of Bulpitt's thesis: informal control if possible and formal control only when necessary. Rose, too, had reached the same conclusion about England and the English: 'to assert an exclusively English identity would be a disruptive claim in a multinational United Kingdom'.[35] The recent literature surveyed here, then, indicates a general scholarly consensus upon many aspects of the United Kingdom as a multi-national state. But it is when we examine the complex interaction of 'Britishness' and 'Englishness' in addition to Welsh, Scottish and Irish perspectives that we can begin to understand why federal ideas achieved the status of a tradition. Their relevance to the respective predicaments of the Scottish and the Irish in the Union is perfectly understandable, but they also appealed conspicuously to English political elites. Clearly, if they offered the prospect of keeping the United Kingdom intact during particularly difficult periods of challenge and change, they could be an attractive proposition.

Federal ideas can be construed therefore as one distinct set of practical political responses to perceived threats to the Union. And, it is worth repeating, the very nature of the Union – its multi-dimensional character and structure – has guaranteed a secure place for the existence of a British tradition of federalism.

We have now discussed in some detail the three dimensions to our analytical framework. Each is important for what it tells us about this strange 'unthinking Union' with no written codified constitution.[36] But before we attempt to build upon this analytical framework, it is important to look separately at yet another feature of the United Kingdom which we have already identified. This is the nature of the United Kingdom as a unitary state. We must briefly explore this conceptual characteristic in order more firmly to establish the British federal tradition.

The unitary state: myth and reality

Among the many paradoxes which lie at the heart of the United Kingdom the phrase 'unitary state' is particularly perplexing. Scholars who have written recently about it seem to veer awkwardly between constitutional theory which is unequivocal and constitutional theory which is ambiguous. This is because although the United Kingdom is a state in terms of international law, it nonetheless has no written constitution. As Rose argued, 'the stateless and nonconstitutional nature of government in the United Kingdom means that questions about its institutions and territorial extent are neither confronted nor resolved'.[37] But Rose remained emphatic that 'the United Kingdom meets the basic definitional criteria of a unitary state. The Crown in Parliament is the sole political authority, and its authority is formally unlimited'. Authority is clearly undivided in a unitary state and where there appear to have been departures from this axiom they have been 'more apparent than real'.[38]

Livingston also recognised the essentially unitary nature of British government. The constitution, he confessed, was 'not federal but unitary'. Indeed, 'the sovereignty of the Queen-in-Parliament is recognized in theory, in fact, and in law'.[39] And in his *Devolution*, Vernon Bogdanor also acknowledged the highly centralised and 'profoundly unitary nature of the United Kingdom, as expressed in the supremacy of Parliament', but he distinguished this from 'the spirit in which this unitary state is administered'.[40] Here centralisation as a force of habit rather than of ideology has permitted a wide diversity of political relationships: 'British politicians have rarely allowed a theory of government to prevent them from constructing new relationships which, whatever the faults to be found in them by strict constitutionalists, nevertheless succeed in providing workable answers to practical problems'.[41] Rose and Bogdanor lead us inexorably to the conclusion that the United Kingdom is a unitary state without a unitary constitution. But the formal trappings of the unitary state have not in practice stifled every attempt at redefining relations between England and Scotland, Wales and Ireland during the last few centuries.

Bulpitt denied that the post-Union structure of government was unitary 'in so far as that term has any meaning'. His thesis emphasised the reluctance of the central authorities to interfere directly in the affairs of local communities and depicted a 'peculiar structure of territorial politics ... characterised by a high degree of constitutional ambiguity'.[42] In summary, then, the authority of the Crown in Parliament has remained intact. The United Kingdom developed as a unitary state in theory but both the instinct and spirit of its practice have been intermittently imaginative and flexible. As Rose remarked, the state was unitary but not uniform.[43] Hence in the absence of an overweening centralist ideology dedicated to cultural uniformity via a single integrated organisation both the myth and the reality of the unitary state have been perpetuated in the United Kingdom. It has remained the archetype of the conventional 'unitary' classification.

But it is not sufficient for our purposes here to leave the discussion of the term 'unitary' in such inconclusive abeyance. The time has now come to jettison this conceptual category. In his *Federalism and Federation*, Preston King has already concluded that 'the whole idea of a "unitary" state would appear something of a myth'.[44] He correctly located the source of the myth in the classical theory of sovereignty:

The reference to a supposed 'unitary' state only really involves an adjustment to the theory of sovereignty. The effect of the adjustment, however, is to render the whole concept redundant. ... Clearly, every government, conceived as a unit, is 'unitary'. This is merely a catch-all category, being less precise than 'sovereign', with its only virtue – and a doubtful virtue at that – being to exclude the newly emergent federations from its purview.[45]

King also noted how far even some of the most ardent proponents of the unitary classification were troubled by its vacuousness. For example, Kenneth Wheare, in his highly respected *Modern Constitutions*, conceded that 'the class of unitary constitutions is so wide and varied, the degree and method of decentralization in practice in unitary constitutions is so diverse, that a good deal more must be known about a constitution described as "unitary" before we can feel we know what it is like'. Its real value was clearly 'limited'.[46]

King's own conclusion was much more trenchant. He believed that it was 'difficult to detect any value in it at all'.[47] In practical terms there was no sovereign state whose power was not in some way, *de facto* or *de jure,* divided. In view of these conceptual problems it might be better to discard the 'unitary' category altogether. King administered his own *coup de grâce* in unequivocal terms:

> The notion of a 'unitary state' is trivial in the sense that every state must be supposed in some sense to be unitary. ... We simply cannot say what a unitary state is, other than trivially or incoherently. ... The notion of a 'unitary' state serves no relevant, useful or coherent purpose.[48]

These considerations suggest that it is not the term 'federal', or 'federation', which is problematic. Rather it is the 'unitary' classification in political science which has outlived its usefulness. The displacement of the unitary category is important because it opens up the possibility of alternative perspectives of the United Kingdom state. Here, however, we must be careful. It is important to remember that during the last century the unitary perception of the state enjoyed a generally unrivalled dominance. This was reflected in the publication in 1885 of Albert Venn Dicey's *The Law of the Constitution*.[49] In this enormously influential book Dicey bequeathed a legacy which served to eulogise parliamentary sovereignty and raised the notion of the unitary state, in direct contradistinction to federation, almost to a deity. Small wonder that his legacy has proved to be troublesome. In what quickly became a classic late-Victorian exposition of British constitutional law, he delivered his famous verdict on federal government in withering terms: federal government meant weak government; federal government tended to produce conservatism; and federal political systems meant, in practice, legalism. Federalism substituted litigation for legislation.[50]

In one sense we are still suffering from this narrow, legalistic interpretation of what constitutes 'federal'. By contrast, the term 'unitary' has escaped serious analytical attention. It has become a conceptual monument to a glorious past. But this framework of ideas about the structure of the state and the nature of its government has been constructed at a cost. It has blinded us to other constitutional possibilities by effectively denying us the incentive to debate the fundamental principles upon which our conduct is based. Nevil Johnson emphasised this constitutional blindness in his own survey of the United Kingdom entitled *In Search of the Constitution*.[51] He lamented the complete dominance of one particular body of ideas about government, namely, the notion of parliamentary government. In England since the end of the seventeenth century there has been no major challenge to what Dicey called 'parliamentary despotism'.[52] For Johnson this was at best only a mixed blessing. The cost was significant:

> there is no alternative or competing political tradition to fall back on, no different view of the basis on which political authority might rest. ... The peculiar problem now presented by the very supremacy of one particular way of looking at the establishment of political authority is that those who may be anxious about the future, sceptical about the continuing vitality of this doctrine alone as a support for a satisfactory political order, have no other tradition to appeal to.[53]

One major consequence of this constitutional blindness has been the perceived illegitimacy of attempts at constitutional reform. A distinct tradition of constitutional conservatism has excluded substantial reappraisal of the British constitution. The reproach likely to be met, according to Johnson, was 'that of importing alien ideas and of pressing for change where, almost by definition, change cannot be made'.[54] The result of this largely English unitary mentality has been the absence of a genuine British constitutional culture. There has been no constitutional stimulus publicly to debate the basic principles upon which the British are governed.

One purpose of this book is precisely to act as a corrective to this misplaced unitary perception of the British state. By establishing the legitimacy of the British federal tradition, it will demonstrate that there is another way of looking at the basis of political authority in the United Kingdom. During the last century there have been many serious attempts at federal constitutional reform, but they appear in the mainstream historical and political science literature to have been random and fitful. Indeed, the general impression conveyed is one of historical and political discontinuity. In consequence, they have been peremptorily dismissed and openly ridiculed as either irrelevant or utopian – or both. In reality these efforts have been neither random nor fitful. On the contrary, they form part of a continuous, unbroken tradition of British federal ideas. During the last century therefore these ideas represent a fundamental continuity in the larger British political tradition.

We have now reached the point where we can begin to build upon the framework of analysis which we have just established. The following chapters will be grouped around the three issue arenas mentioned above, namely, 'Empire, Ireland and Europe'. The book will, in consequence, be divided into three broad sections, respectively identified as Empire, Ireland and Europe. This approach to our subject enables us to focus upon each of these distinct issue arenas separately in order that the essential continuity of the British federal tradition can be confirmed. It is in many ways a task of unmasking what has become a partly hidden dimension to the British political tradition. We will begin our analysis by looking at Empire.

Notes

1. Mogi, S. (1931), *The Problem of Federalism: A Study in the History of Political Theory*, 2 vols, London, Allen and Unwin, vol. I, 208–9.
2. Livingston, W.S. (1956), *Federalism and Constitutional Change*, Oxford, Clarendon Press, 269–71.
3. Rose, R. (1982), *Understanding the United Kingdom: The Territorial Dimension in Government*, London, Longman, 37 and 39.
4. Thomas, K. (1978), 'The United Kingdom', in R. Grew (ed.), *Crises of Political Development in Europe and the United States*, Princeton, NJ, Princeton University Press, chapter 2, 67.
5. Ibid., 79. See also LaPalombara, J. (1969), 'Values and Ideologies in the Administrative Evolution of Western Constitutional Systems', in R. Braibanti (ed.), *Political and Administrative Development*, Durham, NC, Duke University Press, chapter 5, 166–219.
6. Bendix, R. (1978), 'England', in Bendix, R., *Kings or People: Power and the Mandate to Rule*, Berkeley, CA, University of California Press, chapter 6, 198.
7. 'Participation' is one of the five recognised crises of political development, the others being labelled 'Identity', 'Legitimacy', 'Penetration', and 'Distribution'. The general literature on modernisation is vast, but it is best summarised in Binder, L., Coleman, J.S. et al. (1971), *Crises and Sequences in Political Development*, Princeton, NJ, Princeton University Press.
8. Bendix, R. (1978), 'Kings and People in England', in *Kings or People*, chapter 9, 290.
9. Livingston, W.S. (1956), *Federalism and Constitutional Change*, 272.
10. See, for example, Bogdanor, V. (1979), *Devolution*, Oxford, Oxford University Press; Rose, R. (1982), *Understanding the United Kingdom*, London, Longman; Madgwick, P. and Rose. R. (1982), *The Territorial Dimension in United Kingdom Politics*, London, Macmillan; and Keating, M. (1988), *State and Regional Nationalism: Territorial Politics and the European State*, Brighton, Harvester-Wheatsheaf.
11. Rose, R. (1982), *Understanding the United Kingdom*, 5.
12. Barker, R. (1984), 'The Rise and Eclipse of the Social Democratic State', in R.L. Borthwick and J.E. Spence (eds), *British Politics in Perspective*, Leicester, Leicester University Press, chapter 1, 1–18.
13. Rose, R. (1982), *Understanding the United Kingdom*, 47.
14. Rose, R. (1982), 'Is the United Kingdom a State? Northern Ireland as a Test Case', in P. Madgwick and R. Rose (eds), *The Territorial Dimension in United Kingdom Politics*, chapter 4, 128.
15. Barker, R. (1984), 'The Rise and Eclipse of the Social Democratic State', 6.
16. Rose, R. (1982), *Understanding the United Kingdom*, 42.
17. Bulpitt, J. (1983), *Territory and Power in the United Kingdom*, Manchester, Manchester University Press.
18. Ibid., chapter 3.

19. Ibid., 83.
20. Rose, R. (1982), *Understanding the United Kingdom*, 2 and 10.
21. Kearney, H. (1989), *The British Isles: A History of Four Nations*, Cambridge, Cambridge University Press. Here Kearney pressed for a 'Britannic' approach, 4. It is also important to mention Pocock, J.G.A. (1975), 'British History: A Plea for a New Subject', *Journal of Modern History*, 47, No. 4, 601–28 and his (1982), 'The Limits and Divisions of British History: In Search of an Unknown Subject', *American Historical Review*, LXXXVII, 311–36.
22. See Kearney, H. (1991), 'Four Nations Or One?', in B. Crick (ed.), *National Identities: The Constitution of the United Kingdom*, Oxford, Blackwell Publishers, 1.
23. Ibid., 3.
24. Ibid., 4.
25. Ibid., 5.
26. Colley, L. (1992), *Britons: Forging the Nation, 1707–1837*, New Haven and London, Yale University Press.
27. Ibid., 5.
28. Ibid.
29. Ibid., 369.
30. Rose, R. (1982), *Understanding the United Kingdom*, 5–6.
31. Ibid., 15.
32. Kearney, H. (1989), *The British Isles: A History of Four Nations*, 8.
33. Crick, B. (1991), *National Identities: The Constitution of the United Kingdom*, Oxford, Blackwell Publishers.
34. Crick, B. (1991), 'The English and the British', in B. Crick (ed.), *National Identities*, chapter 8, 92.
35. Rose, R. (1982), *Understanding the United Kingdom*, 29.
36. This is the title of one of his sub-sections in Rose, R. (1982), *Understanding the United Kingdom*, chapter 9, 209.
37. Rose, R. (1982), *Understanding the United Kingdom*, 48.
38. Ibid., 52.
39. Livingston, W.S. (1956), *Federalism and Constitutional Change*, 272.
40. Bogdanor, V. (1979), *Devolution*, 7–8.
41. Bogdanor, V. (1979), *Devolution*, 8.
42. Bulpitt, J. (1983), *Territory and Power in the United Kingdom*, 96–9.
43. Rose, R. (1982), *Understanding the United Kingdom*, 54.
44. King, P. (1982), *Federalism and Federation*, London, Croom Helm.
45. Ibid., 138.
46. Wheare, K.C. (1953), *Modern Constitutions* (third edn), Oxford, Oxford University Press, 30.
47. King, P. (1982), *Federalism and Federation*, 138.
48. Ibid., 139.
49. Dicey, A.V. (1897), *The Law of the Constitution* (fifth edn), London, Macmillan & Co. Ltd.
50. Ibid., 162–71.
51. Johnson, N. (1980), *In Search of the Constitution*, London, Methuen & Co. Ltd.
52. Dicey, A.V. (1897), *The Law of the Constitution*, 147.
53. Johnson, N. (1980), *In Search of the Constitution*, 30.
54. Ibid., 31.

PART ONE

Empire

— despite the lack of scholarly discourse, federalism (informal) represents continuity in British political thought

CHAPTER 2

Federalism and the imperial idea, 1870–84

The origins of the imperial federation movement

We have already demonstrated how much of the recent historical and political science literature on the United Kingdom has underlined its contingent unplanned character. It is a union which defies constitutional symmetry. This literature also suggests that elements of federal practice were far from unfamiliar in British political development. Bulpitt acknowledged this when he argued that new bargains between elites could be struck as a series of reconstructions of as much of the old indirect management of the celtic periphery as could be achieved in changed circumstances.[1] As an elite affair such a practice depended entirely upon elite willingness to modify their management of affairs of state. They had first to be convinced that it was necessary.

This chapter will examine the emergence of the federal idea in the specific context of British imperial development in the late nineteenth century. We have already suggested that the making of the United Kingdom had placed federalism among the category of legitimate options and responses available to British elites during difficult periods of change. It is now time to look closely at one of these critical junctures in modern British political development. The mid-Victorian era witnessed a sudden surge in the popularity of the federal idea about 1870. In retrospect, 1870 was an important turning-point in the growing appeal and relevance of federalism in British politics. It furnished all of the ingredients adumbrated by Bulpitt in his hypothesis of a discernible shift from informal to formal empire: perceived economic decline; a significant change in international power relations against British hegemony; the mounting menace of Ireland, symptomatic of a breakdown in elite collaboration; and the challenge to traditional political certainties posed by urban enfranchisement in 1867.[2] In short, the mid-Victorian years between 1860 and 1880 encapsulated a series of major challenges to the old order amounting to nothing less than the modernisation of British politics.

It is important that we begin our examination of this period by clarifying what we mean by 'the federal idea'. In the 1870s the federal idea meant 'imperial federation', an ambiguous phrase which was first used by the Reverend William Arthur, a Wesleyan clergyman, in 1853.[3] But there are several crucial distinctions worth making in the context of the British empire.

Certainly the phrase 'imperial federation', so widely used in the vocabulary of British politics for nearly fifty years after 1870, created many misconceptions and was the source of protracted public quarrels and heated rivalries among British imperial and colonial elites. In hindsight, it was merely a convenient rallying cry for those who sought a much more binding and regulated empire but who could not agree upon the details of how it should be achieved. In practice it was a useful mobilising ploy for the imperialism of consolidation rather than expansion. Most of those who sympathised with this vague ideal did not really believe that utilisation of the federal principle meant superimposing on the empire the full paraphernalia of a federal constitution analogous to that of the United States of America. Such activists who worked to this end were in a tiny minority. But this still left available a very extensive range of empire federalist schemes and proposals which permitted numerous variations of the federal idea.[4]

Ged Martin's important article entitled 'Empire Federalism and Imperial Parliamentary Union, 1820–1870' appeared in the *Historical Journal* in 1973 and did much to establish a revised interpretation of imperial thinking on the consolidation, rather than the expansion, of the empire.[5] But it is also important for our purposes here in clarifying at least two issues which have been persistently misunderstood. First, he focused his attention upon the family of ideas which most imperial historians have dubbed 'imperial federation'. In preference to this vague phrase Martin introduced the terms 'empire federalism' and 'imperial parliamentary union' as being more accurate labels to identify the various strands of thought and opinion about closer imperial union.[6] These, he claimed, boiled down to three broad categories: parliamentary (colonial representation); extra-parliamentary (agents, boards, and conferences); and super-parliamentary ('imperial federation'). Of these various interrelated schemes of empire federalism, colonial representation in the British Parliament has been the most persistent and should be viewed as 'the basic ingredient of empire federalism'.[7]

Martin's second clarification was in many respects more significant than his first. One of the main purposes of his article was to confirm the existence of a continuous sentiment for a federal empire throughout the nineteenth century. He claimed that there was an essential continuity between the mid- and late nineteenth-century empire federalists both in terms of the personnel involved and the content of the public debate. The general significance of his article for our purposes can be appropriately emphasised when we consider the following extract from it:

> In fact, between 1820 and 1870 a debate about the federal nature of the Empire can be traced. ... It is, however, fair to think of one single movement for a federal Empire throughout the nineteenth century. There is a clear continuity in ideas, in arguments, and in the people involved.[8]

This statement, while confirming once again the sense of a real watershed in British imperial thought and opinion about the year 1870, must not be allowed to overlook the peculiar circumstances of the years between 1869 and 1871 which have a special significance for the emergence of the imperial federation movement.[9] Both continuity and change are evident in this particular historical debate. What matters here is the recognition and elucidation of a distinct body of federal ideas linked directly to the evolution of the British empire during the last century. And it is an indigenous body of British federal political ideas which endured until the early 1920s.

The evidence for the rise of the federal idea during 1870–84 is overwhelming. Throughout the 1870s the federal idea, loosely referred to as 'imperial federation', was hotly debated both in the Royal Colonial Institute (originally established as the Royal Colonial Society in 1868), and in the plethora of articles and essays which appeared in the mid-Victorian press and review literature.[10] Indeed, it was used to describe virtually any scheme which promoted closer ties within the empire, irrespective of how widely schemes differed from each other and whether or not a plan actually incorporated the federal principle. There were as many schemes of closer union as there were individuals to propound them. One historian of empire even remarked that imperial federation had become 'the happy hunting ground of cranks'.[11] But it is essential to distinguish this element of heady eccentricity from the first real sign of a new political movement dedicated to the closer union of the empire. This can be detected in 1871.

The public meeting held at the Westminster Palace Hotel in London in the summer of 1871 in order to discuss colonial questions was a landmark in the history of the imperial federation movement which was to have its heyday over a decade later. Meeting between 19 and 21 July 1871, the conference on colonial questions closely followed the publication of two celebrated articles which advertised the cause of the new movement. Entitled 'Imperial Federalism' and 'An Imperial Confederation', these two articles appeared in the January and April editions respectively of *The Contemporary Review*.[12] The author of these somewhat polemical essays was Edward Jenkins, a Canadian expatriate who had already some notoriety as the author of *Ginx's Baby*, a social satire published in 1870. As a former member of the Royal Colonial Society and a future Liberal MP for Dundee, Jenkins' career in the early movement for closer imperial union in 1871 was typical of many of his contemporaries. His importance to the movement must not be exaggerated but he can fairly be credited with the birth of serious discussion on the subject of imperial federation.

The Westminster Palace Hotel Conference was a quite remarkable event in the history of the federal idea in the United Kingdom. Nothing like it had ever occurred before in the debate about the future of the empire. It reflected the mid-Victorian search for a new political and economic relationship with the white self-governing colonies. Once free trade had replaced the old commercial system and the colonies of British settlement had acquired responsible government during the 1840s and 1850s, it had gradually become a common assumption that they would eventually obtain complete independence from the mother country. No specific timetable was envisaged for this event but the ground had been slowly prepared for this shifting emphasis within the imperial relationship. Self-government, self-defence and an overall policy of reduced imperial expenditure fitted the logic of mid-Victorian thinking about empire.[13] As Colin Eldridge observed, 'the question at issue during the middle decades of the nineteenth century was not whether the empire should be preserved but what form a reorganised empire should take in terms of government and defence'.[14] Clearly the public debate about imperial federation in the 1870s was prompted by a strong unsettling sense that the empire had reached a new crossroads. It was time to reappraise and reassess Britain's imperial future.

When Edward Jenkins gave the inaugural address on the evening of 19 July 1871 the company of prominent men from British and colonial circles who were assembled before him was solid evidence of the growing appeal of colonial subjects deemed worthy of serious public discussion. Both the Duke of Manchester and the Earl of Shaftesbury chaired the sessions, while the Earls of Airlie and Lichfield attended together with at least seventeen MPs from both major British political parties. Among the nine Conservative members were Lord Eustace Cecil, Lord George Hamilton, Viscount Sandon, Robert Fowler, and E.B. Eastwick, while Thomas Brassey, Colonel E.T. Gourley, Arthur Kinnaird, McCullagh Torrens and Robert Torrens were among the eight Liberal members who were present. Other notable public figures who attended at various intervals during the three days of debate were Sir Charles Nicholson, Sir George Young and Sir Charles Clifford, while the Colonial Institute was well represented by Frederick Young and C.W. Eddy.[15]

The scope of discussion was comprehensive, with papers on emigration, the reform of the Colonial Office and the complex issue of land transfers. But the interest in imperial federation was especially intriguing. Delivered to such an audience of distinguished MPs, colonists and colonial expatriates, Francis de Labilliere's paper was actually entitled 'Imperial and Colonial Federalism'.[16] Though somewhat vague and idealistic in terms of details, Labilliere's contribution was significant in one particular respect: it symbolised the changed circumstances of British imperial relations. Such a public discussion among practical politicians would have been unthinkable only ten years earlier. Labilliere's paper, if rather crude and superficial in its content, reflected an essentially exploratory purpose. His principal aim was to set the wheels of debate on imperial federation in motion. We will encounter Labilliere again in our later analysis of the Imperial Federation League, which was formed in 1884.

In retrospect, it is understandable that the conference of 1871 has been ignored by historians and consequently forgotten by many students of British imperial ideas. From one viewpoint the conference of 1871 constituted the only visible achievement of the so-called early empire enthusiasts who actively promoted closer imperial union. The promoters actually wanted regular meetings in the future but the Executive Committee, which was given permanent status, was unable to repeat this success. This is often the fate of incipient political movements; they suffer initial setbacks through weak organisation, lack of funds and desultory interest. But it may also be a necessary experience. If the idea behind the movement is fundamentally sound, it will persist and the early activists will learn from the failure. This was the first experience of the imperial federationists. They prepared the ground for later success and it was not long in arriving.

The Westminster Palace Hotel Conference should not be viewed in complete isolation from other developments related directly to the growing public interest in imperial federation. On the contrary, it must be viewed in the overall context of an emergent British federalism. It was not the only evidence of a marked shift of emphasis in the British imperial debate about closer union. Indeed, the subject of imperial federation was ubiquitous in the mid-Victorian literature of the 1870s. In Parliament, too, the impulse to do something about the empire was both evident and novel. Already, in April 1870, a motion was brought before the House of Commons by Robert Torrens calling for a select committee on the political relations between Britain and the colonies.[17] It occasioned a lengthy debate on the colonial question in general and more accurately corresponds to Martin's category of 'Imperial Parliamentary Union' in its content than the specific use of the federal principle. Nonetheless, it signified a noticeable change in the substance of the usual parliamentary debates on imperial questions.

The notion of 'Confederation' was seriously discussed for the first time in the context of closer imperial union during the summer of 1871. Robert Macfie, an intrepid activist in imperial affairs who was a member of the Colonial Institute and a firm believer in imperial federation, moved a resolution for a select committee to consider improvements in existing imperial relations with a view ultimately to 'the permanent maintenance of the best and most cordial interconnection between all parts of the empire'.[18] The ensuing debate, on 12 May 1871, did not focus upon imperial federation *per se*, but it did familiarise the House of Commons with the new mood of consolidationist thinking on empire. Macfie persisted with his efforts to impel the House of Commons to investigate the possibilities of an imperial reorganisation during succeeding debates in 1872 and 1873, but with little success.[19] In Parliament his was an isolated militancy.

Macfie's antics, irritating though they may have been to many members of the House of Commons, do not appear so far-fetched if viewed from a different perspective. Outside Parliament a prominent public figure expressed similar opinions. In June 1872 Disraeli gave his famous Crystal Palace address in which he captured the new public mood about empire.[20] His speech merely paid a timely tribute to ideas which were already circulating about closer imperial union, but it suggested an acute awareness of contemporary change.

He was quick to detect the growing sense of doubt and uncertainty about Britain's changing international position after Russia's unilateral abrogation of the Black Sea Clauses in October 1870 and the sweeping Prussian victory over France which confirmed German hegemony in continental Europe after 1871. These events, which served to undermine Britain's global position, prompted Disraeli to emphasise the link between Britain's continued greatness and her empire: the empire was the solution to halting Britain's perceived decline in power and prestige. Macfie was therefore in good company when, during the early 1870s, he advocated tightening the imperial bonds. The politics of imperial consolidation reflected something distinctly new in mid-Victorian experience: British primacy in industrial, commercial, foreign and military fields was challenged seriously for the first time. These events demonstrate once again the validity of Bulpitt's thesis concerning perceived threats to the Union. They also underline the impact of changes in world politics on the emergence of imperial federation.

Under the editorship of James Froude, *Fraser's Magazine* also took up the cause of closer imperial union in 1871.[21] Two consecutive and anonymous articles appeared in the July and August editions entitled 'Great Britain Confederated' in which the federal solution was propounded as a kind of school catechism for some future generation in the form of questions and answers. Meanwhile, in February 1871, Robert Macfie, as irrepressible as ever, delivered a paper before the Colonial Institute entitled 'On the Crisis of Empire: Imperial Federation' and published his *Colonial Questions Pressing for Immediate Solution* during the same year. In 1873 a small newspaper, *The Colonies*, joined the continuing debate about closer imperial union. Owned by S.W. Silver, a member of the Colonial Institute, the newspaper published a debate between two correspondents in the months of January, February and March who signed themselves 'Philo Colonus' and 'H. de B.H.' and who used the paper's columns to ventilate the possibilities of imperial federation. This debate was extended in 1875 to include letters from Frederick Young, the Duke of Manchester and Francis de Labilliere, and the correspondence was published separately as a book by Young in 1875 entitled *Imperial Federation*. In pursuance of the campaign to tighten the bonds of empire, Labilliere presented a paper to the Colonial Institute in January 1875 entitled 'On the Permanent Unity of the Empire', and during the months of April, July and October 1879 the *Westminster Review* published a series of articles collectively entitled 'The Federation of the English Empire'.[22] Finally, among the articles and papers touching on the subject of closer imperial union a decade after the Westminster Palace Hotel Conference, Alexander Staveley-Hill's 'An Empire's Parliament' was read before the Colonial Institute in February 1880 and Labilliere's 'The Political Organisation of the Empire' was received by the same body in June 1881, thus demonstrating the continuing value of that institution to enthusiasts of imperial federation.[23]

This section has furnished compelling evidence to suggest that the years between 1870 and 1884, when the Imperial Federation League was formally launched, represent a distinctly new mood in favour of imperial federation. The single intellectual tradition of empire federalism at last boasted a political movement to sustain it. Those public men who rallied to the cause of closer imperial union clearly held certain fundamental beliefs in common and possessed a shared view about the urgency of the great imperial debate. They represented the imperial dimension of the British federal tradition. How, then, was such a vague idea as imperial federation eventually translated into practical politics? And what enabled these public men to crystallise and distil it into a formal political organisation in the late-Victorian era? In order to answer these questions we must turn now to examine the contribution to the British federal tradition of one of the most neglected political figures in nineteenth-century British government and politics, namely, William Edward Forster. He it was who gave the embryonic political movement both shape and direction, and it is appropriate to refer to him as a forgotten imperialist.

William Edward Forster: a forgotten imperialist

Forster is remembered chiefly for his important role in the making of the 1870 Education Act and for his dramatic resignation as Chief Secretary for Ireland in Gladstone's second Liberal administration in 1882. These events have obscured his achievements in other areas of public life. One particular aspect of his political career which has been overshadowed by these controversial circumstances is that of imperial federation. In this chapter I will examine Forster's imperial ideas in detail and I will assess his role as a pioneer in the imperial federation movement. Let us begin by situating Forster in the context of the established historical debate about British imperial ideas in the late-Victorian era.

It is certainly true that Forster's early public support for closer imperial union has been well-documented in the standard commentaries of C.A. Bodelsen and J.E. Tyler – the latter in particular paying close attention to Forster's speeches and to his role in the creation of the Imperial Federation League in 1884.[24] But both of these texts are dated and deficient in several important respects. Neither, for example, provides a detailed explanation of the origins of Forster's imperial ideas, and there is also no attempt to explain the motives which drove him to champion the federal cause. Recent accounts of British imperial history which include references to the imperial federation movement and its ideas during the Victorian period have failed to fill this gap. By neglect they have accepted the patchy and incomplete picture of Forster bequeathed by the old school of Bodelsen and Tyler.[25]

The consequence of this benign neglect has been to overlook the important role that Forster played in the history of British federal ideas. Forster the imperial federationist has been ignored and virtually forgotten. Tyler emphasised the links between Forster's liberal political ideology and his advocacy of imperial federation but the precise nature of this connection was not closely investigated. That they were connected in some way is obvious but a detailed analysis of this linkage is necessary if we are fully to understand Forster's imperial thinking and to explain his public actions. Moreover, the nature of his political personality and general political character are two elements which have also been glossed over. Yet they are vital if we are to sketch his career as a leading Liberal statesman of the mid- and late-Victorian years. Indeed, they are crucial in our attempt, as it were, to bring him back to life. Finally two further connections have been understated in the conventional accounts of Bodelsen and Tyler: first, the moral and racial bases of Forster's imperial thinking; and, secondly, the interrelationship between his domestic, foreign and imperial perspectives. This chapter will demonstrate that Forster's imperial ideas were much more complex and deep-rooted than these accounts suggested. And our rehabilitation of Forster will furnish some basis for the pious reference to him as the 'first Liberal Imperialist'.[26]

How, then, did Forster become an imperial federationist? What were the sources of his imperial ideas and how did he translate these ideas into political practice? Forster's early imperial ideas and interests seem to have crystallised in a very piecemeal and cumulative fashion. His father, a Quaker, devoted increasing periods of his life to missionary work for the Society of Friends in the United States during the 1840s and early 1850s, and Forster slowly acquired an intimate knowledge and understanding of American affairs in general and of the slavery question in particular. His biographer, Thomas Wemyss Reid, acknowledged Forster's early interest in Africa and in the opium trade, but it is clear that by the late 1840s two enduring issues competed for his attentions: the slavery controversy in the United States and the Irish problem in the United Kingdom.

According to Reid, Forster's first visit to Ireland in September 1846 'made his name known in many quarters' partly because he had been 'in constant communication with the editors of the great Liberal newspapers both in London and in the provinces', while his own private study of American affairs between 1850 and 1860 earned him something of a reputation as a specialist in that subject. By the time that the 'Bradford wool stapler' drifted into the hurly-burly of British electoral politics in Yorkshire during the late 1850s, then, he had already acquired a limited public prominence as a local dignitary who had 'written many letters to the Leeds Mercury'.[27] And when electoral triumph finally returned him to the House of Commons as the Liberal MP for Bradford in February 1861 (after an earlier defeat in Leeds in 1859), Forster – at the comparatively late age of forty-three years old – was destined to serve that constituency for a quarter of a century.

There is strong evidence that Forster was widely regarded as an eccentric. In both his demeanor and his appearance he certainly cut a strange figure. In Bradford he was held to be 'altogether unconventional in manner and singularly indifferent to outward appearances ... a figure which was certain to strike even the most careless of observers'.[28] Reid's colourful description of him as a man who was 'unquestionably careless in his dress and ... very blunt in his speech' is corroborated by many other vignettes.[29] In Parliament Henry Lucy alluded to his conspicuous disregard for etiquette, while Gladstone's private secretary, Sir Algernon West, referred to his 'want of tact' and Sir Frederic Rogers, the permanent under-secretary at the Colonial Office, observed in a private note that Forster was a 'rough diamond'.[30] His parliamentary credentials were certainly not typical of a man who was destined to reach cabinet status in mid-Victorian Britain: he lacked a university education; he presented a 'somewhat rough and unvarnished exterior'; and (if we are to believe Reid) was 'apt to be absent-minded'.[31] But we must not make too much of Forster's personal foibles for he possessed many redeeming features. Reid refers to his vitality and energy in public affairs, and there were indelible traces of his Quaker heritage in the calculating manner of his decisions which, once taken, were tenaciously defended. It is perhaps not difficult to imagine that Forster's public image as a highly principled politician with a quick sympathy for noble ideals and an essentially practical mind probably endeared him to Gladstone.[32]

The peculiar mix of untidiness, irreverence and willing application that constituted Forster the Bradford radical during the early 1860s did not deter Lord John Russell from offering him his first, albeit minor, government post in 1865. Between November 1865 and April 1866 Forster served as under-secretary at the Colonial Office which he found 'intensely interesting'.[33] But his interest in colonial affairs at this time must not be exaggerated. The public issue which dominated his mind in the mid-1860s was parliamentary reform. What, then, compelled him to organise his thoughts in such a way that closer imperial union began to loom large in his mind? There seems to be no obvious reason why he should suddenly have turned in this direction. It is here that Forster's domestic preoccupations began to merge with his foreign and imperial perspectives to produce a central unifying theme. During the late 1860s and the early 1870s a curious conjunction of circumstances at home and abroad prompted Forster to rivet his attentions upon Britain's imperial future. We have already referred to the so-called 'empire scare' of 1869–71 and Forster lost no time in announcing his belief in British imperial unity. In a speech to his Bradford constituents in January 1870 he identified himself for the first time as an unequivocal supporter of closer union:

> I believe that the time will come when, by some means or another, statesmen will be able to weld a bond together which will unite the English-speaking people in our colonies at present – unite them with the mother country in one great confederation.[34]

In language which bore the unmistakable hallmarks of Sir Charles Dilke's famous travelogue, *Greater Britain: A Record of Travel in English-Speaking Countries during 1866 and 1867*, Forster registered his delight that the 'colonial question' was at last being brought before the British public.[35] The real significance of this small section of his speech lay less in its rhetoric than in its timing. Forster's public remarks were clearly a milestone in his developing interest in closer union, but they were also uttered at a time when the Gladstone government's colonial policy was extremely unpopular. His Bradford speech therefore had a dual purpose: to counteract the damaging separatist criticisms of the Liberal government's colonial policy and to give added weight to the growing debate about how the existing white self-governing empire should be consolidated. Forster, it must be remembered, was a member of Gladstone's government and his own priority was to defend his government's colonial policy while simultaneously calling attention to the merits of empire and its future possibilities.

Foreign events, in particular, weighed heavily upon Forster's mind. While he was busy piloting the Education Bill through the House of Commons, he was also aware of the spectre of mounting foreign competition in several spheres. His correspondence in August 1870 underlined his own personal fears for Britain arising out of continental European events such as the Franco-Prussian War. But it is equally clear from this correspondence that his own antidote for these perceived dangers lay in the 'grand task' of organising 'the English-speaking race'.[36] Educational reform played a key role in his ideas about resisting the growing threat of foreign rivalry in the military, industrial and commercial realms. If Britain's educational system could be effectively modernised and brought within the reach of the mass of the population, this would not only raise the country's standards of literacy and technical competence, but it would also assist towards the larger Gladstonian objective of a major overhaul of British institutions to achieve administrative efficiency. Forster therefore linked the specific need for educational reform to the much larger goal of counteracting foreign competition.[37] Closer imperial union thus emerged as the central unifying theme which cemented these domestic, foreign and imperial perspectives. During the 1870s, as we have already emphasised, this amounted to a vague notion of imperial consolidation as an essentially defensive reaction to shifting global changes which undermined Britain's international position.

When Gladstone's first Liberal government was defeated in the general election of 1874, Forster set off on a long-awaited visit, via Canada, to the United States where his father was buried. He travelled through Quebec and Ontario, and, according to Reid, 'lost no opportunity of preaching increasing union between the mother country and her children on the federal basis'.[38] Forster did not spell out precisely what he meant by closer union between Britain and the white self-governing colonies. His concern that they should somehow reconcile their own growth and development with the maintenance of the 'English' connection certainly acknowledged the twin conceptions of colonial state- and nation-building. It did not of course indicate any clearly conceived idea about the nature of such a union. The use of the term 'federal' merely suggested that Forster believed the adjustment in political relationships must recognise the basic liberal notions of self-government, liberty and equality. No vast constitutional blueprint was intended. Indeed, Forster was just as keen to accommodate the United States in his vague vision of an 'Anglo-Saxon' alliance. In terms which mirrored the assumptions both of Froude and of Dilke, Forster was convinced that all English-speaking communities possessed an organic bond.[39] This was a typical mid-Victorian premise. The cultural union was cemented by a common language and a shared history which even political independence could not completely destroy. The white self-governing colonies might be moving inexorably towards independence but there would always be a particular sense in which they would remain 'Englishmen overseas'. And if Britain and the United States were separate sovereign states with intermittent differences of opinion and interest, they were nonetheless part of that 'Greater Britain'.

Forster's visit to the United States enabled him to canvas these ideas and it served to lay bare the moral and racial assumptions which underpinned his own peculiar brand of closer union. He supported the idea of an Anglo-American alliance in world politics and he believed firmly in the notion of a loose English-speaking union which perpetuated the links between what were basically branches of the English people abroad. Bound together by language and history, 'Greater Britain' was a moral force for good in the world. These experiences in Canada and the United States prompted Forster to speak about the consolidation of the empire when he returned to Britain. In his frequently quoted address given to the Philosophical Institution of Edinburgh in November 1875 entitled 'Our Colonial Empire', he again proclaimed the essential unity of the English-speaking race and reaffirmed his own faith in closer imperial union:

> I believe that our union with our colonies will not be severed because I believe that we and they will more and more prize this union, and become convinced that it can only be preserved by looking forward to association upon equal terms, in other words, I believe that ... we shall welcome them as our partners in a common and mighty empire. ... Who talks now of casting off the colonies? What more popular cry at present than the preservation of our colonial empire? ... May not we and our colonists together ... transform our colonial empire into a federation of peaceful, industrious, law-abiding commonwealths, so that ... our British brotherhood may ... dwell together in unity?[40]

We have already confirmed how far separatist talk had disappeared by the mid-1870s and had been replaced by imperial federation. Forster's challenge to those critics of empire who still opposed closer union to speak out against the colonial connection was not taken up. But what did his speech reveal about his own imperial ideas and how did he seek to include the United States in his 'British brotherhood'? Clearly Forster's increasing propensity to think and speak in terms of the Anglo-Saxon race owed much to the influence

- Dilke, Greater Britain

upon him of Dilke's *Greater Britain*. Both the terms which he used and the assumptions upon which he based his imperial views were so similar to those of Dilke that mere coincidence can be ruled out. Forster's speeches in the United States and at Edinburgh demonstrate that two broad themes – closer imperial union and Anglo-Saxon unity – aligned themselves in his mind as the twin goals of his political actions during the 1870s. The former included only the white self-governing colonies – such as Canada, New Zealand and the Australian colonies – while the latter referred to close, if undefined, Anglo-American relations which would presage an overarching unity of the English-speaking countries. The two themes served to complement each other. They constituted Forster's Anglo-Saxon family.

Rooted among these motives and influences which shaped Forster's imperial views was his own personal antipathy towards slavery. He had long been a bitter opponent of slavery and had supported the North in the American Civil War. Given a wider British imperial focus, Forster easily extended his particular American concern into the larger arena of the general colonial treatment of subject races. Here he was determined to place Britain's civilising mission upon a solid moral foundation. And this intensely moral basis of his imperial thinking was fused with a typically mid-Victorian belief in the supremacy of the Anglo-Saxon race.[41] Dilke's persuasive arguments were fully utilised. They envisaged an Anglo-Saxon alliance or an English-speaking union which included the United States. The moral and racial bases of his views were lucidly expressed in one memorable passage from his *Greater Britain* which underlined the symbiotic nature of Anglo-American links:

> the English element has given language and history to that land; America offers the English race the moral directorship of the globe by ruling mankind through Saxon institutions and the English tongue. Through America, England is speaking to the world.[42]

Forster's advocacy of a 'confederation' of the English race clearly conformed to the mainstream of mid-Victorian intellectual thinking about empire, but the simple logic of his position compelled him to ask his Edinburgh audience why America's inclusion in this confederation should not also be part of their 'Greater Britain' of the future. In this way he attempted to present closer imperial union and a new Anglo-American relationship as part and parcel of his overall goal of Anglo-Saxon unity in the world.

In 1875 Forster stood practically alone among his Liberal party contemporaries in preaching the federation of the empire based upon English racial unity. At this time his reputation for independence from the demands and pressures of party loyalty was noted within the Liberal party leadership. Already in 1874 George Goschen, the First Lord of the Admiralty, had protested to Gladstone about Forster's independent conduct and complained that he seized 'every occasion to follow his own line in speaking'. The Prime Minister agreed, replying that he, too, was exasperated with Forster's behaviour.[43] And shortly after Forster's Edinburgh discourse on the colonies, Granville, the former Liberal Colonial and Foreign Secretary, confided to Gladstone that Forster was 'more Tory' than he was in relation to the colonies.[44] Reid was correct therefore to stress Forster's relatively isolated position within senior Liberal ranks concerning closer imperial union, but this still did not commit him to very much. His membership of the Royal Colonial Institute in 1875 merely labelled him as an active supporter of closer imperial ties. He did not commit himself to any specific scheme of closer union. How and why, then, did Forster play such a pivotal role in the creation of the Imperial Federation League in 1884? Let us begin our explanation with a short recapitulation of the underlying trend of global change which served to undermine British hegemony in the mid- and late-Victorian years.

No single factor explains the formation of the League in 1884. It owed its appearance to a combination of circumstances and events which occurred in the early 1880s. Clearly the background of international change in the 1870s and early 1880s was crucial to the League's creation and we must acknowledge its significance. The changing world which the British viewed with growing alarm in the 1870s has already been noted, but a decade later these perceived challenges to British interests at home and abroad were intensified. J.E. Tyler summarised the new outlook in very general terms:

> The eighteen-eighties have an importance which is all of their own. ... The necessary interval had by this time elapsed for the new forces, which the keen eye of Disraeli and others had discerned ten years before, to have manifested themselves with unmistakable strength. Their influence upon both British thought and British policy was magnified in consequence. ... It was inevitable that the imperialist revival, itself derived from the motive causes of the great change, should enter upon a period of remarkable development and progress.[45]

According to Tyler, the reason for the League's appearance in 1884 was twofold: first, the increasing activity of foreign powers in areas of the world which threatened the safety and independence of British colonies; and, secondly, the persistence of agricultural and industrial depressions in the United Kingdom during the late 1870s and the early 1880s. In short, the potential threats of the 1870s had become actual challenges in the 1880s. The Liberal MP, Sydney Buxton, foreshadowed the later arguments of Tyler when he wrote in the 1880s that it was foreign affairs which dominated these years and that it was foreign policy and 'foreign complications, wars and rumours of wars which embarrassed our finances and injured our trade'. His opinion was that 'all these dangers and adversities ... fostered the feeling that the different parts of the great British Empire could and should be more closely knit together by some system of Federation'.[46]

But the existence of 'foreign complications' does not, by itself, tell us very much. The antagonism between Britain and France over the New Hebrides issue, the British occupation of Egypt, the Sudan imbroglio, and the protests from New Zealand and the Australian colonies prompted by German designs on New Guinea and the Samoan Islands certainly fuelled British anxieties and fears in the early 1880s. However, the Gladstone government's own equivocation and incompetence in its foreign and colonial policies was also a contributory factor in the League's formation. A series of foreign, imperial and domestic problems bedevilled Gladstone's second administration from its very inception in 1880. Personal rivalries and antipathies within the government were aggravated by policy disputes and a clutch of resignations arising principally from Gladstone's decisions about Ireland and Egypt. Indeed, Forster himself resigned from the government as Chief Secretary for Ireland in 1882 in protest at Gladstone's personal bargain with the Irish leader, Charles Stewart Parnell. From this moment he became a confirmed opponent of Gladstone's policies in Ireland and in Egypt. Like many Liberals, he regarded them as damaging to British imperial interests.

One notable Liberal critic of Gladstone's government, Hugh Oakeley Arnold-Forster, was Forster's nephew and adopted son. As one of the two Liberal candidates for Devonport in 1882, Arnold-Forster resigned swiftly in 1883. He was determined to expose the deficiencies in Gladstone's foreign and imperial policies, and he was especially trenchant in his attack upon the government's colonial and naval policies. In an article entitled 'The Liberal idea and the colonies' which appeared in *The Nineteenth Century* for 1883, Arnold-Forster castigated the Liberal government for its neglect of colonial sensitivities and pointed to 'an almost perfect opening for the display of the Liberal statesmanship of the future' which could bring 'the people of this country into close political contact with men of their own race who are seeking the same goal'.[47] His abrupt resignation was accompanied by the warning that 'it may be only a matter of time before this Ministry estranges the colonies and possibly fools away the Empire'.[48]

Arnold-Forster's penetrative criticisms of the Liberal government's colonial policy were extended during 1884 to include its naval policy. In a series of articles which were published by W.T. Stead in the *Pall Mall Gazette* during the autumn of 1884 and entitled 'The truth about the navy', Arnold-Forster created such public concern that the Gladstone government was persuaded to increase naval expenditure in 1885.[49] Thus it was not only war scares and the evidence of intensified foreign activity in areas of the world which threatened British imperial interests that helped to distil the idea of imperial federation into a practical form in 1884. The Liberal government's inability to make firm decisions and its failure to take decisive action in its foreign and colonial policies in particular must also be added to the conjunction of events and circumstances which enabled the imperial federation movement to make organisational progress.

Economic developments also contributed to the changing mood of public unease which characterised late-Victorian society. The bad harvests which had played a significant part in the electoral defeat of Disraeli in 1880 returned to compound the difficulties facing Gladstone. Along with the commercial and industrial depression which hit the United Kingdom during these years, the agricultural recession created an air of stagnation and disillusion. One symptom of the general malaise was the appearance, in May 1881, of the National Fair Trade League. This new political organisation, founded in London and strongly supported by leading figures within the Conservative party, campaigned for reforms in Britain's traditional trading practices. It questioned the sense in pursuing Cobdenite doctrines of free trade in a world where foreign states had adopted protectionist policies. It also favoured imperial preference in order to combat foreign trade rivalry and it thus foreshadowed the commercial federationists of the Imperial Federation League who advocated an imperial customs union or *Zollverein* during the late 1880s. Indeed, many of those who were involved in the Fair Trade League became active members of the Imperial Federation League. Frederick Young, for example, was an ardent federationist who was the Honorary Secretary of the Royal Colonial Institute during 1874–86, while another fair trader, Sir Alexander Galt, was Canada's first High Commissioner in London during 1880–83 and an early member of the Executive Committee of the Imperial Federation League.

Fair trade, like imperial federation, was a defensive reaction and response to the erosion of British hegemony in commerce and trade. D.C. Platt wrote in 1968:

> the renewal of the demand for Protection after the 1870s was not intended, as in the past, to secure a special position for British manufacturers, but to ensure equality of treatment.[50]

But the Fair Trade League was an awkward vehicle for the promotion of imperial federation. Many federationists were, after all, staunch free traders who did not accept that imperial federation necessarily involved a fundamental change in Britain's economic system. And among many of those commercial federationists who advocated either some form of imperial preference or a customs union for the empire, protection *per se* was only a means to an end. Their overriding goal remained the closer union of the empire.

These important foreign, colonial and domestic factors were elegantly synthesised by the most outstanding academic luminary within the ranks of the federationist movement in the early 1880s. Sir John Seeley, who was Regius Professor of Modern History at Cambridge University from 1869 until 1895, lent invaluable intellectual weight to the arguments in favour of imperial federation. In 1881–82 he delivered two series of lectures at Cambridge which, published in 1883 under the title *The Expansion of England*, enjoyed tremendous popularity among empire enthusiasts. Bodelsen claimed that Seeley's book sold 80,000 copies during the first two years of its publication and it is obvious that his belief in the racial superiority of 'Anglo-Saxon unity' touched a responsive chord among many Victorians.[51] Seeley's own interpretation of history enabled him to demonstrate how, by consolidating the empire, Britain could establish a new relationship with the white self-governing colonies which would guarantee her future as a great power. He was therefore able to present a convincing case for closer imperial union as a means whereby Britain's perceived decline in the world could be halted and reversed. But Seeley's persuasive arguments and compelling logic were not confined to intellectual pursuits. He not only provided a firm scholarly basis for the formation of the Imperial Federation League, but he also took an active part in its work, becoming a Council member in 1884 and sitting on the League's Executive Committee as the leader of the Cambridge branch.

As an admirable statement of the case for closer union, Seeley's *Expansion of England* succeeded in popularising the theme of imperial unity in the early 1880s, but it did not create it. In a review of Seeley's book, John Morley claimed just this when he wrote:

> The chances of the time have contributed to make Mr. Seeley's book ... singularly opportune and have given to a philosophical study the actuality of a political pamphlet. ... Mr. Seeley's book has thus come upon a tide of popular interest.[52]

Seeley's contribution to the revival of ideas of closer union, then, must be placed in correct perspective. These ideas, which can be identified in the writings of James Froude at least as far back as 1870, were already in circulation as a result of the conjunction of foreign, imperial and domestic circumstances which have been outlined above.[53] But if Seeley's own imperial ideas lacked originality, they nonetheless possessed an attractive simplicity and were presented forcibly and fluently.

He viewed the various challenges to British hegemony in the late-Victorian years as symptomatic of an inevitable historical process whereby old established states were threatened by new states which sought to surpass them in power, size and influence. Britain, in his opinion, could not stem the tide of foreign rivalry but it had the capacity to come to terms with it. Britain could salvage her future as a great power by tightening the bonds of her existing empire. Seeley's book thus identified the problem and supplied the solution. Far from helping to shape the climate of the times, then, Seeley's *Expansion of England* was itself a product of the new outlook of the decade.

The idea of forming the Imperial Federation League appears to have been that of Francis de Labilliere, a Victorian expatriate living in London who had been active in the field of closer union since the 1860s. We have already encountered this Antipodean figure; he was one of the earliest members of the Royal Colonial Institute and he was prominent among those who had worked relentlessly to promote the federationist cause within the Institute. He summarised some of his campaigning in the following terms:

> The next step forward was the formation of the League for the special advocacy of Imperial Federation. It was evident, when the principle of maintaining the unity of the empire had been so widely accepted, and the idea of its federal union adopted

by so many people, that the time had arrived for a further advance. Accordingly, early in 1884, in a conversation with Sir John Colomb, I suggested the formation of a society with the special object of promoting the policy of Imperial Federation; and we determined to seek the co-operation of some whose sympathies we knew to be warmest in the cause.[54]

Labilliere's idea was translated into practical action by the activities of a small coterie of influential and well-connected men who maintained regular contact with each other via their membership of the Royal Colonial Institute. Some, like Labilliere, William Westgarth and J. Dennistoun Wood, were colonial expatriates living in London, but others, like Colomb, Frederick Young and Sir George Baden-Powell, were British-born empire enthusiasts who supported the basic idea from a mixture of motives. Sir John Colomb, for example, had been a fellow of the Royal Colonial Institute since 1872 and he was a prolific writer on the importance of British naval defence, producing his famous *Defence of Great and Greater Britain* in 1880, while Baden-Powell had been private secretary to Sir George Ferguson Bowen during the latter's governorship of Victoria between 1873 and 1879, and he had also served in the West Indies during 1882–84 as a British Commissioner investigating colonial administration. Colomb hoped that the new League would help to strengthen imperial defence while Baden-Powell believed that it might alert people to the growth of colonial self-government which he opposed.

We can of course never know whether or not Labilliere's conversation with Colomb was the result of a chance meeting. In such circumstances the precise moment of elite decision-making is impossible to determine. What is clear is the importance of the Royal Colonial Institute to the growth of the imperial federation movement. It will be recalled that the idea of closer union had been nurtured in the Institute during the 1870s and the small provisional committee, which Labilliere and Colomb formed in April 1884 to make the crucial preliminary arrangements for creating the new organisation, held all of its meetings in the Institute's rooms in the Strand. Forster was a member of this pivotal group of empire federalists which ensured that the foundation conference of the League, held at the Westminster Palace Hotel on 29 July 1884, was well attended. Here the imperial federation movement transformed itself into a tangible political organisation.

When Forster addressed the opening conference as the chairman in July 1884, the number of prominent people from the political, business and intellectual milieux who assembled in the hotel was an early indication of the potential strength of the new League. Senior politicians from both major political parties in the United Kingdom rubbed shoulders with leading colonial figures and influential colonial expatriates. Besides the long-standing supporters of closer imperial union – Labilliere, Young, Colomb and Westgarth – Lord Rosebery and the Marquis of Normanby, former Governor of Nova Scotia, Queensland, New Zealand and Victoria, attended together with a host of British MPs – James Bryce, Joseph Cowen, Sir Henry Holland,

W.H. Smith, Edward Stanhope and Sir Eardley Wilmot. Among the notable colonial contingent were D'Alton McCarthy, Oliver Mowatt (Premier of Ontario), Sir Charles Tupper (second Canadian High Commissioner), and two agents-general, Captain Charles Mills of Cape Colony and Sir Saul Samuel of New South Wales. In total 104 people attended the foundation conference and over 80 letters of support from prominent politicians, including Sir Michael Hicks Beach, Lord Dunraven, Lord George Hamilton and Sir Henry Drummond Wolff, were received.[55]

This number, by itself, was quite small, but since the members were relatively important and influential public figures – among the leaders of British and colonial societies – it represented a group in the United Kingdom which was potentially a very potent force for almost any cause it might wish to promote. The conference lacked a Gladstone and a Salisbury but, as Tyler commented, 'the names pointed to something more than a hole-and-corner meeting of enthusiastic nonentities'.[56] Forster's role in these proceedings was quietly effective. His political leadership ensured that the main resolution of the conference was simple: 'that in order to secure the permanent unity of the Empire, some form of Federation is essential'.[57] He noted in his diary that the July conference was 'a real success' and, although it underlined the vagueness of the movement's goals, The Times referred to it as 'a sign of the times'.[58]

The League received its public baptism on 18 November 1884. Meeting in the Westminster Palace Hotel – a familiar venue for such conventions – the second conference was similar in size and composition to its July predecessor. The various aims and resolutions of the new League boiled down to one simple goal, namely, the permanent unity of the empire by some form of federation which would not interfere with the existing rights of local parliaments in the conduct of local affairs. Beyond this statement, Forster trod warily. He spoke warmly of 'an alliance for mutual defence' which he took to be 'absolutely necessary'. But he refused to be pushed into the firing line on the highly controversial issue of British trading practices. And although the delicate question of colonial tariffs was broached at the conference, Forster wisely confined his remarks to the innocuous promise of 'more trade between England and her colonies than would exist if there was a separation'.[59] On the similarly difficult question of schemes for the federation of the empire, Forster was equally tactful. He was perfectly aware that there existed as many schemes as there were individuals to propound them. His own priority was to avoid any blueprint for imperial federation which would compromise the League at its outset and irreconcilably divide the membership. Already, at the July conference, he had taken evasive action with the word 'federation':

> What we want is that, agreeing as we do in principle, we should so express that principle as not to give rise to misconception here or in the colonies. In using the word 'federation', we do not by any means bind ourselves to a particular form of Federal Parliament. It may be effected by representation in the Imperial Parliament,

or it may be by a Council of Representatives of the Colonies. We want to convey the notion that ultimately, hereafter, there must be a union, in some form or other, of England with her colonies, on terms of perfect equality to the colonies as well as to England; and I do not know of any word which will better express that notion than the word 'Federation'.[60]

Coming from the movement's guiding spirit, this was an important speech. It suggested that the name of the organisation was a misnomer, inappropriately identifying imperial federation with a much more general and non-committal interpretation of closer union. However, this was the price which had to be paid for action. As a practical man of affairs, Forster was keen that something should be done. He was undeterred by the constraints of terminological accuracy and the temptation to formulate concrete proposals:

> I do not think that it follows that it may be years before we arrive at some conclusion; but it would be most unwise to take the thing into our own hands at once and to sketch out any particular plan.[61]

With the League formally launched, Forster's overriding task was to build up a solid membership. In the early years the League exuded boundless confidence and optimism. It had an enthusiastic and impressive clientele of recognised public figures, MPs from both British political parties and many eminent colonial adherents. In the 1880s its prospects for the future seemed assured and in 1885 Forster wrote optimistically that the movement was growing and that 'the idea possesses men's minds'.[62]

The translation of this idea into practical politics meant that Forster also had to win the argument in support of imperial federation. In two articles advocating and explaining imperial federation in the February and March 1885 editions of *The Nineteenth Century*, the League's Chairman summarised the views and opinions which he had originally expressed at the July and November conferences a year earlier. Entitled 'Imperial Federation' and 'A Few More Words on Imperial Federation' respectively, Forster's articles were an amalgam of principle, expediency and emotion. His chief purpose was to alert informed opinion both to the merits and the urgency of the cause, but he also seized the opportunity to rebuke the Liberal government for its 'halting, half-hearted uncertainty' in failing to give an authoritive lead to closer imperial union.[63]

The basic premise of Forster's argument was that the colonial policy of the Gladstone government amounted to a national disaster. Unless it was quickly reversed the damage would be irreparable and the colonies would be lost forever. The moment had arrived for a bold, constructive initiative. Forster spelled out what he felt was required: 'an organisation for mutual defence and for common control of foreign policy'. Characteristically he declined to fill in the exact details of what this organisation would look like and how it would be instituted. However, he believed that its actual form 'must change from time to time according to the increase of the strength of the colonies, whether absolute or relative'. This was a novel suggestion. In seeking to accommodate the changing interests, needs and relative capacities of the colonies, Forster's remarks anticipated by forty years the thinking of Arthur Balfour who, in the 1920s, argued in a similar vein. Forster was far too adroit to commit himself to a detailed scheme in these articles. Certainly the 'ultimate form of Federation' would have to assume a parliamentary shape: it would be a new and supreme Imperial Parliament replete with subordinate local parliaments 'as that which Congress bears to the American state legislatures or the German Reichstag to the Prussian or Bavarian Landtags'.[64] But this was a vision of the future. From the standpoint of 1885 he was much less sanguine about what could actually be achieved. Constitutional reform of such magnitude was unlikely to win much support from within the British political establishment. Gladstone was privately hostile to imperial federation which he dismissed as 'chimerical if not little short of nonsensical'.[65]

Given that the practical possibilities seemed pitifully few, Forster resorted to what he construed as a halfway house towards the federation of the empire, namely, a Board of Advice along the lines of the India Council. This had the tremendous advantage of practicability. It was both familiar and feasible. Grafted upon existing government structures, it would involve a minimum of fuss. Such a modest proposal would serve two purposes: first, it would be an expedient stepping-stone towards the larger goal of imperial federation and, secondly, it would enable the League to present a concrete scheme to the public. The Board of Advice would be a federal instalment designed to pave the way for an ultimately fully-fledged federal union in the future. This idea of introducing a federal element into the administration of British imperial affairs was certainly not new when Forster discussed it in his two articles. It had, for example, already been canvassed in 1879 by the third Earl Grey and such nostrums were commonplace among empire enthusiasts during these years.[66] But institutional innovation was never likely to cause more than a ripple of public interest. Rather it was Forster's recommendations regarding British trade policy which were guaranteed to arouse public consternation.

In his advocacy of an Imperial *Zollverein* – a customs union for the empire – Forster was on very difficult ground. He recognised the right of the colonies to pursue protectionist trade policies, even against the mother country, if they wished, but he claimed that a Board of Advice would actually combat such actions by argument and persuasion. Indeed, it would be instrumental in advancing imperial free trade. Forster, who was no guardian of Cobdenite beliefs, felt that his 'federal instalment' could meet the objections both of the staunch free traders and of those within League ranks who were increasingly vociferous in the cause of a commercial union of the empire. This was, nonetheless, an awkward position to have to defend. However the idea of an imperial free trade area was promoted and packaged, it could not disguise the reality of being a significant departure from the conventional orthodoxy of universal free trade so sacrosanct to the late-Victorians. The growing challenge to the free trade principle had not then acquired sufficient strength to force a change in official trade policy. This difficult predicament which confronted Forster in the mid-1880s foreshadowed the later controversy over the thorny question of tariff reform promoted by Joseph Chamberlain in the early years of the twentieth century. Forster was on much safer ground when he confined his attentions to imperial defence. This was the subject of his second article published in March 1885.

The March 1885 article on imperial federation was really only a rider to the first. It was prompted by an event which he felt reinforced the case for a Board of Advice. In the early months of 1885 the British government received offers of colonial military assistance in its protracted conflict with the Mahdi in the Sudan. Forster viewed this 'volunteer' aid from Canada and an official contingent of troops from several of the Australian colonies as a signal declaration that the United Kingdom and the colonies were 'one country for the purposes of defence'; it was real 'progress towards Imperial Federation'. The colonies appeared to have taken a momentous step which was 'in advance of a Board of Advice'. Forster envisaged a popular demand at home and in the colonies for a special conference of the British and colonial governments to discuss the reorganisation of the whole British imperial defence system. The colonies had expressed their own collective belief in imperial unity by deeds; Forster was perfectly happy to let such deeds speak for themselves since they assisted the federationist cause 'far more effectually than any possible scheme'. In conclusion, the League's Chairman claimed that 'the ultimate form of Federation' would also have to include 'participation in foreign policy'.[67] His final recommendation was to formalise consultation between the British and colonial governments in matters of common foreign policy. Here again Forster's prescriptions anticipated future British imperial institutional developments. The creation of the imperial and colonial conference system which was first instituted in 1887 symbolised this formal consultation which evolved slowly into shared decision-making and culminated in the Statute of Westminster in 1931.

This survey of Forster's political career as a pioneer of imperial federation shows that in some respects he was remarkably imaginative and innovative. But it also demonstrates quite clearly that he was no visionary. We should certainly not exaggerate his prescience. Many of his ideas and arguments derived directly from broad themes which had circulated during the mid-Victorian era. The threat of foreign powers, the growth of trade rivalry and protection, and the political impact of new technological inventions were popular themes which haunted federationist thinking. Forster was acutely sensitive to contemporary change and his support for imperial federation in the mid-1880s amounted to a plea for action. He was fully aware of the alleged obstacles to closer union and he clearly anticipated most of the objections and the hostility which his views provoked. But Forster was a slave neither to historical precedent nor to revered doctrines. His deep-rooted belief in the progressive forces of change at work in the empire combined with his unshakable faith in the liberal ideas of self-development and self-determination predisposed him to experiment and made him an optimist in his conviction that statesmen could both educate and mobilise public opinion. Imperial federation was just such a great cause which merited public thought and action. A detailed analysis of Forster's ideas and arguments in his articles certainly does not reveal any attempt at intellectual elaboration. But to the extent that he was able to make the underlying connections between intra- and extra-imperial developments in the 1880s and to cement them to his solid liberal beliefs, there was unquestionably a distinct unity of thought in his advocacy of imperial federation.

Leaving aside intellectual analysis, Forster believed in the capacity of an idea to move men's hearts and minds. He remained convinced that imperial federation, however vague, could capture the public imagination. In one of the last letters that he wrote, during the late summer of 1885, he confirmed to Sir George Ferguson Bowen that the idea must not be set back by any 'premature plan', and he insisted upon discovering 'the real views and wishes of leading colonists'. The following remarks were among the last surviving evidence of his own views on how the League should proceed in order to achieve its stated objectives:

> My own impression is that, at first at any rate, we had better aim at concert among the Governments, rather than at an Imperial Parliament. ... We must remember that in order to realise Federation we want only (1) an organisation for common defence (2) a common foreign policy. Practically, great steps have been recently made; not merely as regards defence, thanks to Australian aid, but as regards foreign affairs. I do not believe that any Colonial Secretary will in future venture to disregard any large self-governing colony in negotiating with any foreign government in matters affecting such colony.[68]

Forster's ultimate goal remained a new federal parliament for the empire. He wanted an 'Imperial Parliamentary Union'. But no timetable was ever considered for its attainment. Colonial military aid was deemed a significant advance towards an integrated imperial defence system. Colonial actions had determined British decisions in the South Pacific and contemporary events seemed to march towards imperial federation. When the ill-fated Liberal government finally collapsed in June 1885 Forster viewed the event with an understandable sense of relief. It offered the possibility of more constructive imperial relations. And when the first annual meeting of the Imperial Federation League met in the Mansion House, London under the celebrated presidency of the Lord Mayor on 15 February 1886, the circumstances for Forster's 'great work', as he referred to it, seemed propitious. But the progress achieved and the optimistic expectations of British federalists received a serious setback when, in April 1886, Forster died suddenly. He left behind what appeared to be a thriving political organisation. What had been little more than an idle dream only fifteen years before had become a matter of practical politics by 1886. No plan of federation had been agreed but the movement in favour of closer imperial union had grown and assumed a tangible institutional shape in the form of the new League. For much of this, Forster could justifiably take the credit. Both his dedication to the grand cause of imperial federation and his sound judgement as the first League chairman mark him out as a much more important political figure and early 'Liberal Imperialist' than the standard commentaries of Bodelsen and Tyler seem to indicate.

What, then, are we to understand by Reid's designation of Forster as the 'first Liberal Imperialist'? Clearly Forster was not the first Liberal to value empire. Nor did Reid use the label to describe Forster as a direct forerunner of the 'national efficiency' group of Liberal imperialists led by Lord Rosebery at the turn of the century. Reid's pious biography of Forster is really an apologia of his life and political career, and we must be careful in the way that we interpret it. He was not making a carefully analysed historical assessment when he used the phrase. For a serious assessment of what the label meant, we must look at Tyler's historical portrayal of Forster. In his brief survey of Forster's imperial ideas, Tyler referred to his idea of marshalling and making operative British imperial power as a way of sustaining the forces of liberalism and freedom. This was a 'Liberal Imperialism'. Tyler claimed correctly that imperial federation meant more to Forster than just the consolidation of British power in a more fiercely competitive world. It also symbolised 'the union of forces of freedom in a world given over to militarism and aggression'. It is precisely here that Forster's liberalism comes into sharp focus. He believed that the British empire was the greatest physical and moral force for good in the world and his overriding passion was to defend and maintain 'the vigour of the forces of liberalism and freedom'.[69] His gradual commitment to imperial federation from about 1870 to his death in 1886, then, was based upon his firm conviction that to bind the white self-governing empire closer together was to strengthen it and, in turn, to invigorate and sustain those very forces of liberalism and freedom which constituted the essence of his political beliefs. It was a circular argument in which each of the parts was logically interrelated.

Given this liberal view of empire, it becomes clear why Forster should have seen in federation the solution to his quest. Close analysis of his speeches and articles proves that he never addressed himself to the terminological debate which surrounded imperial federation. He was no great Liberal intellectual. But Forster did have a firm grasp of what the federal principle meant: it provided a form of government which promoted and preserved his liberal faith in self-determination, self-development and self-control in public affairs. It would satisfy the twin requirements of liberty and equality among and between self-governing communities. In this sense his own understanding of federal government sat comfortably with the views of the major liberal intellectuals of his age. Neither Edward Freeman nor Goldwin Smith would have found much to challenge in these beliefs. And Forster's Dilkean pre-conceptions concerning the unity of the English-speaking peoples – with all of its moral content and racial bias – conformed to the mainstream of liberal intellectual thinking in the late-Victorian years. It was only when Forster used the word 'imperial' to qualify 'federation' that he was confronted by a variety of difficult theoretical inconsistencies. But even at this level of debate Forster was not entirely isolated. Most of his assumptions about the white self-governing empire were, after all, synonymous with those of James Froude and Sir John Seeley.

What emerges from this rehabilitation of William Edward Forster is the picture of a senior Liberal statesman who was no stranger to controversy and who, as an early Liberal imperialist, was consistent in his imperial views and genuinely committed to the cause of imperial federation. He understood precisely what federation meant and he championed it as both the instrument and the goal of his political beliefs. The origins of Forster's imperialism and the motives which drove him fervently to support the federal cause were rooted in his perspective of the British empire as fulfilling a great civilising mission in the world. The essentially practical nature of his mind propelled him to popularise the fundamental 'idea' of imperial federation regardless of the many profound theoretical objections to it. This reappraisal of Forster's political career suggests that he should be remembered not only as an architect of educational reform and a renegade from the party of Gladstone, but also as a major apostle of imperial federation. We will turn now to examine both the theory and the practice of imperial federation by examining the formidable intellectual challenge of Edward Freeman and by looking in detail at the activities both of the Imperial Federation League and of its successor, the Round Table Movement. In terms of political ideas, imperial problems and elite activism they underline the continuity of the British federal tradition.

Notes

1. Bulpitt, J. (1983), *Territory and Power in the United Kingdom*, Manchester, Manchester University Press, chapter 3.
2. Ibid., chapter 4.
3. Arthur first used the term in *The London Quarterly Review*, I, (December 1853), 550. See Burt, A.L. (1913), *Imperial Architects*, Oxford, Oxford University Press, 103–14.
4. Cheng, S.M. (1931), *Schemes for the Federation of the British Empire*, New York, Columbia University Press.
5. Martin, G. (1973), 'Empire Federalism and Imperial Parliamentary Union, 1820–1870', *Historical Journal*, XVI, 65–92. See also his 'The Idea of Imperial Federation', in R. Hyam and G. Martin (1975), *Reappraisals in British Imperial History*, London, Macmillan, chapter 6.
6. Martin, G., (1973), 'Empire Federalism', 65–6.
7. Ibid., 66.
8. Ibid., 65.

9. Burgess, M. (1983), 'Imperial Federation: Continuity and Change in British Imperial Ideas, 1869–1871', *New Zealand Journal of History*, 17 (1), 60–80.

10. See Reese, T. (1968), *The History of the Royal Commonwealth Society, 1868–1968*, London, Oxford University Press.

11. Bodelsen, C.A. (1924), *Studies in Mid-Victorian Imperialism* (second edn), London & Copenhagen, Heinemann, 31.

12. 'Imperial Federalism', *The Contemporary Review*, XVI (January 1871), 165–88, and 'An Imperial Confederation', *The Contemporary Review*, XVII (April 1871), 60–79.

13. On the subject of mid-Victorian imperialism and its reappraisal, see Knox, B.A. (1973), 'Reconsidering Mid-Victorian Imperialism', *Journal of Imperial and Commonwealth History*, I, 155–72, and Eldridge, C.C. (1980), *Victorian Imperialism*, London, Macmillan.

14. Eldridge, C.C. (1980), *Victorian Imperialism*, 82.

15. For the attendance list, see the little-known *Discussions on Colonial Questions* (1872), London.

16. Ibid., 72–83.

17. *Hansard*, House of Commons (HC), 26 April 1870, 200, 1817–1908.

18. *Hansard*, HC, 12 May 1871, 206, 750–70.

19. *Hansard*, HC, 31 May 1872, 211, 912–38, and 28 February 1873, 211, 1102–23.

20. On Disraeli's imperial ideas, see Eldridge, C.C. (1973), *England's Mission: The Imperial Idea in the Age of Gladstone and Disraeli*, London, Macmillan, 172–205, and Harcourt, F. (1980), 'Disraeli's Imperialism, 1866–68: A Question of Timing', *Historical Journal*, XXIII, 87–109.

21. See Paul, H. (1905), *The Life of J.A. Froude*, London, Sir Issac Pitman & Sons, and Burrow, J.W. (1983), *A Liberal Descent: Victorian Historians and the English Past*, Cambridge, Cambridge University Press, 231–85.

22. For Labilliere's paper, see the *Proceedings of the Royal Colonial Institute (PRCI)* (1874–75), 6, 36–85.

23. For Staveley-Hill's paper, see *PRCI* (1879–80), 11, 136–77, and for Labilliere's paper, see *PRCI* (1880–81), 12, 346–91.

24. Bodelsen, C.A. (1924), *Studies in Mid-Victorian Imperialism*, 131, and Tyler, J.E. (1938), *The Struggle for Imperial Unity, 1868–1895*, London, Longman, 75–6 and 209.

25. See, for example, Hyam, R. and Martin, G. (1975), *Reappraisals in British Imperial History*, chapters 5 and 6. In the absence of any private papers, historians have had to rely heavily upon Forster's official biography written by his great admirer, Sir Thomas Wemyss Reid. See Reid, T.W. (1888), *The Life of the Rt. Hon. William Edward Forster*, 2 vols, London, Chapman and Hall Ltd.

26. Reid, S.J. (ed.) (1905), *Memoirs of Sir Thomas Wemyss Reid, 1842–1885*, London, Cassell & Co., 318.

27. Reid, T.W. (1888), *Life of Forster*, I, 308.

28. Ibid., 138.

29. Ibid., 140.

30. On Forster's character, see Lucy, Sir H. (1919), *Men and Manner in Parliament*, London, T. Fisher Unwin, 85–6; West, Sir A. (1899), *Recollections, 1832–1886*, 2 vols, London, Smith, Elder & Co., II, 82; and Marindin, G.E. (1896), *The Letters of Frederic, Lord Blachford*, London, John Murray, 258.

31. Reid, T.W. (1888), *Life of Forster*, I, 139–40.

32. Ibid., 34.

33. Forster to his wife, 11 January 1866, quoted in ibid., I, 391.

34. *The Times*, 18 January 1870.

35. Dilke, Sir C.W. (1868), *Greater Britain: A Record of Travel in English-Speaking Countries during 1866 and 1867*, 2 vols, London, Macmillan & Co.

36. Forster to Sir Arthur Helps, 26 August 1870, quoted in Reid, T.W. (1888), *Life of Forster*, I, 510–11.

37. See, for example, Forster's remarks in the House of Commons on 22 July 1870 during the parliamentary debate on the Elementary Education Bill, *Hansard*, HC, 264, 757–62.

38. Reid, T.W. (1888), *Life of Forster*, II, 68.

39. Like Dilke, Froude believed in the unity of the white Anglo-Saxon race and canvassed his views most clearly in two famous articles entitled respectively 'England and her Colonies' and 'The Colonies once more' which were published in *Fraser's Magazine* in 1870. They were subsequently republished in 1890 in his *Short Studies on Great Subjects*, 4 vols, London, Longmans, Green & Co. He also published his *Oceana, or England and her Colonies* in 1886, Longmans & Co. and became Regius Professor of Modern History at Oxford during 1892–94.

40. Forster, W.E. (1875), 'Our Colonial Empire', Edinburgh, unpublished, 5.

41. On the broad subject of mid-Victorian beliefs in Anglo-Saxon racial superiority, the following sources can be read with profit, Parker, C.J.W. (1981), 'The Failure of Liberal Racialism: The Racial Ideas of E.A. Freeman', *Historical Journal*, 24, 825–46; Burrow, J.W. (1983), *A Liberal Descent*; and Collini, S. et al. (1983), *That Noble Science of Politics: A Study in Nineteenth Century Intellectual History*, Cambridge, Cambridge University Press.

42. Dilke, Sir C.W. (1868), *Greater Britain*, 227.

43. Goschen to Gladstone, 15 June 1874, quoted in Spinner, T.J. (1973), *George Joachim Goschen*, Cambridge, Cambridge University Press, 45.

44. Granville to Gladstone, 16 December 1875, in Ramm, A. (ed.) (1952), *The Political Correspondence of Mr. Gladstone and Lord Granville, 1868–1876*, London, Camden Society, 81, 478.

45. Tyler, J.E. (1938), *The Struggle for Imperial Unity*, 27.

46. Buxton, S. (1888), *Finance and Politics: An Historical Study, 1783–1885*, 2 vols, London, John Murray, I, 302–3. Buxton was Gladstonian Liberal MP for the Poplar Division of Tower Hamlets, 1886–1914 and Under-Secretary of State for the Colonies, 1892–95.

47. Arnold-Forster, H.O. (September 1883), 'The Liberal idea and the colonies', *The Nineteenth Century*, XIV, 391.

48. Arnold-Forster, H.O. (1910), *The Rt. Hon. Hugh Oakeley Arnold-Forster: A Memoir. By his Wife*, London, Edward Arnold, 50–1.

49. Whyte, F. (1925), *The Life of W.T. Stead*, 2 vols, London, Jonathan Cape, I, 145–55 and Arnold-Forster, (Wife), *A Memoir*, 52–61.

50. Platt, D.C. (1968), *Finance, Trade and Politics in British Foreign Policy, 1815–1914*, Oxford, Oxford University Press, 83.

51. Bodelsen, C.A. (1924), *Studies in Mid-Victorian Imperialism*, fn 5, 151. On Seeley's life, see Wormell, D. (1980), *Sir John Seeley and the Uses of History*, Cambridge, Cambridge University Press.

52. Morley, J. (February 1884), 'The Expansion of England', *MacMillan's Magazine*, XLIX, 241–2.

53. For sources on James Anthony Froude, see note 39 above.

54. Labilliere de, F. (1894), *Federal Britain*, London, Macmillan, 28.

55. For the attendance list, see the *Report of the Westminster Palace Hotel Conference, 29 July 1884* (1884), Rhodes House Library, Oxford, 9–24.

56. Tyler, J.E., (1938), *The Struggle for Imperial Unity*, fn 5, 108.

57. *Report of the Westminster Palace Hotel Conference*, 54.

58. *The Times*, 30 July 1884.

59. *Report of the Adjourned Conference, 18 November 1884* (1884), Imperial Federation Pamphlets, Rhodes House Library, Oxford, 12–13.

60. *Report of the Westminster Palace Hotel Conference*, 46.

61. *Report of the Adjourned Conference*, 12.

62. Forster to Sir George Bowen, undated, quoted in Reid, T.W. (1888), *Life of Forster*, II, 609.

63. Forster, W.E. (February 1885), 'Imperial Federation', *The Nineteenth Century*, XVII, 216.

64. Ibid., 204–7.

65. Sir Edward Hamilton, Gladstone's private secretary, recorded the Prime Minister's words in his diary on the day following the official launching of the League, 19 November 1884, *Hamilton Papers*, British Museum, London, Add. Mss. 48638, 58.

66. Grey, Lord (June 1879), 'How Shall We Retain The Colonies?', *The Nineteenth Century*, V, 937–54.

67. Forster, W.E. (March 1885), 'A Few More Words on Imperial Federation', *The Nineteenth Century*, XVII, 552–6.

68. Forster to Sir George Bowen, dated 'August 1885', in Lane-Poole, S. (1889), *Thirty Years of Colonial Government: A Selection from the Despatches and Letters of Sir George Ferguson Bowen*, 2 vols, London, Longmans & Co., II, 359–60.

69. Tyler, J.E. (1938), *The Struggle for Imperial Unity*, 209; Bodelsen, C.A. (1924), *Studies in Mid-Victorian Imperialism*, 131. Forster was also described as a 'Liberal Imperialist' in Reese, T.R. (1968), *The History of the Royal Commonwealth Society, 1868–1968*, 68.

CHAPTER 3

Imperial federation: theory and practice, 1885–1917

Edward Freeman and imperial federation

We have already seen that the idea of 'imperial federation' was vague but simple to grasp. It committed its adherents to nothing more than strengthening the bonds of empire. Most of those public men who rallied to the cause of imperial federation during the 1870s and 1880s were not genuine believers in an imperial reorganisation founded upon federal principles. The wide diversity of opinion within the British political elite as to what constituted 'imperial federation' did not permit it. Most League members never gave serious thought to the terminological meaning and analytical implications of applying federal principles to a major reorganisation of the British empire. Those who did so, like William Forster and Francis de Labilliere, were a tiny minority within the League. The deliberate policy of studied vagueness which was the hallmark of the League during its infancy, however, soon caught up with the movement.

Within a year of the League's establishment the first signs of a serious intellectual confrontation and undisguised academic hostility were manifested when Edward Freeman's article entitled 'Imperial Federation' appeared in the April 1885 edition of *MacMillan's Magazine*.[1] In hindsight this important and influential article was a milestone in the evolution of British federal ideas during the late nineteenth century because it presaged the great academic debate about federalism and empire which persisted up until 1917. Indeed, it is possible today to look back upon this intellectual debate on the consolidation of the British empire during the heyday of the League as integral to the distinctly British tradition of federalism. The epic debate about imperial federation, we are reminded, should be seen as part of a century of British federal ideas which links empire, Ireland and Europe in a continuous, unbroken tradition. Let us turn now to Edward Freeman's swingeing foray against imperial federation in 1885 and see how he unwittingly enriched the emergent federal tradition in the United Kingdom.

As an established historian of some considerable repute and the new Regius Professor of Modern History at Oxford, Freeman had already devoted some of his time to an historical study of federalism which, though never wholly completed, was nevertheless published in 1863 as a single volume.[2] Convinced that historical study did more than anything else to lead the mind to a definite political creed, and recognising his own predilections in foreign and domestic politics, Freeman had set himself the task of exhibiting the actual working of federal government throughout history rather than attempting to deal with the subject as a contemporary reality which merited practical examination. However, this particular approach to the subject still demanded a definition of federalism if only for historical purposes. He concluded that a federal union was: 'The most finished and the most artificial production of political ingenuity':

> A Federal Union will form one state in relation to other powers, but many states as regards its internal administration. This complete division of sovereignty we may look upon as essential to the absolute perfection of the Federal ideal.[3]

Freeman had thus established himself as an acknowledged authority on the question of federalism in late-Victorian England. His unequivocal hostility towards the idea of imperial federation and his ruthless condemnation of the movement's leaders in 1885 therefore took the League by surprise. The pioneers of imperial federation had not anticipated opposition from such quarters and they were unprepared for Freeman's intellectual artillery. Let us look briefly at the structure of his main arguments against imperial federation.

In the article in *MacMillan's Magazine*, Freeman's detailed analysis of imperial federation represented the most scathing and merciless attack that federationists had ever encountered. His passion for accuracy and lucidity of statement coupled with his own clarity of conception and exact precision in the use of words had a devastating effect upon the League. Imperial federation for Freeman was a branch of enquiry which was directly connected with history and his approach to the investigation was simply to trace it to its origins and expose it as having no historical basis. In this way he could dismiss federationists as either confused thinkers or careless writers. The following extract from his article serves as a useful example of Freeman's knife-sharp critique of imperial federation:

> First, there is the name: then there is the thing. It may be some objection to the name that it is altogether meaningless, or rather that it is a contradiction in terms. ... It tells a little against the name of the scheme that what is 'Imperial' cannot be 'Federal', and that what is 'Federal' cannot be 'Imperial'. It tells a little against its substance that none can expect the scheme to carry out its professed purpose except those who have forgotten the existence of India and the existence of the United States.[4]

This was candour indeed. Freeman, with a characteristic eye to philological purity, summarily dismissed imperial federation as simply 'unhistorical'. It made no sense. Empires were empires and federations were something completely different. They were republics in which citizens were able fully to determine their own lives for themselves by democratic means. To qualify the word 'federation' by the word 'imperial' was palpably indefensible. But to the imperial federationists the precise meaning of the terms was not as important as the general desire to convey the urgency of closer relations between Britain and the white self-governing colonies. Let us look a little more closely at the intellectual debate between these protagonists.

It was a common argument of federationists that since some shadowy form of federal relationship already existed between Britain and her colonies, the vague aspiration of imperial federation would not involve any major constitutional upheaval. Indeed, the emphasis of this line of thought was that it would be an almost imperceptible transition which would render the whole operation painless. Freeman, however, wasted no time in exposing the shallowness of this presumption. First, he complained that this reasoning had no historical basis because there existed no voluntary union of independent states keeping some powers to themselves and granting other powers to a central authority of their own creation. As the mother country, Britain was a central authority much older than the colonies, which were recipients of certain powers granted to them. Hence when federationists claimed that an American state had no more of a direct voice in the foreign affairs of the American union than a British colony had in the foreign affairs of the British empire, they overlooked the simple fact that a British colony was a subject community which had never had a voice in such matters, whereas an American state had no direct voice in foreign affairs simply bacause this was one of the powers which it had ceded to the federal authority. Secondly, the unswerving logic of Freeman's position enabled him to point to the fact that the British colonies had no voice, either direct or indirect, in choosing representatives in the British Parliament who were responsible for foreign affairs, whereas the American states and their citizens did have a voice in selecting those who were responsible for foreign affairs. Thus the citizens of the several states, as citizens of the United States of America, had an indirect voice in choosing the President, while the states comprising the American union chose the representatives in the Senate. In short, the difference between the position of an American state and the position of a British colony was simply the difference between federation and subjection. The British colonies had never been in a position to cede certain powers to a central authority; they possessed only such powers as Britain had chosen to grant them. Clearly, such a condition of affairs was 'imperial', but it could not be 'federal'.

Not content with exposing the abuse of terminology regarding the existing state of things, Freeman also surveyed the intentions of federationists when he observed:

The question in truth comes to this: shall an 'empire' break up or shall it be changed into a federation? To speak of changing an imperfect federation into a perfect one gives a false idea of the case. What is really proposed to be done is not to change a lax confederation into a closer one or an imperfect confederation into a perfect one. It is to bring federation, as a perfectly new thing, where at present there is no federation, but its opposite, subjection. And it is proposed to bring in federation, not only as a perfectly new thing, but under circumstances utterly unlike those under which any of the present or past confederations of the world ever came into being. The proposal that a ruling state ... should come down from its position of empire, and enter into terms of equal confederation with its subject communities, is a very remarkable proposal, and one which has perhaps never before been made in the history of the world.[5]

By exposing the novelty of such a literal intention, Freeman successfully focused attention upon an aspect of the subject which continued to embarrass federationists engaged in debating the future of the empire. While William Forster preached the gospel of a 'complete and equal and perfect federation',[6] critics of the movement suspected imperial federation of being a ruse designed to perpetuate British hegemony rather than a scheme based upon the division of sovereignty between distinct and coordinate governments. Several months before Freeman's great critique appeared, Sir Charles Adderley, a former under-secretary at the Colonial Office during the Conservative administration of 1866–68, had conveyed his opinion of the United Kingdom's role in the proposed federation in language which was remarkably similar to that used by Freeman:

> There is about as much chance of the English people turning their ancient Parliamentary system into such a Constitution, as of their deliberately restoring feudalism or the Heptarchy. ... A Minister coming down to the House with a proposal for abolishing Parliament, and issuing writs for a Federal Congress, would be immediately consigned to Bedlam.[7]

The thrust of these arguments lay in their sense of the absurd and therefore of the impracticable. By depriving imperial federation of any historical experience to recommend it, the project was marooned as a chimerical notion which could be judged only on its abstract merits and not according to any bogus precedent.

Freeman and other believers in terminological exactitude were clearly annoyed by the pretentious way that imperial federation was espoused. If there was to be any real hope of achieving closer union, a more meaningful phrase than 'imperial federation' was obviously desirable from the standpoint of theoretical accuracy. There was a good deal of wisdom in the advice that if 'federation' meant some wholly new device which the world had never witnessed in its history at any time, then it was better to discuss the merits of the new device by calling it by some new name of its own, and not by using old established names in a strange way which only distorted their accepted meaning and served merely to confuse rather than clarify. Here Freeman felt that he had unmasked what he considered to be an intellectual self-deception of his time. If the idea of imperial federation was allowed to go unchallenged it might become respectable by default. He was determined that serious analytical discussion of the subject would not be neglected.

Freeman arrived at the heart of the controversy when, having effectively exposed the spurious nature of the terminology, he turned his attention to the real practical implications of applying federal principles to the British empire. His conclusions, he felt, were at variance with what federationists pictured as somehow making Britain greater. In past federal unions, such as Switzerland and the United States of America, the member states gained in political stature by joining the union, but it involved a simultaneous loss of sovereignty and position with regard to the right, for example, to maintain war and peace. In many of the past examples of federal unions, however, the states had never known separate independence, and, in any case, any nominal loss in power and position was always fully compensated for in other ways. Argued in terms of a crude balance-sheet of gains and losses, therefore, it was less obvious that Britain stood to gain from forfeiting her position as a ruling power in order to become a component part of a larger federal state. In short, it meant the emasculation of the British Parliament which would have to give up its widest and greatest powers as the Imperial Parliament to some other, yet imaginary, assembly. Doubtless most federationists had not ever thought of such a prospect and even those who had, such as William Forster, could offer only a modicum of comfort by the prediction that Britain's future in a more competitive and hostile world might be less bleak if she was prepared formally to reassess her relationship with her own empire. This not only illustrated yet again the fundamentally defensive nature of imperial federation as a strategy designed primarily to address Britain's relatively declining world status and influence, but it also revealed the implicit assumption that the residuum of imperial powers would remain in the hands of Britain alone. Thus was the image of imperial federation reinforced as essentially an act of magnanimity – a gift to the colonies from the mother country of a share in those affairs which had hitherto been her own exclusive preserve. And this conundrum was simply the product of attempting to reconcile a position of predominance with the status of equality, as expressed by Freeman's famous dictum that what was 'imperial' could not be 'federal'.

Clearly, then, if the self-governing colonies were to be admitted into a federal relationship with Britain as a method of effecting a closer union between the head of an empire and its subject colonies, the reality of such a proposal meant that the Parliament of the United Kingdom would perforce be content with jurisdiction over the purely local affairs of the United Kingdom and the sending of representatives to some new grandiose institution which could administer the affairs of the empire. Here Freeman was obviously on strong ground. Historical experience certainly seemed to vitiate imperial federation at its source. Its practical implications were so far-fetched that hope and sentiment were all that was left to the defenders of imperial federation. These were poor substitutes for real arguments.

Freeman, however, was not easily given to hope and sentiment. He preferred to translate the vision of the British empire, reformulated by federal principles, into practical terms. He wanted to consider exactly what would be involved. In one of his earliest letters on this subject to James Bryce, the jurist, historian and Liberal MP for South Aberdeen during 1885–1906, Freeman stated his views with characteristic candour:

> To me Imperial Federation seems to be, not an intelligible proposal which one deems unjust or inexpedient, and therefore argues against, but a mere heap of vague, meaningless and contradictory phrases, pure and mere babble in short. ... What is Imperial Federation? ... Some say, a Federation of the British Empire, the Queen's dominions, or something of that kind. That means a Federation in which we all shall be outvoted by Hindoos and Mahometans. Some say (as if it meant the same thing) a Federation of the English-speaking people. That, indeed, gets rid of the barbarians; but it implies the partnership of the United States which will hardly be got for an 'Imperial' concern. ... In either case, the Kingdom of Great Britain and its Parliament will have to sink to the level of the State of Rhode Island and its Legislature.[8]

The assertion that the supremacy of the British Parliament would disappear and that it would have no more power than the legislature of a Swiss canton or of an American state did not really correspond with the august conception of a greater Britain which federationists were so often keen to delineate. Indeed, if federal principles were to be strictly applied to the British empire, there was considerable weight in the additional argument that the British empire would simply cease to exist. It all depended upon what was understood by the epithet 'Greater Britain'. As Freeman argued:

> Is the people of Great Britain, is the Parliament of Great Britain, so delighted with the existence of what in the cant of the day is called a 'Greater Britain', as to be ready to give up to that Greater Britain all that has hitherto made Britain great in a wider sense than the original one of being geographically greater than the lesser Britannia of the mainland?[9]

What did 'Greater Britain' really mean? We have already traversed this conceptual landscape in Chapter 2 when we looked in detail at the imperial views of Dilke and Forster. Here it had a bifurcated meaning: it referred to Britain either as the existing undisputed ruling power of a vast and universally venerated empire or, in an entirely new and different sense, as part of a constitutional union of states and citizens which would guarantee a future greatness that would far outstrip its own present and past. The former was a known experience, rooted in history, while the latter was merely a future possibility. Moreover, the novel metamorphosis involved a change in kind as well as in degree, but this was obscured by the inappropriate use of the phrase 'imperial federation'. In short, the runic terminology concealed a qualitative as well as a quantitative change in the objective to be gained.

The academic debate which persisted in the 1880s as to the meaning of imperial federation also touched upon the danger of encouraging separatism in the United Kingdom. Given that the watchwords of the 1880s were Ireland and empire, the investigation of the meaning of imperial federation occasionally followed the path which led to the public debate on the Irish controversy, but it also raised the question of how far the application of federal principles to the British empire would allow a Parliament of the United Kingdom to exist. Freeman had warned in his article that it would be far more in keeping with the federal principle for England, Scotland, Ireland and Wales to enter the new union as separate states with their own separate state legislatures than for them to enter collectively as the United Kingdom.[10] However, there could be little doubt that separatists in these communities would have regarded a separate legislature as nothing more than a stepping-stone, or halfway house, towards complete independence from England. It hardly needs to be emphasised that Freeman was totally opposed to the break-up of the United Kingdom. In his masterly *History of Federal Government in Greece and Italy*, which first appeared in 1863, he had already referred to this spectre in unequivocal terms:

> No one could wish to cut up our United Kingdom into a Federation, to invest English counties with the rights of American states, or even to restore Scotland and Ireland to the quasi-Federal position which they held before their respective Unions. A Federal Union, to be of any value, must arise by the establishment of a closer tie between elements which were before distinct, not by the division of members which have been hitherto more closely united.[11]

Logically consistent, as he invariably was, Freeman insisted that federation should amalgamate what was separate, not sunder what was already united. Here he called attention to the role of federation in building new states rather than in reconstructing old ones. In his view there was simply no reason to destroy the United Kingdom so that its constituent parts could acquire the status of a Swiss canton or an American state within a 'federal empire'.

As the foremost literary critic of imperial federation whose arguments and reflections it has been expedient to utilise for the purposes of this chapter, Freeman could hardly fail, finally, to focus his attention upon the scope of the proposed federation as part of his relentless condemnation of the movement and its theory. The purview of imperial federation was an important aspect of the debate to which most critics of the movement regularly referred, and it involved some vital points of detail. For example, the place of India in the proposed federation was of particular interest as the celebrated jewel in the crown of empire, and the fate of such colonies as Malta, Gibraltar and the West Indian islands was repeatedly questioned. Clearly, if the scope of federal principles was restricted to the white self-governing colonies, then the place of India, and indeed of any other part of the empire which fell outside this category, would be subject to the United Kingdom and the white self-governing colonies. Such an arrangement might certainly have been imperial, but it would not have been federal.

In the concluding part of his great diatribe on imperial federation Freeman pointed to the fact that India was the most prized imperial possession, yet it was conspicuous by its absence when the advocates of closer union discussed the federal future:

> In truth, in this particular argument, India, so present to every mind in every other argument, India, the choicest flower of the Empire, the brightest jewel in the imperial crown ... seems suddenly to be forgotten.[12]

India had not been forgotten; it had been deliberately ignored. Its omission was not difficult to explain. It did not figure in the arguments and plans of most federationists simply because it was widely acknowledged that India was ruled permanently and solely by the British and that it was therefore a more obvious example of 'empire' than the white self-governing colonies. In this respect, it was generally believed that India's connection with the United Kingdom had a quality of permanence which was in marked contrast to the United Kingdom's historically changing relationship to the white self-governing empire.[13]

In reality, a federal relationship with India was simply absurd and Freeman was probably correct to emphasise the point that nobody had ever meant to support such a proposal. Yet if India was not to be admitted to federal rights in an imperial federation, critics of the movement persisted with the view that it was nevertheless too important to be neglected. Most federationists doubtless wanted the best of both worlds: to apply federal principles to the white self-governing colonies and the United Kingdom, but to maintain India's position as a foreign dependency under the suzerainty of the United Kingdom. It is true that a handful of federationists did try to accommodate India in their various schemes of imperial reorganisation in the 1880s, but it was generally accepted that the problem of India was one which merely added to the already immense difficulties standing in the way of the practical realisation of imperial federation.[14] Nobody ever seriously contemplated a situation whereby all the English-speaking parts of the empire could be outvoted by Hindus.

The debate upon the role of India in an imperial federation revealed yet another significant feature of the federationists' semi-coherent ideology. Without doubt, their conception of the empire was racial. Indeed, this was probably the only aspect of the theory to acquire unanimity among the advocates of closer union. The idea of a closer union between the mother country and her self-governing colonies based upon a community of race, religion, language and culture did at least have an aura of credibility about it in late-Victorian Britain. We can still appreciate today how far such an ideal must have appealed to the sentiments of even the most ardent opponents of imperial federation. Even Freeman demonstrated a warmth of feeling for the idea of a 'lasting friendly union of the English and English-speaking folk' in contrast to the maintenance of the British empire.[15] But his reference to the prospect of harmonious relations with the United States of America as a symbol of the unity of the English-speaking peoples – while it chimed with the British racial spirit of the age – was merely a rhetorical flourish. He knew perfectly well that most federationists did not include the United States in their vision of closer union. The conundrum of advocating a 'federation of the English-speaking peoples' and 'Anglo-Saxon unity' which did not include the United States was the final outcome of using words without attempting to define their real meaning.

Freeman's devastating analysis both of 'the name' and 'the thing' received no convincing rebuttal. Federationists were simply at a loss to know how to counter his impressive logic. In terms of theoretical consistency Freeman demonstrated clearly that the logical limit of using such terms as 'Anglo-Saxon unity' and 'English-speaking union' meant the inclusion of the United States as well as the white self-governing colonies in what was misleadingly referred to as 'imperial federation'. But while the incomplete theory of imperial federation was obviously overtly racial, it did not provide for the inclusion of Americans and this was further evidence of how far federationists had no clear idea of what their terminology meant. Freeman had repeatedly exhorted them to avoid using terms loosely. It only created difficulties for those who wished to use them accurately about past events and it merely caused confusion and misunderstanding about contemporary events. In retrospect, then, the task which Freeman in particular had set himself was first to expose the spurious nature of the terminology and then to demonstrate the real practical consequences of applying federal principles to the British empire. His approach was simply one of elucidation.

It is true that the theory of imperial federation was never convincingly defended, but this should not be taken to mean that it was indefensible. Quite the reverse. Freeman's historical approach to the subject was certainly not without its weaknesses and his mid-Victorian perception and understanding of federation – a view which did not change during the late-Victorian years – was narrow. Let us consider first his damaging analysis of imperial federation and then investigate what he took federation to be.

According to Bryce, Freeman's quest for terminological precision and his method of assessing contemporary events in the light of historical origins embodied a fundamental flaw. It did not equip him fully to appreciate constructive statesmanship looking forward and trying to find solutions to difficult problems.[16] He was anchored in the past and this explains why his own dictum about history and politics prevented him from sympathising with the imperial federation movement. Bryce, for example, wrote that 'he sometimes made history present politics as well as past'.[17] In contrast, Bryce, while accepting the criticisms of inaccuracy and logical absurdity levelled at the terminology, nonetheless believed that the movement was worthwhile and merited his support: 'It is not mere babble, although it is admittedly at present vague. There is a sound idea at the root, and only to that idea is anyone who joins it committed'.[18]

Clearly vagueness did not deter Bryce. His willingness to join a movement whose name he regarded as a misnomer and whose objectives he believed were confined to retaining the political connection of the colonies to the United Kingdom while preparing for a major readjustment of that connection in order to preserve imperial unity, and Freeman's total aversion for anything 'unhistorical', was simply the difference between the practical politician and the theoretical academic. The leisured private scholar who lived in easy circumstances did not have to address the practical problems which regularly confronted active politicians. Consequently the terminological stipulations of the word 'federation' and the theoretical implications of the phrase 'imperial federation' did not bother Bryce. They were merely a convenient slogan or watchword for closer imperial union.

The first of Freeman's weaknesses was personal: it lay in his lack of any practical experience of public life. Apart from fighting, unsuccessfully, two parliamentary elections, acting as a conscientious magistrate, and playing a leading part in the anti-Turk agitation of 1877–78, he lived essentially as a private scholar.[19] However, it is his intellectual shortcomings which are more important here. Freeman, as we have seen, was apt to make history present politics as well as past. But one historian of the Victorian era has gone even further in his criticism of Freeman's historical method. John Burrow claimed that 'Freeman did not simply inject his contemporary politics into history; it would be truer to say that apart from history he had no contemporary politics at all. All his opinions were rooted in history; they were derived from his conceptions of the past'.[20] Accordingly, his interest in English politics was 'feeble and flickering' and contemporary politics intrigued him only by 'being seen as part of the historical continuum, part of an unfolding and recognisable historical pattern'.[21] Freeman's abiding interest – the goal of his academic life – lay in unmasking the 'unity of history'.

Burrow also claims that Freeman's interest in federalism was 'the nearest he ever came to a practical political concern' and that even here it was only a fragile concern originating principally in 'a philhellene devotion to Athenian democracy' and an 'English predisposition in favour of the institutions of local self-government'.[22] The classical scholar never seems to have tired of building his intellectual attacks upon the historical experience of the Achaean League, the Swiss cantons and the Italian city states of the Middle Ages. Indeed, there seems to be sufficient evidence to suggest that Freeman's real interest in federalism derived mainly from his belief that it offered a chance of perpetuating at least some vestiges of the early civic humanist notions of republican virtue. Federation would enable citizens to achieve moral self-fulfilment via active participation in the polis; it was Freeman's own idealised vision of the distant past which federation would go some way to recapturing.[23]

We can see from this short survey of Freeman's intellectual weaknesses that in striving constantly to rekindle – some might be tempted to say, recreate – the past he was frequently imprisoned by it. The imperial federationists were unfortunate in having him as their main antagonist. His analytical approach was narrow but methodical, his style was righteously apocalyptic and his prejudices were both contradictory and suffocating. Nonetheless, his critique of imperial federation was as important as it was influential. It never received the convincing intellectual rebuttal which it deserved. But in hindsight Freeman did, albeit unwittingly, enrich and strengthen the intellectual tradition of British federalism. His own particular contribution was indirect: it added to the mainstream scholarly literature on the subject; it forced federationists to think more clearly about their goals; and it ensured above all that serious analytical debate about one of the nostrums of the age was not neglected.

Given the somewhat threadbare theory of imperial federation just sketched, it seems rather strange to prod the reader towards what must now be viewed as its practice. Yet this is precisely what we must do. We will look at how imperial federation was translated into practice by a detailed analysis of the federal plan of the Imperial Federation League which was presented to W.E. Gladstone, the British Prime Minister, in November 1892. It is a little-known but quite extraordinary chapter in the overall evolution of the British tradition of federalism.

The federal plan of the Imperial Federation League

It will be recalled that at the Westminster Palace Hotel Conference of November 1884, which officially launched the Imperial Federation League, William Forster, its first chairman, spoke of the need to avoid concocting specific proposals and schemes of imperial federation. His words are worth repeating here:

> I do not think that it follows that it may be years before we arrive at some conclusion, but it would be most unwise to take the thing into our own hands at once and to sketch out any particular plan.[24]

How was it, then, that this important political organisation with an enigmatic title about which few of its members could agree found itself promoting just such a plan only eight years after its official inception? Furthermore, what was the intellectual process by which the League arrived at a definite set of proposals for the federation of the British empire? Upon what assumptions did it formulate its scheme? And how was federation understood by the public men who worked together to consolidate the British empire? The answers to these searching questions are of crucial importance to the establishment of the British tradition of federalism. They are based entirely upon empirical evidence from the League's Minute Books which were released for scholarly analysis only recently.[25] What follows, then, constitutes a late nineteenth-century survey of elite opinion about federal principles within the Imperial Federation League itself. Let us look first, however, at how the League crossed the Rubicon.

In June 1891 an official deputation of the League waited upon the Prime Minister, Lord Salisbury, to urge him to convoke a second colonial conference along the lines of the first and highly successful Colonial Conference of 1887. Salisbury's reply that it would be pointless unless there was 'some definite scheme of our own' to put before such a conference led indirectly to the League, at Sir Charles Tupper's initiative, appointing a Special Committee 'to submit to the Council, for the consideration of the organization of the League throughout the empire, definite proposals by which the object of Imperial Federation may be realised'. Established in July 1891, the Special Committee comprised eleven League members and solicited the opinions of thirty-nine people 'specially qualified' to raise 'the principal points involved in any form of federation'.[26]

Having committed itself – unwisely in the view of many federationists – to producing a concrete scheme of imperial federation, the League certainly set about its task with great gusto and impressive intellectual organisation. It produced a detailed survey of elite opinion concerning the essential elements of federation, together with the political strategy required to achieve it. We will begin our investigation by identifying the key elite figures and then look at the nature of the enquiries. This will be followed by an assessment of the many replies to the questions posed. On the basis of this quantitative and qualitative sample of elite opinion about federation, we will be able to understand the intellectual process by which the League formulated its ill-fated plan.[27]

Composition of the Special Committee

1.	Lord Brassey	7.	Sir Lyon Playfair MP
2.	James Bryce MP	8.	James Rankin MP
3.	Sir John Colomb MP	9.	Sir Rawson Rawson
4.	Sir Daniel Cooper	10.	Lord Reay
5.	H.O. Arnold-Forster	11.	Sir Charles Tupper
6.	Lord Lamington		

List of persons to whom Enquiries of the Special Committee were sent:

1.	W.M. Acworth	12.	Oscar Browning
2.	Sir William Anson	13.	Rev. Canon Dalton
3.	Edward A. Arnold	14.	Professor E.A. Freeman
4.	Talbot Baines	15.	R.R. Dobell
5.	Sir Henry Barkly	16.	Lord Dunraven
6.	Robert Beadon	17.	Major-General Sir J. Bevan Edwards
7.	E.W. Beckett MP	18.	Sir William Farrer
8.	Thomas Belshaw	19.	Sandford Fleming
9.	S.B. Boulton	20.	Sir Alexander Galt
10.	J.C. Bourinot	21.	Principal George Grant
11.	T.A. Brassey	22.	Rev. William P. Greswell

23.	Major-General Sir R. Harrison	32.	G.W. Rusden
24.	Lieutenant-General Sir W. Jervois	33.	Professor J.R. Seeley
25.	Captain Charles Johnson	34.	James Service
26.	D'Alton McCarthy	35.	P.V. Smith
27.	Archibald McGoun, Jr	36.	Sir Leonard Tilley
28.	S.V. Morgan	37.	Sir Julius Vogel
29.	Professor A.S. Napier	38.	Sir Frederick Young
30.	George Parkin	39.	David Wark
31.	Professor Cyril Ransome		

*Replies to the Special Committee: Interrogatories issued by
the Special Committee, 11 August 1891*

Points for Consideration:

a) To broadly define what are the essentials of the federation to be aimed at.
b) To suggest by what gradual process they can be approached.
c) To indicate the steps in that process which it is now practically possible to take.

Interrogatories:

I.   Whether it is desirable to have contributions from the self-governing colonies to imperial defence?
II. What should be included in a proper scheme of imperial defence?
III. On what basis should contributions be apportioned?
IV. What method should be adopted for raising the money?
V.   What system of administration should be adopted in order to give the self-governing colonies a share in it?
VI. Whether influence over, or a share in, the control of foreign policy should follow?
VII. How that control, if granted, should be exercised by the colonies?

Outline of Replies to Interrogatories:

I.   (a) The following eleven respondents agreed that colonial contributions to imperial defence were 'essential' – with responsibility and power should go the burden undoubtedly:

Lord Lamington   James Bryce MP
Sir William Farrer   H.O. Arnold-Forster
S.V. Morgan   W.M. Acworth
S.B. Boulton   W.P. Greswell
Archibald McGoun Jr   Sandford Fleming
Talbot Baines

(b) Major-General Sir Richard Harrison agreed in the form of:

(i) maintenance of local forces;
(ii) facilities for migration;
(iii) 10% preference on British goods, proceeds to go to the Navy.

(c) Professor Cyril Ransome disagreed – not desirable until the Central Representative Body has been formed.

(d) Sir Henry Barkly agreed – but the point should not be pressed until the Council has been formed.

II. (a) Lord Lamington, James Bryce MP, Sir Frederick Young, T.A. Brassey, Major-General Sir J. Bevan Edwards (the distribution of the navy).

(b) Lord Lamington, Sir William Farrer, James Bryce MP, Sir Frederick Young, H.O. Arnold-Forster, T.A. Brassey (the protection of ports and coaling stations).

(c) Lord Lamington, Sir William Farrer, W.P. Greswell (the defence of trade routes).

(d) Lord Lamington, Sir Frederick Young (the disposal of land forces).

(e) Lord Lamington, Professor Cyril Ransome, T.A. Brassey, Major-General Sir J. Bevan Edwards (plans of attack and defence).

(f) H.O. Arnold-Forster (defence of India).

III. (a) Sir William Farrer, S.V. Morgan, Professor Cyril Ransome, Sir Henry Barkly, S.B. Boulton, Archibald McGoun Jr, H.O. Arnold-Forster, W.M. Acworth, W.P. Greswell (on the basis of population).

(b) S.B. Boulton, Archibald McGoun Jr, T.A. Brassey (on tonnage entering and leaving British ports).

(c) Archibald McGoun Jr, Major-General Sir J. Bevan Edwards (on aggregate trade).

(d) Archibald McGoun Jr (on the basis of risk).

(e) Talbot Baines, James Bryce MP, W.P. Greswell (on the established resources and wealth of each country).

IV. (a) Major-General Sir Richard Harrison, S.V. Morgan, Professor Cyril Ransome, Archibald McGoun Jr, H.O. Arnold-Forster, W.M. Acworth, Sandford Fleming (the Hofmeyr proposal advocated at the 1887 Colonial Conference).

(b) Sir William Farrer (specially appropriated revenues from each country).

(c) S.V. Morgan, H.O. Arnold-Forster (duties on drink).

(d) S.V. Morgan (tonnage dues).

(e) Professor Cyril Ransome, Sir Henry Barkly, Talbot Baines, James Bryce MP, W.M. Smith, W.P. Greswell, Major-General Sir J. Bevan Edwards (each country to find its own contribution in the way it likes).

V. (a) Major-General Sir Richard Harrison (an Imperial Council of Delegates).

(b) Sir William Farrer (an Imperial Council of Delegates for foreign policy followed by a Common Council for all purposes).

(c) S.V. Morgan (two Imperial Houses: Upper by nomination, Lower by election).

(d) S.B. Boulton (a Council of State with colonial representation).

(e) Archibald McGoun Jr (a Representative Executive Government, responsible to an Imperial Parliament).

(f) James Bryce MP, T.A. Brassey (an Imperial Council of Defence).

(g) W.M. Acworth (a Committee of Defence with Colonial Representation).

(h) W.P. Greswell (some constitutional representation of all parts of the empire).

VI. (a) Major-General Sir Richard Harrison, Sir William Farrer, S.V. Morgan, Professor Cyril Ransome, S.B. Boulton, Talbot Baines, James Bryce MP, H.O. Arnold-Forster, T.A. Brassey, W.M. Acworth, Sandford Fleming (yes).
(b) Lord Lamington (no).
(c) Sir Henry Barkly (yes – to an extent).
(d) Archibald McGoun Jr (yes – eventually).

VII. (a) Sir William Farrer (cannot be decided yet but should follow the USA example).
(b) Professor Cyril Ransome (through the Imperial Parliament when constituted; at first through the Colonial Committee of the Privy Council).
(c) Sir Henry Barkly, S.B. Boulton (a Council of the Empire to be formed).
(d) Archibald McGoun Jr (control to be exercised by an Imperial Council advised by Colonial Representatives).
(e) H.O. Arnold-Forster (by the Colonial Council and by the introduction of colonists into the administrative and diplomatic posts of the empire).
(f) James Rankin MP (by developing the principle of representation).
(g) T.A. Brassey (by colonial representation in the Council of Defence).
(h) W.M. Acworth (by the UK Government acting under the advice of the colonial representatives).
(i) Major-General Sir J. Bevan Edwards (cannot be decided until after the Conference).

Summary of Replies

(a) Generally speaking the answers are to the effect that the essentials to be aimed at are:

I. Common Citizenship.
II. Common Action for Common Objects.
III. The organization of the empire as a whole against foreign powers or, in the words of the League's Constitution: 'The combination of the resources of the empire for the maintenance of common institutions and the defence of common rights'.
IV. The principal object to be attained is the strengthening of the empire by unity of action and the principal object to be avoided is the break-up of the empire which is the inevitable result of the continuance of the present system.

The means whereby the objects sought may be obtained are primarily representation combined with responsibility and the delegation of certain powers by individual states within the empire to a common executive for the common good of the empire.

The points especially dwelt upon by contributors may be briefly summarised:

I. The preservation of the unity of the empire.
II. The inauguration of a common foreign policy.
III. The organization of a common system of defence.
IV. The institution of a Representative Assembly dealing with a common fund.
V. A Supreme Judicial Tribunal.

In addition to these, some individual contributors advise the establishment of an Imperial *Zollverein*, either immediately or ultimately, an assimilation of the laws of marriage and the regulation of Commercial and Criminal Law. All contributors are agreed in recommending that there should be no interference whatever with the internal administration of any part of the empire save by the direct consent of its inhabitants.

(b) There is general agreement that a preliminary conference should be summoned to make arrangements for a permanent Council to be created subsequently. There are various views as to the constitution of this conference but the general opinion appears to be that it should be composed of representatives of the United Kingdom and the Agents General or, in lieu of the latter, delegates provided *ad hoc* by the Colonies. The work of this conference should be to discover a basis upon which a permanent body could be created, such body to deal primarily with questions of imperial defence and secondarily with all such questions as may from time to time fall within its scope.

(c) A Council and a Minister of Defence to be appointed, Colonial Judges to be added to the Judicial Committee of the Privy Council; a greater share in the administration of imperial affairs to be given to the Colonies. It is generally held that while defence should take a first place, other matters, such as preferential tariffs, and the regulation of emigration should ultimately be dealt with.

Original Draft Report Explaining the Origins and Purposes of the Exercise

It was decided to circulate to persons specially qualified to give their opinions, a series of carefully considered questions raising the principal points involved in any form of federation. The questions were sent to some thirty gentlemen who were invited to furnish replies to the Committee. From most of the gentlemen so addressed replies were received. Many of these are elaborate and valuable documents, and there can be no doubt that, taken together, the papers embody the result of much time and thought, and form an important collection of opinions upon the main points connected with the federation of the empire.

Nature of Replies

It has been the duty of your Committee to carefully examine the replies in which the unanimity of suggestion with regard to many of the points at issue is as remarkable as it is satisfactory. There is an absolute agreement with regard to the object of federation which may be correctly expressed in the words of the original Constitution of the League adopted in 1884.

Your Committee, after duly considering these replies, have drawn up the following proposals which appear to them to embody the main principles that must prevail in any federal or quasi-federal organisation of Britain and her Colonies. In presenting these proposals your Committee wish it to be understood that they have not dealt with the question whether there exists a desire on the part of the various countries concerned to form a federation but have assumed a general wish for a consolidation of the empire, neither have they considered, whether any particular feature in the proposals will or will not be acceptable to any particular country or countries, but they have throughout regarded only the welfare of the empire as a whole.

Essentials of a Federated Empire

(a) That the voice of the empire in peace, when dealing with foreign powers, shall be the united voice of all its autonomous parts.
(b) That the defence of the empire in war shall be the common degree of all its parts, by the forces and resources of all its parts.

Measures Conducive but not Essential to Federation

In addition to the 'Essentials of a Federated Empire', there are other measures which, though non-essential, may be regarded as conducive to the same end. Some of these would become immediately practicable on the fulfilment of the essential conditions, others, if not so at once, might become so later in consequence of the permanent character given, by the fulfilment of those conditions, to the imperial relationship. Among those that would be immediately practicable are:

(i)   The admission of colonial securities to the category of British Trust Funds.
(ii) The imperial guarantee of local loans raised for purposes subservient to imperial ends, such as dry docks, strategic cables, railways, etc.
(iii) The opening of the administrative services of the empire, outside the UK, by holding local examinations for the Indian, Diplomatic and Consular services, as now done for the Army and Navy and the appointment to Governorships and other high posts of fit persons in whatever part of the empire they may be domiciled.
(iv) Uniformity in certain branches of Statute Law, especially Commercial Law, such as Bankruptcy and Merchant Shipping, including facilities for the execution of legal processes.
(v)   Uniform Imperial Postage and special arrangements for telegraphic service under the control of the Council.

The uniformity contemplated under heads (i), (iv) and (v) can only be attained by local legislation at the invitation of the Council, since these matters are at present subjects of local legislation, with which no scheme of Britannic Confederation should interfere.

A detailed analysis of these conclusions which were reached in June 1892 is interesting for what it reveals about the structure of the arguments used both for and against federation. It is also useful for affording us a rare glimpse into late nineteenth-century British thinking about federation and its preconditions. Both the meaning of federation and the assumptions upon which it was understood are laid bare by this compelling historical evidence of a century ago. When the plan was finalised it contained a total of forty separate sections but Articles X to XXVIII formed the kernel of the League's report and it mirrored the general recommendations outlined earlier by the Special Committee.[28]

Put simply, the essential precondition of a federation of the empire was deemed to be imperial defence. The whole report was built around this proposition. Articles X and XI committed the League to proposing both a representative body and common property in the means of defence concerning the self-governing colonies, while Article XII emphasised imperial naval communications as the sphere where the common interest loomed largest. But Articles XIII to XX arrived at the heart of the constitutional reform: arrangements for a Council of the Empire. It would be composed of members appointed by Britain and the self-governing colonies. Britain, Canada and the Australian and South African colonies would be directly represented while India and the Crown Colonies would be only indirectly represented by the appropriate secretaries of state in charge of their affairs. The Council might include – in addition to the representatives of the three great self-governing groups of colonies – the British Prime Minister, Foreign Secretary, Colonial Secretary, First Lord of the Admiralty, Chancellor of the Exchequer and the Secretaries of State for War and India.

The report fought shy of detailing the proposed Council's functions. It was assumed that they would evolve slowly in the future according to changing circumstances. But it is clear that they were to deal primarily with imperial defence and foreign policy. Defence meant naval defence, but the report took on board the recommendations of the report of the Hartington Commission of 1890 which advocated a corporate perception of naval and military defence.[29] This meant, for example, the coordination of military and naval strategy to produce a combined plan of operation for imperial defence together with a joint assessment of service estimates in relation to overall imperial needs. It also stated somewhat obscurely that the Council might receive such information relating to matters of foreign policy as would enable it to deal adequately with questions of defence. In matters of defence the Council could supervise the appropriation of any finance provided for the defence of the empire by the common contribution of Britain and the colonies. On this sensitive matter the report trod very carefully. It was felt that the method of raising contributions would at the outset be left to each individual self-governing colony but that future developments might eventually reveal an agreed means of raising the money according to some 'uniform principle' throughout the empire.

Overall the general principle was crystal clear: the rapid development of the colonies (interestingly alluded to as self-governing 'states') suggested that they would, in the future, be prepared to share in the increased cost of the general defence of the empire provided that they were given 'a proper share in the control and expenditure of the common fund'. This enhanced cost of their own defence as an integral part of a larger overall imperial system, it was emphasised, would be much smaller than the cost they would incur if they remained outside such a system. And what would induce them to participate in this scheme? In language which was later to be echoed by twentieth-century scholars of federalism, the report stoutly declared that these inducements sprang from 'the identity of the populations of the Mother Country and the self-governing Colonies in all the essentials of a common nationality and from the existence of a common danger which united defence alone can avert'.

In order to ascertain the views of the various self-governing colonies, Article XXIX of the report urged that an Imperial Conference should be summoned *ad hoc*. But it also warned that such a conference should be formally convened by the British Government only when it was deemed opportune. This conference would be sustained by a complete statement of the defence necessities of the empire, buttressed, if desired, by a Royal Commission survey of imperial defence requirements. No claim was made about the proposals being conclusive. On the contrary, it was intended that an Imperial Conference would use them as debating points in order to mould an acceptable scheme into shape.

What, then, are we to make of this plan to federate the empire in 1892? Was it a genuine federal plan and did it have any lasting significance? Edward Freeman certainly did not think much of it. His own reply to the Special Committee was couched in characteristically caustic terms: he did not see how the process helped to explain what imperial federation was and he remained at a loss to understand 'how the same thing' could be 'two contradictory things'. Nonetheless the very preparation of such a comprehensive blueprint as a focal point for public discussion was itself clearly no small achievement. Several parts of the report were conspicuous for their studied vagueness, especially those concerning colonial contributions to imperial defence, the question of commercial union (relegated to Articles XXXVI and XXXVII), and foreign policy, but the League had never undertaken to resolve these thorny questions. The League's journal, *Imperial Federation*, while making no claim to finality, roundly declared that it had at last defined what imperial federation really meant: it included all the principles laid down in the 'working' portion of the report which referred to the 'Essentials of Federation'. And while it also acknowledged that the political arrangements proposed were impartial and tentative, the journal described the report as 'the most important advance made in the history of the Imperial Federation movement since the League was established'.[30]

There can be no doubt that there was an intellectual process at work in arriving at this federal plan. The anatomy of this process is clear. It can be divided into three separate sections: the goal of federation; the strategy required to achieve it; and the immediate tactics or approach deemed practicable in the existing circumstances. Those who supported the federal cause clearly understood both the 'Essentials of Federation' and the 'secondary' factors 'conducive' to its attainment. They did not seek recklessly to reconstruct or redesign the British state but simply to graft upon it a new institutional device. It nonetheless accorded with federal principles in the extent to which it addressed the task of accommodating the constituent elements of the white self-governing empire in the central (imperial) decision-making process. And in the sense that the imperial federationists confronted the awkward problem of the preconditions or prerequisites of federation, they anticipated the scholarly arguments of both Kenneth Wheare and William Riker by at least half a century.[31]

The federal plan of 1892 was, in reality, only a federal instalment. It was also a pyrrhic victory for the League. A strong body of opinion within the League had been consistently opposed to it supporting a particular scheme, and their fears were justified when in April 1893 Gladstone, the British Prime Minister, rejected both their plan and their request for an *ad hoc* imperial conference. Gladstone, who in 1884 had privately dismissed imperial federation as 'chimerical if not little short of nonsensical', mounted a written assault upon the League's proposals.[32] He raised a whole series of searching questions about the federation of the empire by enumerating his queries and expressing his doubts in a collection of comments scribbled on the facia of the report.[33] He asked the following pointed questions: What was the position of those colonies which did not possess self-government? On what basis was the burden of imperial defence to be adjusted? What securities existed for the punctual and steady working of a financial system? Was the prerogative of peace and war to be devolved upon the Imperial Council? What were colonial members supposed to do in an emergency situation? Would colonial members be invested with powers to bind their respective governments or would they have to refer all decisions for the ratification of their home governments?[34]

It seems ironical, in retrospect, that these typically incisive remarks of Gladstone's suggested not that the report was too ambitious but that it was both vague and deficient in certain important respects. It was lacking in the sort of details which he had expected of such a report. Indeed, he went even further in his thinly veiled criticisms. He referred to the impact which a federation of the Australian colonies might have upon the larger goal of imperial federation, he wondered whether or not common contributions to imperial defence would be voluntary or fixed, he questioned the ability of the Imperial Council to legislate and he expressed concern about its relationship to the Crown, the House of Commons and each colony respectively. His most damning indictment of the report, however, was couched in seemingly innocuous language: 'public opinion has yet to be exercised and matured'.[35]

When Gladstone met the League's deputation on 13 April 1893, his opposition to their request for another colonial conference was based upon four main considerations: that neither he nor the Cabinet would countenance the abandonment of free trade which was implied by articles XXXVI and XXXVII of the report; that such an initiative would throw too great a burden of responsibility upon the government; that the League's proposals did not amount to the scheme which Lord Salisbury had requested in 1891; and that the time was inopportune for holding such a conference.[36] Gladstone had, in effect, given the proposals a decent burial. This verdict seemed to indicate that the movement to federate the empire had finally reached its nemesis in 1893. At this time the League maintained thirty-one flourishing branches throughout England and Scotland with a total membership of approximately two thousand. Moreover, it had succeeded in establishing branches in the Australian colonies, Canada, New Zealand, Cape Town, Barbados and British Guiana. And although it achieved only modest public support, it had been effective in promoting federation as a subject worthy of public debate for nearly a quarter of a century.

Historians have usually dismissed the Imperial Federation League as merely a footnote in the overall evolution of the British empire. Their conventional view is that it had only a marginal significance in the history of British imperial relations. But they have been looking at the League from a particular perspective. If we adopt a different perspective it assumes a new importance. In the British tradition of federalism neither the Imperial Federation League nor the political movement which it represented should be depicted as a mere interlude in British imperial history and politics. In reality the League has its proper place in a long tradition of British federal ideas which begin with empire and culminate in Europe.

The political ideas and influence of the Round Table movement

After the abrupt collapse of the Imperial Federation League in 1893, federal ideas for the empire did not disappear with it. On the contrary, their resilience was manifested in the variety of small pressure groups which sprouted in the United Kingdom during the 1890s. Apart from the Royal Colonial Institute, which had nurtured such ideas for a generation, the United Empire Trade League in 1891, the Imperial Federation (Defence) Committee in 1894 and the British Empire League in 1896 each championed different aspects of the politics of imperial consolidation. The cause of closer imperial union was consequently channelled along several separate routes.[37]

At the turn of the century, then, the cause of imperial unity had been effectively reorganised along more specific lines. But federal ideas about empire soon resurfaced in more robust shape during the first decade of the twentieth century when the Round Table movement was formed during 1909–10. Destined to dominate British intellectual thinking about empire–commonwealth relations until the early 1920s, the movement served as the crucial repository of imperial federationist ideas in the United Kingdom. It also represented a basic continuity of thought and action between the late nineteenth and early twentieth centuries in terms of the reorganisation of the British state.

Imperial federation was the link which ran beneath the surface of the activities of public men like Lionel Curtis and Philip Kerr, later Lord Lothian, who were among the founders of the new political movement in Edwardian England. This connection was expressed by the nebulous phrase 'organic union' but it is clear that 'the discovery of some form of federation which shall be at once effective and acceptable' was the main focus for their energies.[38] Their main strategy, like that of the Imperial Federation League, was to popularise the federal idea and to influence official thinking; but there the similarity ended. They avoided the mistakes of their predecessors. Concentrating less on mass agitation than on influencing political leadership, they recognised that popular support was valuable only after politicians had raised the issue. This, as Ged Martin observed, determined their tactics: 'Major policy problems, like the role of India in a federal union, were thrashed out in secret memoranda. Lobbying was confined to the powerful'.[39] And as the historian of the movement, John Kendle, remarked 'the movement, particularly the London group, did have some influence in governmental circles in Great Britain and in the Dominions, not least because its members came from the affluent, the well-placed, the intellectual, and generally the most acceptable members of society'.[40]

Curtis and Kerr agreed that the purpose of 'organic union' was to achieve some form of imperial consolidation but they did not see eye to eye on the question of federation. Curtis's own mystical faith in the empire and his almost doctrinaire commitment to the cause of imperial federation was not shared by Kerr. The latter believed fervently in empire but he was less than sanguine about attempts to 'fit the Empire into the constitutional ideas which have suited the United Kingdom and the self-governing colonies in the past'.[41] This, in his view, would be to court destruction. The empire would be lost forever. But Kerr did share Curtis's interest in a major reorganisation of the imperial structure and he concurred about the need for a common policy in defence and foreign affairs. He was fully alive to the strength and sensitivities of colonial nationalism, however, and this awareness made him cautious about what precise form the new political system should take. He preferred merely to acknowledge the desire for a closer, more binding, imperial union.

With the exception of Curtis, the Round Table movement determined not to force the pace unnecessarily. Under Kerr's influence as editor of the journal, *Round Table*, the movement preferred to educate British and colonial public opinion in the need for constitutional reform. Kerr characteristically felt much more comfortable when specific schemes and blueprints were eschewed. They were both premature and unhelpful. Only when international circumstances changed and after a long period of discussion between the British and colonial governments were concrete initiatives and proposals liable to be well received. Meanwhile, federal ideas would continue to circulate and form part of what he viewed as the crucial preliminary intellectual spadework necessary to alter official attitudes and perceptions regarding constitutional change.

As with the imperial federationists of the late-Victorian years, many Round Table enthusiasts favoured the idea of colonial representatives sitting in the British Parliament, while others sought to devise new executive machinery to facilitate more effective cooperation and consultation in defence and foreign policy. In this matter the Round Table was unanimous: if the white self-governing colonies (now called 'Dominions') were to have an effective voice in imperial policy, the quadrennial colonial conferences of the Edwardian years were palpably inadequate. Lionel Curtis was adamant about this. Curtis, a former town clerk of Johannesburg, dubbed 'the Prophet' by his admirers, launched himself with single-minded determination on the path towards a federal reconstruction of the empire. His famous *Green Memorandum,* published and widely circulated in 1910, outlined the movement's aims and assumptions, and sketched out a detailed plan of imperial federation which acknowledged the separation of domestic and imperial affairs. The new institutional framework would include an Imperial Parliament, distinct from Westminster, with a directly elected lower house and an upper house of states based upon equal representation together with an impartial tribunal to decide disputes over legislative jurisdiction between the federal authority and the constituent governments. These far-reaching reforms entailed the creation of a much more narrowly based domestic government for the United Kingdom (since the new federal government would deal only with imperial matters and not with the internal affairs of the United Kingdom) and the adjustment of British status, concerning internal affairs, with regard to Canada, Australia, New Zealand and South Africa. Various concessions to national sovereignty were incorporated in Curtis's scheme. He was, for example, scrupulously careful to leave the regulation of tariffs alone and he devised an ingenious method for the raising and collecting of revenues for imperial purposes. Curtis's plan, in short, contained virtually all of the institutional checks and balances which were conventionally associated with a modern federation.[42]

A strong sense of mission propelled Curtis into the dominions during 1910 with a threefold purpose: to disseminate the movement's ideas; to establish Round Table groups among the elite and professional classes; and to maximise the impact of his own memorandum. He met with varied success. His influence appears to have been greatest in Australia and New Zealand where he was able convincingly to depict 'the Imperial Problem' as 'the Empire in danger', successfully exploiting Antipodean anxieties about both German and Japanese expansionist designs. The threat of war certainly focused dominion attention upon the deficiencies of the existing imperial/colonial conference system of consultation, and there was undoubtedly a growing belief in the dominions that a constitutional void existed which could be successfully filled only by new executive machinery devised to respond smoothly in times of crisis. One particular response to this perceived deficiency in imperial decision-making was that of Sir Joseph Ward, the New Zealand Prime Minister. With audacious enthusiasm, Ward laid bare his detailed scheme of imperial federation as the last peacetime initiative to reconcile dominion self-government with imperial unity at the Imperial Conference of 1911. We will look briefly at this interesting proposal for federal constitutional reform which emanated from the dominions and which became part of the British tradition of federalism, but first let us be reminded of the background context to this remarkable event.

The 1907 Colonial Conference had recognised the need to convene regular conferences in order principally to discuss questions of common interest among the white self-governing members of the empire. At this time, the balance of the imperial relationship, according to Hancock, consisted of two main elements: the local autonomy of individual governments and the broad authority possessed and exercised by the United Kingdom.[43] The 'Imperial Problem' for those, like Curtis and Kerr, who sought a more formally regulated and binding union of states was to arrive at a new institutional arrangement which would facilitate common defence and foreign policies and thereby reverse the trend towards imperial decentralisation. Their aim, in short, was to centralise the direction of local affairs. They deemed the Conference system to be too weak to arrest the process of decentralisation which they viewed as leading ultimately to the disintegration of the empire into wholly independent states. 'Federate or perish' was the familiar proposition which aptly summarised this view. It was a watchword which stretched back at least to the imperial federationists of the 1870s. In the early years of the twentieth century, many politicians and intellectuals, like their immediate forebears, reflected upon the possibilities of reconstituting the imperial relationship by reintegrating the parts into the whole. These predispositions derived their strength, yet again, from the sense that another crossroads had been reached in the evolution of the empire.

This belief in the urgent need to do something about the empire before it finally and irretrievably fell apart prompted Sir Joseph Ward to take an initiative which even today seems quite astonishing. The details of his federal scheme were put forward as tentative suggestions designed to create a favourable atmosphere and to demonstrate that a new central authority, empowered to legislate on specific subjects, was feasible. It would halt imperial disintegration, widen the burden of imperial defence and give the dominions a direct voice on subjects hitherto the sole responsibility of the United Kingdom. What, then, did Ward propose to the sceptical representatives assembled before him at the 1911 Imperial Conference? How would his version of imperial federation work?

The scheme was founded upon a logical, coherent argument: the need to coordinate and harmonise naval defence by establishing a uniform system which would formally accommodate the component units of the empire in the decision-making centre. To achieve this, Ward advocated an 'Imperial Parliament of Defence' composed of two houses: an 'Imperial House of Representatives' elected for five-year terms with one member for every 200,000 of the constituent populations of the United Kingdom, Canada, Australia, New Zealand, South Africa and Newfoundland; and an Imperial Council of Defence or 'Senate' providing equal representation to the six governments, resulting in a Council of twelve and having only limited consultative and revisory functions. The executive would consist of up to fifteen members of whom not more than one would be chosen from the Senate. In this way the dominions would acquire an entrenched voice in naval defence, treaty negotiation, foreign relations and questions of peace and war, but without seriously threatening British supremacy.[44]

Ward's proposal met with the sort of indignant disbelief customarily reserved by governing elites for radical reform blueprints. In retrospect, his bold initiative seems naive. It had no real chance of being accepted. Yet it was not without significance both from the standpoint of the federal idea and as a serious proposition directed at imperial reorganisation. According to Hancock, the New Zealand Prime Minister took 'less than an hour to discuss the proposal', but he nonetheless sparked into life a real debate about imperial federation and its institutional implications among the practical men of affairs assembled before him.[45] I have included some key extracts from this remarkable debate because it affords us a useful glimpse into the intellectual and practical arguments about federalism from an unusual perspective:

Sir Joseph Ward: The people of these dependencies are not yet citizens of the Empire. ... Is not the time now ripe for the consideration of conferring it? ... I, as representing New Zealand, ... am entitled ... to emphasize the need of some Imperial Council properly accredited to coordinate and harmonize these policies of naval defence, and of the still greater question of naval supremacy. ... I would ask the Conference to look facts broadly and candidly in the face, and if independent naval policies ... are to continue on the part of the overseas Dominions, ... this does not make for a strong position in connexion with the Imperial ties being maintained. ... I have explicitly called the scheme I propose to outline an Imperial Parliament of Defence. Defence is above all other questions the one in which every part and subject of the Empire is vitally concerned.

The President (Mr. Asquith): Just a moment. The words used in your Resolution are: 'An Imperial Council of State'; you spoke just now of an Imperial Parliament of Defence. I do not find any such phrase in the resolution.

Sir Joseph Ward: I do not mind what the name is – an Imperial Council of State or an Imperial Parliament of Defence, or a Defence Council.

The President: They are practically synonymous, you think?

Sir Joseph Ward: Yes. Perhaps I ought to use the term Imperial Council of State. Defence is above all other questions the one in which every part and subject of the Empire is vitally concerned. It is the great vital topic which can be treated only by a proper Council of State. ... The day for partnership in true Imperial affairs has arrived, and the question which now emerges is – upon what basis is that partnership to rest? It certainly cannot rest upon the present relationship. No partnership deserves the name which does not give to the partners at least some voice in the most vital of the partnership concerns; and what I am endeavouring to bring out is: how is that voice to be heard and how is it to be made effective?

I desire to avoid any minor controversial questions at this time; but I am entitled to express, as I do now, my profound conviction that, if there had existed some true Imperial Council of State in which defence could be dealt with – I attach no importance to the name, whether it is an Imperial Council of State, or an Imperial Parliament of Defence, or an Imperial Council – separate naval policies ... would be today, if not non-existent, at least more completely harmonized and made integral with the Imperial Navy. ...

I recognise that there must be given up by the constituent self-governing parts of the Empire to any central Imperial Council only such power as is absolutely necessary to deal with questions essentially imperial in their nature, questions which cannot be dealt with satisfactorily or at all unless through collective deliberative action, and I would make the framework of the Imperial Parliament of Defence, or Imperial Council of State, as elastic as is consistent with efficiency and durability; but I am impressed with the belief that some such framework we must have. ...

Sir Wilfrid Laurier (Canada): There is a difference between a council and a parliament. What do you propose, a parliament or a council? I want a proper definition of what you mean, because you have proposed neither so far.

Sir Joseph Ward: I prefer to call it a Parliament of Defence.

Sir Wilfrid Laurier: Very well.

The President: That is a very different proposition to the one in your resolution. Your resolution is 'An Imperial Council of State' – nothing about defence – 'advisory to the Imperial Government'. It is limited, as I understand the resolution, to giving advice.

Sir Joseph Ward: I would point out that the resolution is: 'with representatives from all the self-governing parts of the Empire'.

Sir Wilfrid Laurier: But you say 'Council'. Is it a council, or is it a parliament? It is important that we should know exactly what is the proposal.

Sir Joseph Ward: I prefer to call it a parliament.

Sir Wilfrid Laurier: Very good, then. Now we understand what you mean.

Sir Joseph Ward: I prefer to call it a parliament, although I admit that there is a good deal in the name.

Sir Wilfrid Laurier: There is *everything* in the name.[46]

These extracts, from what was a very detailed and wide-ranging debate on imperial federation, reveal a colonial prime minister who became increasingly isolated and embattled in his own personal struggle to persuade the Imperial Conference to consider some permanent form of imperial reorganisation. His failure adequately to clarify the institutional details of his own scheme did not augur well for public support and it is fair to say that Ward's initiative never stood a realistic chance of acceptance in 1911. Indeed, if the text is read in full today, the discussion appears unreal. Ward's defence of his proposal sounded more like an apology. But while criticism is easy, initiatives are not. His scheme, despite its deficiencies, had the merit of confronting the real practical problem not only of imperial defence *per se*, but also of imperial relations in their larger purview. Moreover, even as he rejected the proposal, the British Prime Minister, Herbert Asquith, was compelled to confess to the dominion premiers that he had received a memorial signed by some 300 British MPs who had called for the formation of a representative advisory council. And we should also remember that the dominion premiers did not approach the issue with identical motives. The conclusion to this whole episode must be that no government was prepared to sacrifice local interests for the sake of a common policy. Hancock's assessment was both accurate and succinct: 'The Empire had become too decentralized to permit "imperial solutions" to "imperial problems"'.[47]

The crisis the Round Tablers had waited for arrived in 1914 with the onset of the First World War. Here, at last, was an opportunity to confront the basic lacuna in the British imperial system. Sir Joseph Ward's peacetime complaint – that the dominions would be supporting foreign policy decisions over which they had no control – was suddenly thrown into sharp relief. What would the British imperial response be? In 1916 Curtis published *The Problem of the Commonwealth*, which emphasised the urgent need for a common foreign policy. With Lord Alfred Milner, the Round Table's inspiration and idol, entering Lloyd George's Cabinet in 1916, and both Philip Kerr and Waldorf Astor joining the Prime Minister's 'Garden Suburb' in the same year, the prospects for the federal idea at the forthcoming Imperial War Conference to be summoned in 1917 seemed highly promising. No supreme federal organ emerged, however. The Conference did produce the Imperial War Cabinet with (briefly) executive powers in which all autonomous governments were represented. It just outlasted the war, to represent the empire at the peace conference. With it faded the vision of a common imperial government. It would be difficult to take issue with Ged Martin's conclusion: '1917 marked both the greatest triumph and the final defeat of the imperial federation movement'.[48]

Conclusion: federalism and empire

The creation of the Imperial War Conference and the Imperial War Cabinet in 1917 brings to an end the examination of imperial federation as part of the British tradition of federalism. We have demonstrated that in the years between 1870 and 1917 the continuous public debate about empire prompted an equally sustained debate about federalism. The relationship between empire and federalism was always muddled and confused. In a strict sense imperial federation remained punk theory. How, after all, could an empire realistically be transformed into a federation of its constituent parts? How could a constitutional relationship founded upon subordination and inequality be converted into one based upon coordination and equality?

This theoretical conundrum explained the peculiar difficulties encountered by those who used the label 'imperial federation' to search for a practical way to save the empire from disintegration. It also explained why so many different schemes and blueprints proliferated in this period. The theoretical hurdle invited practical responses. Many of them of course were hopelessly impracticable and suggested that the imperial federationists were out of touch with reality. But some of them, like colonial representation and an Imperial Council, were feasible proposals which implied only modest constitutional tinkering. In hindsight, the theoretical objections had the unwitting merit of revealing the many institutional and policy variations inherent in the federal idea. They actually served to enrich the British tradition of federalism.

We must not lose sight of the fact that the thinking behind imperial federation had a compelling logic. The imperial federationists were aware that they were living in an age in which both extra-imperial and intra-imperial relationships were rapidly changing. They sought merely to influence the direction of the imperial destiny. Some mistakenly viewed the federal idea as a means to perpetuate British imperial hegemony, but others were attracted to it simply because it seemed increasingly consonant with the spirit of the age. It promised simultaneously to preserve colonial self-government *and* consolidate the union. To these men it mattered little that the empire would no longer be an empire, but a new union of states and, possibly, of citizens. But this would be for the future. They sensed a more urgent pressure. The constitutional principles of representative and responsible government, which had been bestowed upon the colonies of white settlement during the mid-Victorian years, were about to run their logical course. Complete independence beckoned. Looked at from this historical perspective, the imperial federationists were far from utopian in their aspirations. These movements of men and ideas certainly represented a basic continuity of federal thought and practice, but they also conform to Bulpitt's thesis of a series of internal and external challenges to the integrity of the United Kingdom. During this period the British empire – and the politics of imperial consolidation – could never be divorced from the question of the Union.

Before we conclude our survey of British federal ideas and the problem of imperial unity, it is important that we do not overlook the contribution which these ideas have made to the development of the Commonwealth. It is often remarked that although the British have a genuine fear and dislike of federal systems for themselves, they have been the greatest exporter of such systems for others. Imperial federation may not have succeeded but colonial federation did. Canada, Australia, India, Malaysia, and Nigeria are examples of successful federal systems, while both New Zealand and South Africa utilised some federal devices at different periods in their constitutional evolution. Furthermore, the federal experiments of Rhodesia and Nyasaland and the West Indies, though abortive, confirm the view that 'federal constitutions ... could scarcely have been born without the long-continued interest and support of British officials'.[49] And as Ronald L. Watts remarked in his superb study of new federations in the Commonwealth, 'there is some evidence to suggest that British colonial policy after 1945 was actually characterized by a general policy favouring closer territorial association in the colonial areas'. Successive British governments played a major role in constitution-making and 'a general policy of encouraging inter-colonial federations was carried forward by both major British political parties'.[50] British federal ideas moved easily from empire to Commonwealth.

Notes

1. Freeman, E.A. (April 1885), 'Imperial Federation', *MacMillan's Magazine*, 430–45.

2. His *History of Federal Government* (1863) was republished posthumously in a new form in 1893 edited by J.B. Bury and entitled *The History of Federal Government in Greece and Italy*. The latter work was a reprint of the original volume but with the addition of a new chapter on Italy and a new fragment on Germany which were discovered in Freeman's papers and intended for his second volume.

3. Freeman, E.A. (1893), *History of Federal Government*, New York, Books for Libraries Press (1972), 3.

4. Freeman, E.A. (April 1885), 'Imperial Federation', 430.

5. Ibid., 435–6.

6. Forster, W.E. (February 1885), 'Imperial Federation', *The Nineteenth Century*, XVII, 201–18.

7. Adderley, Sir C. (September 1884), 'Imperial Federation: Its Impossibility', *The Nineteenth Century*, XVI, 505–16.

8. Freeman to Bryce, 16 December 1886, Bryce Papers, Bodleian Library, Oxford, Mss. 7, ff. 256–8. This letter can also be found in Stephens, W.R. (1895), *The Life and Letters of E.A. Freeman*, 2 vols, London, Macmillan, II, 356–7.

9. Freeman, E.A. (April 1885), 'Imperial Federation', 440.

10. Ibid.

11. Freeman, E.A. (1893), *History of Federal Government*, 70.

12. Freeman, E.A. (April 1885), 'Imperial Federation', 444.

13. See Mehrotra, S.R. (1961), 'Imperial Federation and India, 1868–1917', *Journal of Commonwealth Political Studies*, No. 1, 29–40.

14. See Young, F. (1876), *Imperial Federation*, London, publisher unknown, 64, and his (1902), *A Pioneer of Imperial Federation in Canada*, London, George Allen, 148–9. See also Labilliere, F.P. de (June 1881), 'The Political Organization of the Empire', *Proceedings of the Royal Colonial Institute (PRCI)* (1880–81), 12, 355–6.

15. Freeman, E.A. (April 1885), 'Imperial Federation', 445.

16. Bryce, J. (1903), quoted the historian, S.R. Gardiner, in his *Studies in Contemporary Biography*, London, Macmillan, 274.

17. Ibid., 274–5.

18. Bryce to Freeman, 24 December 1886, *Bryce Papers*, Mss. 9, ff. 259–62.

19. Burrow, J. (1983), *A Liberal Descent: Victorian Historians and the English Past*, Cambridge, Cambridge University Press, 155–6.

20. Ibid., 164.

21. Ibid., 164–5.

22. Ibid., 166.

23. See Collini, S. et al. (1983), *That Noble Science Called Politics: A Study in Nineteenth Century Intellectual History*, Cambridge, Cambridge University Press, 219–25.

24. *Report of the Adjourned Conference, 18 November 1884* (1884), Imperial Federation Pamphlets, Rhodes House Library Oxford, 12.

25. The Minute Books of the Imperial Federation League were released in 1983 by the League's bankers, Messrs C. Hoare & Co. with whom the League's records had been deposited in 1894. *The Imperial Federation League Archive (IFLA)*, 1884–94 is now in six volumes held at the British Library (BL), London, Add. Mss. 62778–83.

26. *Imperial Federation*, Vol. VI, July 1891.

27. What follows is based entirely upon *IFLA*, Add. Mss. 62783, vol. VI.

28. The League's report, endorsed by the General Council in November 1892, is reprinted in full in *Imperial Federation*, Vol. VII, December 1892.

29. For further details, see Johnson, F. (1960), *Defence by Committee*, Oxford, Oxford University Press.

30. *Imperial Federation*, Vol. VII, December 1892.

31. Wheare, K.C. (1963), *Federal Government* (fourth edn), Oxford, Oxford University Press. It was first published in 1946. See also Riker, W.H. (1964), *Federalism: Origin, Operation, Significance*, Boston, Little Brown & Co.

32. Sir Edward Hamilton, Gladstone's private secretary, recorded the Prime Minister's words in his diary on the day following the establishment of the League, 19 November 1884, *Hamilton Papers*, British Museum, London, Add. Mss. 48638, f. 58.

33. Gladstone's comments on the report by the Special Committee of the Imperial Federation League, 12 April 1893, Gladstone Papers, British Museum, London, Add. Mss. 44775, ff. 114–25.

34. Ibid., f. 118.

35. Ibid., f. 120.

36. For a full report of the deputation, see *Imperial Federation*, Vol. VIII, May 1893.

37. For futher information on these organisations, see Miller, M.G. (1980), 'The Continued Agitation for Imperial Union, 1895–1910: The Individuals and Bodies Concerned, Their Ideas and Their Influence', DPhil, Oxford University.

38. Kendle, J. (1975), *The Round Table Movement and Imperial Union*, Toronto, University of Toronto Press, 64.

39. Martin, G. (1975), 'The Idea of Imperial Federation', in R. Hyam and G. Martin, *Reappraisals in British Imperial History*, London, Macmillan, chapter 6, 133.

40. Kendle, J. (1975), *The Round Table Movement*, 305.

41. Ibid., 68.

42. For the contents of the *Green Memorandum*, see ibid., 74–80.

43. Hancock, I.R. (October 1966), 'The 1911 Imperial Conference', *Historical Studies: Australia and New Zealand*, 12, 356–72.

44. For the details of Ward's scheme together with the debate, see Keith, A.B. (1933), *Selected Speeches and Documents on British Colonial Policy, 1763–1917*, 2 vols, London, Oxford University Press, II, 247–303.

45. Hancock, I.R. (October 1966), 'The 1911 Imperial Conference', 359.

46. Keith, A.B. (1933), *Selected Speeches*, 247–71.

47. Hancock, I.R. (October 1966), 'The 1911 Imperial Conference', 372.

48. Martin, G. (1975), 'The Idea of Imperial Federation', 134.

49. Livingston, W.S. (ed.) (1963), *Federalism in the Commonwealth: A Bibliographical Commentary*, London, Cassell, introduction, xii.

50. Watts, R.L. (1966), *New Federations: Experiments in the Commonwealth*, Oxford, Clarendon Press, 63–4.

PART TWO

Ireland

CHAPTER 4

Federalism and the Irish question, 1870–1920

Ireland and imperial unity

In the late nineteenth and early twentieth centuries the Irish question dominated British government and politics. According to Bulpitt's thesis, it was part of the major challenge of modernisation which undermined and radically altered the traditional territorial order. Indeed, Bulpitt construes two specific historical periods – the 1880s and the years between 1910 and 1926 – as amounting to 'conditions of territorial crisis' in the United Kingdom.[1] Michael Keating has also identified these years as 'The Crisis of the United Kingdom'. The Irish question forced those who wanted to keep the United Kingdom intact 'to consider the meaning of the Union and its intellectual justification'.[2] And in a recent study of Ireland and the federal idea, John Kendle has reinforced this interpretation with the argument that the question of Irish self-government provoked a much larger constitutional discussion about the territorial structure and the distribution of power within the United Kingdom.[3]

The Anglo-Irish relationship from the Act of Union of 1800 to the Government of Ireland Act of 1920 may be characterised as a seedbed of constitutional reform ideas and proposals. Dissatisfaction with the union of Ireland with Great Britain proved fertile ground for a wide range of constitutional initiatives which included local government reform, devolution, home rule, federation and the outright repeal of the union. In a recent essay George Boyce has even gone as far as claiming that 'British federalism is an Irish invention'. 'Without the Irish case', he argues, 'it is safe to say that federalism would hardly have merited serious political discussion in the British Isles; or at least would not have moved beyond discussion and into the policy process'.[4] He was wise to qualify this statement. Clearly, the very structure of the United Kingdom – and of Great Britain before it – has always rendered elite discussions of the federal idea perfectly intelligible and legitimate. And as part one of this book has already demonstrated, federalism and the Irish question could never be completely divorced from the imperial dimension. The problem of Ireland was always viewed in terms of the integrity of the United Kingdom, but during the period surveyed here it was also intimately linked to the wider question of imperial unity. Indeed, it is important to emphasise the imperial dimension at the very outset: 'Given the resurgence of interest in the federal idea in the colonial and imperial settings in the 1840s, it is not surprising that a few Irish and English politicians speculated about its possibilities as a solution to the problems inherent in the Anglo-Irish relationship'.[5]

The relationship between Ireland and empire was always complex, not only because of its strategic significance and general security implications, but also because of the gradual reshaping of a distinct British identity. Michael Keating referred to those who defended the Union as being unable to draw on an 'existing theory of the state or what it meant to be British'.[6] This is interesting for what it suggests about the evolving sense of an overarching national identity in what was indisputably a multi-national, imperial state. How could a resurgent and revitalised Irish nationalism be safely accommodated in such a state? The threat of Irish nationalism and the way in which it forced an assortment of constitutional reform ideas and proposals on to the agenda for public debate was perplexing for the late-Victorians precisely because it occurred during a critical period of historical change which Bulpitt has called 'the modernisation of territorial politics'.[7] During these years the United Kingdom experienced major internal social, economic and political change while simultaneously confronting external challenges to its economic, naval and military supremacy, and increasing pressure from its white self-governing colonies for a serious reappraisal of the imperial relationship. In short, all of the elements necessary for a bout of introspection concerning the notion of 'British' were present.

It is often easily forgotten just how important the very existence of the empire was for this constantly changing sense of British national identity. Consequently, the internal threat to the integrity of the United Kingdom posed by Irish nationalism must also be viewed in terms of an imperial perspective. How could the British consider greater autonomy for Ireland – let alone Irish independence – without seeing it as tantamount to imperial disintegration? How could they retain the empire when they could not even prevent the break-up of the mother country itself? This was a difficult equation for those British politicians who searched for new constitutional remedies to resolve. It was difficult precisely because it went to the very core of British national identity. Could Ireland ever really fit into the evolving sense of 'Britishness'? The Irish problem underlined this conundrum. We have already encountered Linda Colley's admirable historical analysis of the forging of a British nation and it is useful here to remind ourselves how far 'Britishness' was always composed of many varied elements which changed over time. Ireland was always a problem from this standpoint chiefly because its predominantly Roman Catholic population could never be effectively integrated into an otherwise 'common investment in Protestantism'.[8] But because empire was increasingly bound up with British identity any attempt to reorganise the United Kingdom itself met with fierce accusations of imperial, and *ipso facto* national, dismemberment.

The key to understanding the politics of constitutional reform during these years, then, lies in the complicated relationship between the United Kingdom and its empire. They could never be effectively disengaged. In this light, all proposals for constitutional reform had to be consistent with imperial unity. George Boyce may have been correct when he observed that 'Federalism gave the Irish problem a British dimension, and the British problem an Irish dimension', but it also added another, imperial, dimension.[9] In this context the federal idea was both resilient and ubiquitous precisely because it bridged the three dimensions of constitutional discourse: the imperial; the (multinational) United Kingdom state; and the constituent sub-state national territories of England, Scotland, Wales and Ireland. Small wonder that this Rubik's Cube of its day should lead political elites to misuse terms and treat 'home rule', 'devolution', and 'home rule all round' as if they were synonymous with 'federalism'. Imperial federation itself suffered as much from this confusion and misunderstanding as it did to perpetuate it.

It is important to remember that the federal idea was perceived by its advocates to be a means of consolidating, rather than breaking-up, the United *consoli-dation!* Kingdom. They viewed it as an inherently flexible concept which was capable of accommodating a fairly extensive range of constitutional reforms. We have already seen how, in the imperial context, this could include *inter alia* colonial representation in the British Parliament or an advisory council of agents-general. It usually did not mean a fully-fledged federation in the strict sense of the United States of America. Most proponents of the federal idea sought merely a modest constitutional revision rather than a wholesale root-and-branch reconstruction of the United Kingdom. But even a modest reorganisation of the British state was likely to alter hitherto settled intra-state relations. For example, Keating's argument that there was no obvious constitutional ground on which to object to Irish home rule because parliamentary sovereignty, 'the only immutable principle of the constitution', was 'unaffected by the proposals' misses the point.[10] Gladstone's first Government of Ireland Bill of 1886, by excluding Irish members from Westminster, would have significantly affected relations between the constituent parts of the United Kingdom. It was simply not possible to deal with the Irish problem in complete isolation; there would always be a ripple effect upon the rest of the United Kingdom.

The relationship between Ireland and imperial federation was probably the most illuminating route into this aspect of the British federal tradition. Let us look a little more closely at it. From the perspective of a federal empire, it was perfectly possible to situate Ireland in two opposing strategic positions. Indeed, the imperial federationists were divided very much along these two lines. The first of these two approaches viewed Irish self-government as a necessary prerequisite for the establishment of a wider scheme of imperial federation. This interpretation did not equate Irish self-government with Irish separation; it meant simply the reconciliation of local autonomy with imperial unity. The second imperial federationist position took the rival view that Irish self-government would present an obstacle to a federal empire. The grant of home rule to Ireland would weaken the United Kingdom and create a new dependency, the majority of whose population wanted complete independence. There were, however, several nuances to these opposing positions and since they involved a federal United Kingdom and 'home rule all round', they are of interest.

Some federationists, like Sir George Ferguson Bowen, believed that the simultaneous pursuit of imperial federation and Irish home rule was a way to resolve two intimately connected problems. In his view, imperial federation would be the best means of achieving 'some measure of local autonomy for Ireland' because the Irish question would have to be handled in an imperial, rather than just a domestic, context.[11] Sir Alexander Galt, on the other hand, represented a school of thought which linked imperial federation, via Ireland, to 'home rule all round'. In 1883 he had stated unequivocally that Irish home rule was an indispensable precondition of imperial federation; in 1886 his opinion had travelled as far as proposing local parliaments for England, Scotland, Wales and Ireland and an imperial legislature in which the colonies would be represented.[12] Murray Finch-Hatton, the Conservative MP for Spalding, Lincolnshire, shared Galt's imperial conclusion, though not his belief in Irish home rule *per se*. He outlined a scheme of imperial federation in which Ireland – and the other parts of the United Kingdom – would have control over their domestic affairs while 'every part of the empire' would be represented in an imperial parliament sitting at Westminster, according to their respective burdens of taxation. For Finch-Hatton, federalism meant 'an entire solution', not only of the Irish question, 'but of many other great questions that affected the empire'.[13] Banister Fletcher, the Liberal MP for Chippenham, Wiltshire, also put the case for 'home rule all round' and envisaged the various MPs from the constituent parts of the United Kingdom meeting at Westminster to discuss 'imperial work alone' – a stepping-stone towards imperial federation.[14]

These gradations of thought about Ireland and imperial unity underline the cross-currents of political opinion about a complex relationship in which there were many different and often competing priorities. The structure of the United Kingdom and an empire at the crossroads combined to produce a heady mixture of constitutional reform ideas and proposals. But in seeking to define the precise nature of this relationship it was important to understand what the practical implications would be. There was of course no better exponent of the art of scholarly elucidation than Edward Freeman and we will return to his views on Ireland shortly. First, however, it is appropriate to prepare the ground for his intellectual appraisal by looking briefly at William Forster's imperial conception of Irish home rule.

Forster did not live long enough to witness the introduction of Gladstone's first home rule bill in the spring of 1886, but he did comment upon the

relationship between the Irish question and imperial federation in a letter to
Sir George Ferguson Bowen shortly before his death:

> There are two marked differences between our relations with the colonies on the
> one hand and with Ireland on the other hand: (1) Ireland has already what the
> colonies have not, viz. her voice in foreign affairs and her share in the common
> defence; (2) but she has not the independent home government which the colonies
> have. The great difficulty, however, is that whereas we propose and hope by federa-
> tion to tighten the bond with our colonies, Home Rule in Ireland would, at any rate
> at present, be used as a lever for loosening the bond which unites the two islands –
> probably even for severing the Union.[15]

Forster had made two important observations which helped to clarify the
relationship between Ireland and imperial unity. First, Ireland could not be
treated as a self-governing colony because it was part of the United Kingdom
and subject to the British Parliament in which it had elected representatives.
Secondly, this fact of parliamentary representation gave Ireland at least a
theoretical voice in the approval and administration of British foreign and
defence policies – something denied to the white self-governing colonies. The
first Chairman of the Imperial Federation League and former Irish Secretary
in Gladstone's Liberal government appeared to suggest that Irish home rule
would weaken imperial unity and that there was no necessary connection
between imperial federation and the Irish question.

In an important and influential article entitled 'Federalism and Home Rule'
which was published in the *Fortnightly Review* in 1874, Edward Freeman had
already prepared the ground for the clarity of thought which Forster was
later to demonstrate. He acknowledged that neither dependence nor quasi-
independence nor incorporation had resolved Anglo-Irish difficulties, and he
was quick to concede that 'home rule' was increasingly the cry. But what was
'home rule'? It appeared to mean an imperial parliament for the resolution
of imperial questions (issues which were common to England, Scotland, Wales
and Ireland), and a separate Irish parliament for purely Irish affairs. Freeman
wasted no time in exposing the difficulties inherent in this arrangement. What,
he asked, was to happen to those matters which pertained solely to England
or to Scotland or which concerned the whole of Great Britain but not Ireland?
Would there also be separate parliaments for England and Scotland? If not,
Irish members would be able to vote on English and Scottish affairs while
English and Scottish members would not be able to vote on Irish matters. It
would also be extremely hard to define what was English, Scottish and Irish
business. And even with an Irish parliament the Irish members would still be
inferior at Westminster since they would be able to vote only at certain times
on specific issues whereas the others would be entitled to vote at all times on
every matter, except those assigned to the Irish parliament. In short, 'home
rule' would be difficult to administer and it might not solve the problems for
which it was intended.[16]

There was an Arctic ruthlessness about Freeman's simple logic which did not leave much room for ambiguity. We have already seen how he summarily dismissed imperial federation. But the Irish problem presented him with a different analytical framework. Here the federal idea could be relevant. Indeed, he admitted in a later article, entitled 'Prospects of Home Rule' and published in the *Fortnightly Review* in 1886, that federation would be one way of resolving the Irish difficulty. But he complained once again that the words 'federal' and 'federation' had been used too loosely and too vaguely. It was not possible to have a federation of Great Britain and Ireland since 'two members are not enough for a federation'. Freeman's logic compelled him to disaggregate the United Kingdom:

> Its different members might agree to vest certain powers in purely English, Scotch, Irish assemblies, and to vest certain other powers in an assembly common to the whole body. The establishment of such a federation would be a very singular event in history. For federations in general have been formed by an exactly opposite process, the union of several smaller members into a greater whole, not by the splitting of a greater whole into several smaller members. Still this relation also is perfectly conceivable.[17]

But the practical implications of applying federation to the United Kingdom, even in its proper sense, still harboured great difficulties. How, for example, could such a federation operate without England dominating it? The only answer would be to disaggregate the Union even further. This meant cutting up the constituent parts of the United Kingdom into several smaller units. Freeman wondered what the people of England, Scotland and Ireland would think about this proposition. None the less, he wrote to Bryce in July 1886 hoping that if Gladstone won the next election he would:

> ... either bring in the old bill in its main features – 1. Parliament at Dublin 2. No Irish at Westminster – or else make something quite different – federation if he likes; there seems to be more tendency to it in Great Britain than I had fancied. I don't want it, because I am sure that England, Ireland, Scotland, Wales would not do; you would want smaller centres, and I do care for the integrity of the Kingdom of England, though not for that of any absurd 'Empire'.[18]

This brief survey of Ireland and imperial unity emphasises just how difficult it was to define the nature of what was a tangled and convoluted relationship. But we can nevertheless appreciate just how significant this complicated relationship was for the British tradition of federalism. Its very complexity served to sustain a vigorous constitutional debate and ensured that the 'tendency to federation' would continue to grow in British political discourse until the end of the First World War. In this light it probably makes sense to regard the 'crisis of the United Kingdom' in British constitutional politics as a continuous, unresolved crisis rather than a series of episodic crises. Keeping this view in mind, let us turn now to look at how Joseph Chamberlain responded to the threat which Irish home rule posed to the integrity of the United Kingdom. His role in the British federal tradition is interesting because, although it was largely unintended, his activities were the catalyst for a major reappraisal of the various policy alternatives available to successive British governments in their quest to solve the Irish question. The hub of these arguments of course was Gladstone's first home rule bill of 1886.

Joseph Chamberlain, federalism and Ireland

Joseph Chamberlain's role in the Liberal party split of 1886 has been the subject of constant debate and reappraisal by historians. He played a crucial role in the failure of Gladstone's first home rule bill in the House of Commons in June 1886 and subsequently, along with Lord Hartington, led the dissentient Liberal Unionists into permanent opposition to Gladstone's policy for Ireland. But while most of the facts about Chamberlain's views on the Irish question have long been well known, the overall significance of his federal ideas has been underestimated. Furthermore, there has also been a tendency in the mainstream literature to gloss over Chamberlain's growing sympathy for imperial federation. Both of these dimensions to his political views – and the way that they came to be related – merit further research and investigation. Here we will focus primarily upon the years 1885–86 in order to demonstrate how far federal ideas became entwined in the epic public debate about Ireland.

Chamberlain's federal ideas appear to have developed in a somewhat haphazard fashion. They were both confused and confusing. This was doubtless because they crystallised under the sudden pressure of the Irish problem in 1885 but much remains unexplained. His main political strategy was to defeat the Gladstone bill rather than to promote an alternative scheme. None the less, there was sufficient consistency in Chamberlain's thinking to suggest that federalism was more than mere opportunism. His support for the federal solution to Irish home rule can be traced back at least to 1874 when he approved Isaac Butt's proposal, called a 'federal arrangement', and an advanced form of devolution was firmly incorporated in the famous Radical Programme of 1885.[19] Here the primary aim of what was a drastic reorganisation of British government was the devolution of parliamentary business which would improve the efficiency of legislation by freeing the imperial parliament to confine itself to foreign affairs, trade, defence and Indian and colonial matters. Let us look in a little more detail at the background to Chamberlain's goals and priorities.

We can begin by noting the remarks of a recent biographer, Richard Jay, who claimed that 'many historians have attempted the ultimately fruitless task of providing Chamberlain with perfect consistency throughout his career'.[20] We are confounded in our search for motives by 'Chamberlain's own tendency to extreme inconsistency in his comments'.[21] In a later essay Jay confessed that 'there is some question about whether Chamberlain himself was altogether seriously committed to ... a constitutional overhaul, or whether "federation" was merely an effective political counter for a politician seeking to display his Liberal credentials while in open conflict with mainstream Gladstonian Liberalism'.[22] It should not surprise us, then, if today Chamberlain continues to maintain 'a peculiar fascination for historians', but this verdict clearly does not make our task at all easy.[23] Indeed, if we consider the contrary view of John Kendle, who has recently claimed that Chamberlain was genuinely committed to 'some reform of the constitutional relationship between Ireland and Great Britain' since 1879, it makes it much more difficult.[24] Mindful of these contending interpretations, we must try to pick our way carefully through a veritable minefield of historical detail and interpretation. In order to understand both how and why Chamberlain came to see in federal ideas a potential remedy for the Irish problem, it is necessary first to establish his position with respect to the growing Irish demand for greater control of their own affairs. The emergence of federal ideas, after all, cannot be examined in complete isolation from their context.

Chamberlain's whole approach to the Irish problem was elaborately explained in two key articles published in the *Fortnightly Review* for July 1885 and February 1886.[25] His fundamental premise, although it remained shaky, was to deny the Irish nationhood. In a communication to Sir William Harcourt he stated this view:

> I do not think that Ireland can be recognised as a nation without conceding separation. Ireland is a province and the cardinal difference between Mr. Gladstone and myself is that he has treated the question from the point of view of the separate Nationality of Ireland while I have regarded it from the point of view of a State or Province.[26]

Given this basic assumption about Ireland, Chamberlain refused to follow the Gladstonian home rule line which treated it as both a separate nation and a discrete problem. His own policy preference was completely different. Recognition of nationality did not mean recognition of nationhood. The article entitled 'Local Government and Ireland', which was written by Thomas Escott and George Fottrell, appeared in the *Fortnightly Review* for July 1885 and was publicly endorsed by Chamberlain. It situated the Irish problem in terms of local government reform for the whole of the United Kingdom: 'The problem here is to entrust Wales, Scotland and Ireland with the free and full administration of those of their internal affairs which do not involve any Imperial interest'.[27] Parliamentary government was clearly overburdened with work. The problem could be simply stated:

> The enormous complexity of modern legislation, to say nothing of difficulties caused by obstruction and party politics, indefinitely postpone many measures of reform. ... (and) parliamentary congestion ... has long since become a national calamity. ... How can the work of legislation and administration in the United Kingdom be so

adjusted as to secure the integrity of that kingdom, while giving to each of its component parts the best means of providing for its own public wants and developing its own resources?[28]

The answer was to establish both County Boards and National Councils. All local matters pertaining to counties would be administered by the elected County Boards while elected National Councils would be created for those larger domestic affairs which necessarily transcended individual counties but which could be satisfactorily accommodated within England, Scotland, Wales and Ireland. With specific regard to Ireland, the following statement summarised Chamberlain's position:

> The establishment of a National Council, elected by the Irish people and endowed with national authority, would enable the Imperial Parliament to delegate to a body of sufficient weight, capacity, and power, duties which Parliament now endeavours to perform, but the performance of which necessitates the neglect of other and more important matters upon which the attention of the great legislative assembly of the Empire should be concentrated. By the creation of County Boards and National Councils we should secure in the United Kingdom a rational division of the duties and labours of government. The Imperial Parliament, the National Councils and the County Boards would together form, so to speak, a hierarchy of legislative and administrative authority, all based upon the only true principle of government, free election by the governed. For all parts of the United Kingdom the establishment of such a system of government would be advantageous. For Ireland it would mean the beginning of a new life; it would substitute a government founded upon trust of the people in the place of one founded upon distrust and coercion. ...
>
> It is expedient, then, to recognise and satisfy, as far as may be done without danger to the integrity of the Empire, the natural desire of the Irish people to legislate for themselves on matters of purely Irish concern.[29]

For Chamberlain this scheme had many merits. In particular, it freed the Irish from an overweening British interference in their domestic affairs. Irish legislation had to be 'domestic' in its origins and not 'foreign'. In a nutshell, Ireland should have domestic control of purely domestic affairs. Parliament, too, would be liberated; it would be relieved of the burdens of 'strictly local discussions' in the House of Commons. And, above all, parliamentary sovereignty would remain unimpaired. Chamberlain believed that a separate parliament for Ireland was superfluous. The return of Grattan's Parliament would be 'a white elephant' since it would add little to the essentially practical advantages which this scheme offered. The article concluded by broadening the context of the benefits which would accrue:

> It would signify for Great Britain the redemption from an Imperial approach, and a substantial addition to our sources of Imperial strength. We live in an epoch when our relations with our dependencies and our whole scheme of Imperial administration is undergoing close scrutiny. Upon what terms is the mother country to be associated with her colonies? How far are the latter to be represented in the

Government of the former? In what proportions are the burdens of empire to be divided between the two? ... Let it be always remembered that an alienated Ireland means a weakened England, and even a weakened Empire.[30]

It is certain that by the autumn of 1885 Chamberlain's mind had begun to contemplate the federal idea. Kendle acknowledged that he was by then 'familiar with federal systems' partly because of the refusal of the Irish national leader, Charles Stewart Parnell, to entertain Chamberlain's preference for County Boards and National Councils.[31] Parnell wanted an Irish parliament. Chamberlain, however, remained implacably opposed to this goal:

> The powers he claims for his separate Parliament are altogether beyond anything which exists in the case of the State Legislatures of the American Union, which has hitherto been the type and model of the Irish demands; and if this claim were conceded, we might as well for ever abandon all hope of maintaining a United Kingdom.[32]

Chamberlain, we are reminded, was determined not to offer Ireland anything more than he would concede to either England or Scotland. In these difficult circumstances – where there seemed to be no meeting of minds between Chamberlain and Parnell – it should not surprise us to learn that the federal idea began to present itself as a possible solution. There is no other way of explaining Chamberlain's sudden willingness during 1885–86 to give serious thought to some form of federation for the United Kingdom. In the following letter to his radical contemporary, Henry Labouchere, he considered the adoption of the American Constitution:

> 1. Separate legislation for England, Scotland, Wales, and possibly Ulster. The three other Irish Provinces might combine.
> 2. Imperial Legislation at Westminster for foreign and colonial affairs, Army, Navy, Post Office and Customs.
> 3. A Supreme Court to arbitrate on respective limits of authority. Of course the House of Lords would go. I do not suppose the five legislations could stand a Second Chamber a piece. Each would have its own Ministry responsible to itself. There is a scheme for you. It is the only one which is compatible with any sort of Imperial unity, and once established it might work without friction. ... I am not going to swallow separation with my eyes shut.[33]

He also wrote to his radical partner, Charles Dilke, in similar vein, acknowledging that federation would necessitate 'the entire recasting of the British Constitution and the full and complete adoption of the American system'.[34] Despite Dilke's repudiation of 'any scheme of Federation whatsoever', Chamberlain insisted in supporting 'the principle of federation' and made no secret of where he felt the central issue lay:

> The retention of the Irish representatives is clearly the touchstone. If they go, separation must follow. If they remain, federation is possible whenever local assemblies are established in England and Scotland.[35]

What are we to make of this apparent change of heart? Did Chamberlain really abandon his earlier belief in devolution, parliamentary sovereignty and imperial unity? Kendle claimed that 'it is not fully clear what Chamberlain meant by "federalism", although it would seem that, for a time at least, he did seriously consider a true division of sovereignty'.[36] This view contrasts sharply with that of Jay who believed that there were 'grounds for doubting his seriousness in advocating it'.[37] It is vital that we consider the context of this seemingly abrupt departure of policy. In mid-December 1885 Herbert Gladstone's revelation that his father was giving serious thought to home rule threw the political world into turmoil. Given these exceptional circumstances which called for an urgent response, only one explanation seems likely: Chamberlain was prepared, at least theoretically, to experiment with the British constitution in a way that Gladstone refused even to contemplate. Between December 1885 and June 1886 therefore, Chamberlain was 'casting around for an alternative solution to justify his resistance to Gladstone' and found none.[38] His personal correspondence during these critical months reveals a despairing effort to consider a wide range of constitutional possibilities. He did not object to the federal idea; indeed, it had certain obvious attractions to him. But he knew that it would involve the abolition of the House of Lords and ultimately of the monarchy. In practical terms therefore, it was only a remote prospect. None the less he can be credited with the attempt to have fully thought through the implications of a federal scheme.

This background context is important to a proper understanding of Chamberlain's subsequent parliamentary observations. His willingness to champion the federal idea in the House of Commons stemmed directly from his collision with Parnell and his resolute opposition to Gladstone's new Irish home rule policy. Indeed, he preferred Irish separation to this scheme. Federation at least had the merit of logical coherence; it would have resolved the thorny question of Irish representation (which Gladstone's policy failed to do); it would have helped to put the financial basis of the union on a more secure footing since each of the parliaments would have had the same taxing powers; and in general it would have treated each part of the United Kingdom equally.

It is clear that federalism emerged as one of the most significant features of the momentous debate on Irish home rule in the House of Commons in 1886. Chamberlain certainly played a key role in this shifting emphasis. Indeed, his memorable parliamentary announcement on 9 April 1886 that the solution to the Irish problem might be found in 'some form of federation' kindled a fire which spread rapidly throughout the House.[39] But in this respect it was also something of a confused debate. The Irish problem prompted many MPs to comment upon the perceived merits and deficiencies of the federal idea. However, they did so in ways which revealed much misunderstanding about the idea. In retrospect, perhaps this is not surprising. As we have seen, the constitutional issues at stake were related in an extremely complex way. And Chamberlain's overall contribution to the growing prominence of the federal idea did little to clarify matters. He himself was struggling to come to terms with the notion of a federal United Kingdom and sent out many misleading signals to his contemporaries.

The other aspect of Chamberlain's political career which continues to provoke disagreement among historians is his sympathy for imperial federation. Jay claimed that the reasons for Chamberlain's firm opposition to Gladstone's home rule bill are 'by no means clear' but that they are certainly not due to his belief in closer imperial union. Indeed, 'he had never shown the slightest interest in, or support for, imperial unification'.[40] But if his resistance to home rule was not based upon 'imperial unification' this is not to argue that 'there was no continuity between his basic perspective on Home Rule and his later espousal of imperial federation'.[41] It is important to clarify this point. In opposing Gladstone's home rule bill, Chamberlain understandably aligned himself to what was the popular cry, namely, 'the empire in danger'. Gladstone's critics viewed his home rule bill as far too separatist; it was tantamount to imperial dismemberment. But this was a general view and support for it did not have any necessary implications for imperial federation. Jay's observation that 'the plausibility of this claim is enhanced by Chamberlain's subsequent career, but not by his earlier one' furnishes an interesting area for further research.[42]

It is not appropriate to pursue this line of enquiry very far here, but it is useful to reflect upon the relationship between two separate developments which were present in Chamberlain's mind at this time: first, his willingness to consider a wide range of constitutional policy alternatives to Gladstone's home rule bill; and, secondly, his emergent views on closer imperial union. The origins of Chamberlain's support for imperial federation in the years after 1886 are still disputed by historians. After all, he was never associated in any way with the Imperial Federation League and the movement which it represented. But there is some evidence to suggest that the critical events of 1886 constituted something of a turning-point in his imperial views. William Strauss's classic study of Chamberlain's imperial beliefs which was published in 1942 took a firm position on this:

> ... the roots of Chamberlain's imperialism were apparent in the earlier years, although his chief concern was with the Radical program of domestic reform. But with the casting of the die in 1885 the Empire assumed larger and larger proportions in his thinking. ... Before the Irish struggles Chamberlain appeared to have formulated no definite ideas about Imperial policy. During the course of the Home Rule fight, however, circumstances forced him to consider certain problems heretofore neglected. ... It was Chamberlain's opinion that Ireland must be bound closer to England than by mere sentimental ties if Imperial Federation was ever to succeed. ... Chamberlain's stand on the Irish question ... signalled the awakening of an Imperialist. This later imperialism grew naturally from the ideas that he expressed during the Irish struggle.[43]

Two separate developments are worth more than a moment's reflection. Barely a month after the parliamentary defeat of Gladstone's first home rule bill, Chamberlain made his first public speech in support of imperial federation. When he addressed Liberal Unionist supporters in Rawtenstall, Lancashire, on the subject of Ireland and the colonies on 8 July 1886, his imperial vision was unmistakable:

> I hope we may be able sooner or later to federate, to bring together, all these separate independencies of the British Empire into one Supreme and Imperial Parliament, so that they should all be units of one body.[44]

Later the same month the estranged radical leader displayed a much more specific commitment to imperial federation. Writing to Sir Alexander Galt, an imperial federationist and recognised advocate of tariff reform, Chamberlain agreed with Galt's emphasis on 'the great importance of securing a commercial union with the colonies as a preliminary step towards a closer federation'.[45] This, it should be emphasised, was never a scheme of Chamberlain's and Garvin was quite correct to claim that Chamberlain regarded actual schemes of imperial federation to be premature. He had certainly not arrived at any detailed plan of imperial federation himself. But there is sufficient evidence here to warrant further investigation into the linkage between his willingness to accommodate constitutional experimentation concerning Ireland and his shifting support for closer imperial union.

How, then, should we assess Chamberlain's contribution to the British federal tradition? It would be wrong to portray his actions in this period as those of a confirmed convert to the federal cause. Historians remain divided about many aspects of his turbulent political career, but there is agreement about this. The scholarly consensus would seem to be that Chamberlain did wrestle with federation as a potential solution to the Irish problem but only briefly and under extenuating circumstances. None the less, he was personally responsible for the discernible shift towards serious parliamentary discussion of the federal idea in 1886. Moreover, he was one of the few among his contemporaries to consider the question of Irish minority rights in a constructive way. Many critics of home rule identified the loyalist population of Ulster as a central objection to any plans for genuine Irish self-government. But they rarely construed Ulster as a positive incentive for thought about how the Irish minority might be satisfactorily accommodated in any new constitutional settlement. Jay's assertion that 'almost alone, Chamberlain in the 1880s grappled with the idea of separate assemblies for Dublin and Belfast' is a useful reminder of the Birmingham radical's imaginative boldness.[46] It is a reminder, too, of the important legacy which he left for succeeding politicians who were to tackle the Irish question a quarter of a century later.

Chamberlain was a practical politician rather than a man of ideas. His contribution to the British federal tradition must be viewed in this light. He knew that just as British public opinion was firmly opposed to Gladstonian home rule, it was also not prepared to support a genuine federal scheme. Despite this he introduced the federal idea into the public debate about Ireland and widened the scope of the debate to include England, Scotland and Wales while broadening the context to encompass the imperial implications. In hindsight Chamberlain's political activities gave impetus to the wider debate about federation in the United Kingdom during the late 1880s and the 1890s.

After 1886 strong pressure grew in the Liberal party for a revised home rule scheme for Ireland. In 1889 Lord Rosebery wrote to Gladstone that the longer the Liberals prevaricated in working out the details of the next home rule bill the more it would 'approximate to the federal principle'.[47] Another Liberal imperialist, Ronald Munro-Ferguson, preferred to see home rule as 'an item in the Imperial Federation Scheme'.[48] Hugh Childers, who represented a Scottish constituency, wrote to Gladstone that in his opinion the great question that must be decided was 'are we to have an Imperial Parliament for all the Imperial affairs of the Empire, with separate Legislatures for England, Scotland, Ireland & Wales, or is Ireland alone to be dealt with'. The 'Federal Idea' had been gaining ground in Scotland where Scottish Home Rule was growing rapidly, and he felt that federalism had to be either adopted or repudiated by the Liberal party once and for all.[49] In Wales, too, many Liberals were in favour of home rule for imperialist reasons. Tom Ellis, the Liberal MP for Merioneth, agreed that 'the tendency of the Home Rule question' was 'towards Federalism'.[50] Childers eventually warned Gladstone in October 1889 that he did not see how 'in the present state of Scottish and Welsh opinion, saying Aye or No to the federal idea' could be long deferred.[51] Gladstone, however, was unmoved and immovable. He determined to treat Irish home rule in isolation from other, larger questions concerning the United Kingdom and the empire. Gladstone's determination to pacify Ireland continued into his fourth administration during 1892–94 when he resigned and subsequently retired from public life. The second Irish home rule bill went some way to meet the main criticisms and objections of its predecessor, particularly with regard to Irish representation at Westminster, and it was formally approved by the House of Commons. But the bill was emphatically rejected by an obdurate House of Lords in 1893 and the prospects for another Irish home rule bill disappeared with the restoration of Conservative governmental hegemony until 1905.

Despite the continuity of federal ideas in British constitutional politics at the end of the nineteenth and the beginning of the twentieth centuries, Bulpitt is correct to emphasise the enduring success of the Conservative party's own 'operational code for territorial politics'. Lord Salisbury's management of territorial politics kept the new, emergent social, economic and political forces which challenged the traditional order effectively at bay. It was not until after 1910, 'when a very real territorial crisis developed', that federal ideas resurfaced with renewed vigour in the public debate about Ireland.[52]

Federalism under the shadow of home rule, 1910–20

The events between 1910 and 1920 led to a partial disintegration of the United Kingdom. The Government of Ireland Act received the royal assent on 23 December 1920, the Stormont Parliament was formally opened on 7 June 1921 effectively establishing partition and the Anglo-Irish Treaty was narrowly approved by the Dail Eireann on 7 January 1922. The overall effect of these dramatic events was to create the independent Irish Free State comprising twenty-six of Ireland's thirty-two counties. The remaining six counties formed the province of Northern Ireland which remained within the United Kingdom.

The years between 1910 and 1920 were convulsive in British politics. Leaving aside the impact of the First World War, Bulpitt identified five main forces which challenged the old order: the positive state ideology of the new liberalism; the advent of a formally democratic constitution as a result of the Parliament Act, 1911, and the Representation of the People Act, 1918; the third Irish Home Rule Bill of 1912 and the concurrent idea of 'home rule all round'; the new industrial and political power of the labour movement; and the Sinn Fein revolution in Ireland after 1916 and the consequent demand for an independent republican Ireland.[53] Together these developments produced a 'very real territorial crisis' in the United Kingdom polity.[54] They combined to recreate the conditions of territorial political instability which in terms of sequential development had given rise to the three original unions, namely, the Anglo-Welsh, the Anglo-Scottish and the Anglo-Irish spanning three centuries. In other words, in the period surveyed here, there existed a perceived decline in the autonomy of the state from external forces, prolonged political instability which included a distinct lack of elite consensus at the centre and ubiquitous constitutional reform notions, and the attenuation of peripheral collaborative arrangements resulting from the activities of the Ulster Unionists, Sinn Fein and the emergent Labour party. But this time, Bulpitt added, there was an additional condition: 'peripheral dissidents possessed what appeared to be plausible alternative ideas regarding the nature of the Union'.[55]

The Irish question must be situated in the context of a United Kingdom polity which was subject to extraordinary constitutional turbulence and upheaval during this period. From about the year 1910, moreover, it is important to make a distinction between two separate sets of political events and circumstances. First, a highly influential federalist pressure group, known as the Round Table movement, emerged in British politics and played a significant role in the reappearance and reshaping of federal ideas. It represented the intellectual dimension to the new political environment identified by Bulpitt. Secondly, the idea of 'home rule all round' finally entered the domain of practical politics. During the years between 1910 and 1918 the notion of separate local parliaments for England, Ireland, Scotland and Wales situated alongside a genuine, overarching imperial parliament for the whole of the

United Kingdom – which might also facilitate 'imperial parliamentary union' – was seriously debated and considered by British political elites. The Irish question, once again, prompted a continuous stream of constitutional reform ideas and proposals which spanned both sides of the traditional British party political divide. These innovative ideas and proposals were not confined to the outer reaches of the British parliament. On the contrary, they penetrated to the very heart of executive cabinet government, reaching the inner sanctum of the British Prime Minister's own office. Both Asquith and Lloyd George were compelled to respond to the British federal tradition.

The activities of the Round Table movement have been well documented in the work of John Kendle.[56] Both in its origins and its inspiration it was very much an organisation with partisan Unionist sympathies. Inspired by Philip Kerr, later Lord Lothian, and Lionel Curtis, it viewed the Irish problem as an imperial question. From about 1910 it attracted other former members of Lord Milner's 'Kindergarten' as well as a number of influential outsiders, including Frederick Scott Oliver, Lord Robert Cecil and Leopold Amery. Kerr and Curtis are of special significance to the British federal tradition because together they made an enormous contribution to the overall evolution of British political ideas which straddled a generation. Their own federal ideas emerged from genuine attempts to resolve British imperial problems, the Irish conundrum and, later, European relations. Empire, Ireland and Europe were the catalysts for change, but change which produced a continuity of ideas.

Clearly the Round Table group were concerned about Ireland only in so far as it presented a real obstacle to their main goal of imperial federation. To this extent, the Irish problem was always more than merely a domestic political problem. And it was here, once again, that 'home rule all round' represented a convenient panacea for many of the United Kingdom's outstanding difficulties. One of the movement's most ardent supporters abroad was Earl Grey, the Governor General of Canada from 1904–11, and it was he who influenced Curtis, among others, with his own strong ideas about Ireland:

> My view is, ... that it is in the United Kingdom that the chief educational work has to be done. Before the road is cleared for the Federation of the Empire we have to put the United Kingdom straight. The time is approaching, if it is not already here, for getting this work done. ... Provincial Legislatures of the Canadian rather than the South African type for 1. Ireland 2. Scotland 3. Wales 4. England (4. North 5. South?) with a Federal Parliament armed with powers of disallowance sitting in London. Each Provincial Unit to be represented in the Federal Parliament in proportion to its population. ... When the Irish are thus reduced in the Federal Parliament of the United Kingdom to their proper proportions we can begin to talk Imperial Federation.[57]

On this subject, however, opinion was divided. Many believed that Ireland would not be able to support the financial burdens involved in home rule. In a determined effort to have the whole question thoroughly ventilated, Kerr attempted to influence those politicians who represented the Unionist cause at the constitutional conference assembled to find a solution for the conflict between the Commons and the Lords during June and November 1910. Notwithstanding Unionist preferences, he was convinced that major constitutional reform had to be considered on its merits. In a letter to Curtis he indicated what he thought was likely to happen:

> I believe that whether the constitutional conference is a success or not a proposal for the solution both of the Irish and of the House of Lords questions by federating the United Kingdom will be authoritatively put forward by one or other party or both together, in connection with the Coronation, so that it may be considered calmly and without party bias. ... This will probably be in about a year's time. ... For the moment we can do nothing.[58]

These attempts to persuade key political figures about the need for a royal commission to examine the whole constitutional machinery, however, failed. The movement had to be satisfied with its own private study. Part of its discussions were subsequently published as articles in the *Round Table* in August and December 1911 and the whole study was issued anonymously as a book in 1912 entitled *An Analysis of the System of Government Throughout the British Empire*.[59] There is strong evidence to suggest that Kerr gradually came to adopt a more cautious approach to the subject, being unsure as to how far 'home rule all round' would be a necessary step on the road to 'organic union' of the empire. And it is also clear that the so-called 'federal' ideas which circulated at this time were really varieties of devolution. Kerr himself acknowledged the instrumental nature of the federal bandwagon; the term 'federation' was a misnomer, for an imperial parliament would always remain supreme and under no scheme would there be a court to interpret the constitution:

> But it is a good fighting word to begin with. Devolution has noisome associations. Home Rule all round, worse. Federalism has been a success everywhere and people will therefore not be inclined to fight shy of the word.[60]

Kerr eventually came to regard imperial federation and 'home rule all round' as two entirely separate ideas and proposals. The former was not dependent upon the latter.

Besides Kerr and Curtis, the contribution of F.S. Oliver to the British federal tradition is especially interesting. A Unionist and much respected political thinker, Oliver had immersed himself in the problem of constitutional reform during 1910 and he became one of the most enthusiastic and forceful advocates of federalism during these years. As a prolific and highly readable writer of books, pamphlets, periodical articles and letters to newspapers, he saw his role as attempting to exert pressure behind-the-scenes in order to advance his own causes. While never holding political or administrative office, nor any formal position in the Unionist party, 'he made himself the confidant of leading figures in the party, and he strove to bring influence to bear on the men who took decisions, using his considerable literary talents as a substitute for ordinary political leverage'.[61] Along with J.L. Garvin, editor of *The Observer*, and Lord Northcliffe, who supported the federal cause in *The Times* and the *Daily Mail*, he carried his campaign into the heart of Unionist circles. While Garvin used his newspaper to support the federal goal and continuously bombarded leading Unionists with lengthy letters and memoranda on the Irish question and 'home rule all round', Oliver infiltrated the Unionist camp with his federal ideas by approaching both Austen Chamberlain and Arthur Balfour directly. Using the pseudonym 'Pacificus' he also published a short series of letters in *The Times* calling for a truce between the political parties at odds over Ireland. His influence in helping to shape the intellectual climate was clearly considerable; he had, in Kerr's words, 'ploughed the hard soil' so as to prepare it to receive Round Table ideas later on.[62]

Other notable Unionists who were strong supporters of a federal settlement for the United Kingdom were Lord Selborne, Thomas Allnutt Brassey and Moreton Frewen.[63] But what of the Liberal government and party? The considerable interest which 'home rule all round' evoked in Liberal circles during 1910–14, as Patricia Jalland remarked, has tended to be overlooked:

> The Unionist advocates of federalism have received far more attention than the Liberals. ... Yet it won far more sympathy from Liberal than from Unionist leaders, and gained strong support from the Liberal backbenches, especially among the Scottish Nationalists.[64]

According to Jalland, there were two distinct groups of Scottish Liberals which advocated 'home rule all round' for different reasons. The first group could be described as Scottish home rulers who were independently aggressive and eager to use the renewed Liberal interest in Irish home rule as a lever for pressing Scotland's demands. Many Scottish Liberals resented the priority given to Irish home rule and saw a larger federal scheme as a means of promoting Scotland's prospects more rapidly. Certainly their overriding pre-occupation was with Scottish home rule rather than with either Ireland or a constitutional settlement for the United Kingdom. One prominent Scottish Liberal, Captain Duncan Vernon Pirie, MP for North Aberdeen, claimed that as many as sixty out of the seventy-two Scottish Liberal MPs favoured Scottish home rule. The second group of Scottish Liberals, however, championed 'home rule all round' on its own merits. They included Captain D.V. Pirie, William Henry Cowan, MP for East Aberdeenshire, Arthur Ponsonby, Alexander MacCallum Scott, Ronald Munro-Ferguson, J. Cathcart Wason and J.A. Murray Macdonald.[65]

This political background is important when we consider the great success which Lionel Curtis scored on his own terms in 1912. He persuaded the young Winston Churchill to consider the federal ideas circulating within the Round Table. Churchill, however, was already sympathetic to these ideas, having just presented, along with Lloyd George, federal proposals to the official cabinet committee on home rule when it commenced its deliberations in February 1911. The Round Table could perhaps be forgiven for failing to anticipate Churchill's apparent conversion to their cause in a major public speech during September 1912 in which he urged his Dundee constituents to consider a federal United Kingdom. His conception of a reconstructed Albion included national parliaments for Ireland, Wales and Scotland and regional legislatures within England – all subordinate to an imperial parliament. Churchill's own version of 'home rule all round' would, he argued, solve the Irish problem and facilitate the Dominions in a new central government of the empire. Empire, Ireland and federalism were thus indissolubly connected in his mind. Kendle noted that Churchill spoke speculatively and not as a cabinet representative, but his speech had 'wide reverberations' and he 'helped in making federalism a major talking-point once more in party and intellectual circles; and it remained at the forefront of the political stage until the early summer of 1914'.[66]

The cabinet committee on home rule comprised seven members: Augustine Birrell, Lloyd George, Winston Churchill, Herbert Samuel, Sir Edward Grey, Lord Haldane and its chairman, Lord Loreburn. According to Jalland, 'United Kingdom devolution was the only alternative to the Gladstonian approach under consideration in 1911, and it received substantial support'. Consequently 'federalism and finance obsessed the Cabinet in 1911'.[67] Only Churchill and Lloyd George actually presented federal proposals to the committee. Churchill circulated two memoranda in February and March, proposing a full-blown scheme of 'home rule all round'. It spelled out a United Kingdom divided into ten segments, each with its own assembly for legislative and administrative purposes, and we can see how far this concrete scheme foreshadowed his famous Dundee speech of September 1912. Lloyd George's proposal was far less radical. It acknowledged that general devolution should be the ultimate goal, but recommended that Irish home rule be implemented immediately while bills relating exclusively to England, Wales and Scotland should be dealt with by grand committees of the regional members concerned.[68] Neither plan was accepted, although Lloyd George's 'grand committee' suggestion was actually incorporated in the August 1911 draft of the home rule bill, but subsequently dropped. When the third Government of Ireland bill was eventually introduced by Asquith in the House of Commons on 11 April 1912 there was no reference made at all to any future federal scheme. 'Home rule all round' appeared to have been summarily dismissed as impracticable. It was deemed by its critics to be too ambitious, too complex, irrelevant and ultimately lacking in public support.

Asquith did, however, make at least a token gesture to the federal idea. When he introduced the third home rule bill he indicated that the government considered it 'the first step, and only the first step, in a larger and more comprehensive policy'.[69] In practice the scheme that Asquith outlined was a very modest home rule proposal. The bill proposed the establishment of an

Irish parliament of two Houses, a House of Commons consisting of 164 elected members and a Senate of forty nominated members. In addition, Ireland was to be represented in the United Kingdom parliament by forty-two elected members, a retention of Irish members which left open a federal solution for the future. The Irish parliament was to be completely subordinate to Westminster. As in 1886 and 1893, a huge range of powers and responsibilities were witheld from the Dublin parliament including defence, foreign affairs, treaties, peace and war, treason, naturalisation, trade with any place outside Ireland, merchant shipping, coinage, trade marks, copyright, patents and lighthouses. The Irish were also denied control of customs and excise (though they were allowed extremely limited powers to vary customs and excise duties), and the policy areas of old age pensions, national insurance and labour exchanges were initially reserved to the imperial parliament until the Irish requested their transfer. In contrast, land purchase and the collection of taxes were reserved in perpetuity. In summary, then, the Gladstonian approach was adopted largely by default, in the absence of any clearly defined alternative.

Jalland has argued that Asquith played a shrewd tactical game in paying lip-service to the federal principle. It enabled him to retain the support of the Welsh and Scottish Liberal nationalists and those Liberals who were lukewarm about Irish home rule. It also allowed him to leave open a line of approach to the Unionists in case deadlock over the Irish proposals made compromise negotiations a necessity. Consequently, the Liberal government 'never entirely rejected the federal idea after April 1912 because its tactical advantages remained significant'. It remained 'a powerful negotiating gambit'.[70]

The two main obstacles to the future federal organisation of the United Kingdom contained in the third home rule bill, namely, the financial provisions and the failure to deal with the Ulster question, were also the two weakest features of the bill. Leaving aside the financial arrangements, which seemed to many Liberal federalists to be frankly incompatible with a larger federal scheme, it was the problem of Ulster that more than any other issue threatened to torpedo the home rule bill. Ulster, it will be recalled, had not received special attention in either the 1886 or the 1893 home rule bills. Gladstone had certainly been aware of the serious nature of the problem, but he had abandoned the idea of making special provision for Ulster for several reasons. First, it was a particularly thorny issue. Given that neither the Nationalists nor the Ulster Unionists favoured partition, it was difficult to see how their obvious socio-cultural differences could be satisfactorily accommodated in a home rule package. Secondly, few people took the Ulster Unionist threats of civil war very seriously in 1886 and 1893. Thirdly, Gladstone was undoubtedly among the majority of the cabinet in not seeing Ulster Unionist demands as particularly urgent. He preferred to leave the question open for consideration during the parliamentary debates. By 1911, however, the extent of Ulster's hostility to Irish home rule, especially a scheme which treated

Ireland as a single unit, was evident for all to see. Since the Ulster question was obviously crucial both to the success of the Liberal government's home rule bill during 1911–14 and the possibilities of a federal settlement for the United Kingdom, we will look at it in a little more detail.

During the years between 1870 and 1920 Ireland was increasingly characterised by a comprehensive dualism which separated the nine county province of Ulster from the rest of the country. The most significant empirical features of Ulster Unionism were its regional status, the uniformly sectarian character of its following and its integration of all the major classes in Protestant Ulster.[71] These distinctions produced a corresponding set of divisions which were mutually reinforcing: a regional dualism (Ulster versus the rest of Ireland); a religious dualism (Protestants versus Catholics); and a political dualism (British Unionism versus Irish Nationalism). The upshot of this corrosive constellation of social, economic, and cultural forces was a political divide which seemed intractable. There were, moreover, additional complications. Within the nine counties of Ulster there was an uneven geographical distribution of the two major religious groups in Ireland. The Protestants were concentrated in the six north-eastern counties of Ulster where they comprised about 66 per cent of the population in 1901. The sense of difference was further accentuated by significantly divergent modes of production. The north was predominantly characterised by industrialisation, while the south relied upon extensive commercial farming. Finally, the separate identity of Ulster Protestantism derived from its common sense of kinship, religion and culture, reinforced by the historical traditions of evangelical Protestantism. After 1886, 'political and religious lines of division increasingly coincided' so that the former differences between Protestants were papered over in the face of an assumed Catholic threat.[72]

This, then, was the political reality which confronted Asquith and his Liberal government in their attempt to deal with Irish home rule after the passage of the Parliament Act in 1911. Given the serious nature of the Ulster challenge during 1912–14, the British Prime Minister's relative indifference to it, up until the eleventh hour, remains quite remarkable. He seems to have believed that the insertion of safeguards for the Protestant minority into the home rule bill was enough to satisfy the Ulster Unionists. But the question of Ulster's exclusion from the Irish home rule bill was important from a different perspective. Churchill's famous Dundee speech had, as it were, opened a can of worms. His support for 'home rule all round' had weakened the government's position on Ulster. After all, if a senior minister could seriously propose ten or twelve parliaments for England, then it was equally feasible to contemplate at least two for Ireland. The logical conclusion to draw from this was that a strong case could be made for offering Ulster separate treatment.

Churchill was not the only Liberal to make the connection between the Ulster problem and 'home rule all round'. As we have already seen, there was also a small but vocal group of Scottish and Welsh Liberal nationalists who favoured individual parliaments for all parts of the United Kingdom. And in 1913 the revival of Liberal enthusiasm for a federal solution was manifest when Loreburn in the Lords and Murray Macdonald and Arthur Ponsonby in the Commons combined to urge the government to agree to an all-party settlement along the lines of United Kingdom devolution. When, in the same year, they were joined by a prominent group of Unionist federalists led by T.A. Brassey and Lords Dunraven and Grey, who advocated a genuine representative non-party conference to search for an agreement by consent, it is clear that a discernible convergence of informed opinion, cutting across major party lines, had crystallised in favour of a United Kingdom solution. Indeed, from March to May 1914, the Round Table movement seized the opportunity, which the Curragh incident and the intensified threat of civil war evident in Ireland provided, to launch a renewed campaign for a federal solution. A fresh House of Commons appeal for the exclusion of six Ulster counties until United Kingdom devolution was established attracted the support of seventy-eight Liberal MPs and fifty-six Unionist MPs.

The party leaders – Asquith, Lloyd George, Sir Edward Carson, Bonar Law, and Sir Austen Chamberlain – certainly expressed interest in the idea, but refused to take any practical steps in that direction.[73] In September 1914 the third Irish home rule bill became the Government of Ireland Act. However, a Suspensory Act, passed simultaneously, guaranteed that Irish home rule would not be implemented until after the First World War. As Jalland remarked, the outbreak of the war enabled Asquith to escape the consequences of his Irish policy and 'there is no evidence to suggest that a political solution would otherwise have been reached, given a little more time'.[74]

With the outbreak of war the Irish question rapidly became a secondary consideration for most politicians. Federal ideas understandably disappeared from public view. Everyone was preoccupied with the war. But 'home rule all round', devolution and imperial federation were gradually resurrected during 1917–18. According to Kendle, the chief driving-force behind this revival was F.S. Oliver. His personal influence upon leading Unionists in general and upon Lloyd George, Sir Edward Carson, Sir Austen Chamberlain and Lord Selbourne in particular, seems to have been crucial. Once again his personal contacts were of vital importance and his single-minded commitment to the federal cause ensured that 'the main topic of conversation was federalism'.[75] Chamberlain was especially amenable to the idea which he regarded as 'the best compromise available'. Federal schemes received wide coverage in the British press and figured prominently in both Scottish and Welsh home rule circles. Indeed, such was the ubiquity of this mode of thinking in the United Kingdom that Oliver himself estimated that about fifty Unionists, ninety Liberals and an uncertain number of Labour MPs wanted 'federalism for its own sake'.[76] This assessment of support for the federal idea in March 1918 may actually have seriously underestimated the real figure. A personal survey conducted for Lloyd George in May 1918 to weigh the strength of the federalists put their numbers at around 340 MPs stretching across virtually the entire party political spectrum.[77]

In hindsight, 1918 represented yet another crossroads in the overall evolution of the British federal tradition. It was the year when federalism reached its apogee in terms of elite opinion and the public policy agenda. Both Lloyd George and Austen Chamberlain agreed that a revised scheme of Irish home rule would have to 'fit in with a Federal plan' – it would have to be consistent with 'home rule all round'.[78] On 26 June 1918 the British Prime Minister met a very impressive all-party deputation led by T.A. Brassey (later Lord Hythe) which urged him to consider the federal solution. Lloyd George wanted to hear what suggestions the deputation had and to see how much support it commanded. This would enable him to decide whether or not to create a new committee of the House of Commons or a joint committee of both Houses to consider federalism.[79] Chamberlain observed that 'the outside movement in favour of federalism grows in numbers and strength' while 'the inside opposition shows signs of weakening'.[80] And *The Times*, which held out considerable hope for the success of Brassey's deputation, suggested that 'the future is clearly with the federal solution'.[81]

Lloyd George's response to these circumstances and events was understandably cautious. He had other pressing affairs of state on his mind, especially the conduct of the war in its final phase and vital questions concerning economic resources. Moreover, 'it was only with the virtual breakdown of negotiations over the home rule question in early 1918 and the apparent need to introduce conscription to Ireland that federalism began to seem a reasonable alternative to many British politicians'.[82] Lloyd George was also exposed to conflicting views within the War Cabinet. While opinion within the Irish Committee – set up by Lloyd George to draft a home rule bill acceptable to all the interested groups – hardened in the direction of a federal system, the War Cabinet had no desire to embark upon a full-scale overhaul of the United Kingdom. And if there was probably a majority for it in Wales and Scotland, there was clearly no popular demand for it in England. Lloyd George's objection merely echoed the remark made by Gladstone some thirty years earlier: England remained the stumbling-block to a federation of the United Kingdom.

In conclusion, then, 1918 represents a strange paradox in the history and development of British federal ideas. At this time the federal idea was undoubtedly a *zeitgeist*. Public interest in federalism did run high in the country. The British government came under considerable pressure from both executive and parliamentary elites in favour of the federal solution and it was compelled to consider a practical federal arrangement for Ireland. And if we examine the nomenclature of federalists who actively promoted federal ideas in this period the list is both long and eminent. Apart from the more prominent Round Table activists, like Curtis, Kerr, Earl Grey, Amery, Brand and Lord Robert Cecil, there existed a critical mass of Unionist, Liberal and Labour party sympathisers whose intermittent support and overlapping activities kept the federal idea alive. These included Lords Selbourne, Dunraven, Charnwood, Haldane and Loreburn, while in the House of Commons Walter Long, T.A. Brassey, Sir Austen Chamberlain, Moreton Frewen, Sir Edward Grey, William O'Brien, W.H. Cowan, Captain D.V. Pirie, Arthur Ponsonby, E.T. John, R. Munro-Ferguson, T. Agar-Robartes, J.H. Thomas and Arthur Henderson were among the most well-known enthusiasts of the federal solution. In addition, in the summer of 1918 the annual Labour party conference carried a resolution submitted by the executive in favour of a federal system for the United Kingdom and for the British Commonwealth as well. It must also be remembered that both Winston Churchill and Lloyd George had proposed practical schemes of United Kingdom devolution earlier in their political careers and the support of both J.L. Garvin and Geoffrey Dawson had been unwavering throughout the period. Finally, it would be hard to over-estimate the political influence of F.S. Oliver during the momentous years between 1917 and 1918. He more than anybody else supplied the ideas and the arguments in favour of federalism, and worked tirelessly to keep them within the realm of practical politics.[83]

None the less, the impressive groundswell of elite opinion in favour of the federal idea by 1918 did not bring it to fruition. As Kendle observed, 'federalism had become topical and possible because of the Irish problem but ultimately it was the Irish problem which made it impossible to either adopt or examine the proposition seriously'.[84] The obstacles to its implementation at any particular moment during 1910–18 were simply too great. Before we bring this brief historical analysis of Irish home rule and British federal ideas to a close it is worth reminding ourselves about the relationship between 'home rule all round' and federation. Devolution is not federation. This was openly acknowledged by the Speaker's Conference on Devolution which was appointed in October 1919 to devise a practical scheme of devolution for the United Kingdom.[85] When its report was eventually submitted to Lloyd George in April 1920, it did not indicate agreement upon a general recommendation. But the very existence of such a conference at this time was itself indicative of the impact of constitutional reform ideas upon parliamentary opinion. And if devolution was not federation, it could easily be construed as movement in that general direction. In his masterly account of the Speaker's Conference of 1919–20, Wan-Hsuan Chiao made the following observation, which is pertinent here:

> It is impossible to create a federal system by a mere delegation of powers to local legislatures such as is contemplated by devolution. ...
> Devolution may, however, resemble federalism in one respect, namely, in its practical operation. So long as Parliament should, on grounds of policy or expediency, abstain from interfering with the powers of the local legislatures of England, Scotland and Wales, the new system under devolution would work on federal lines. ... This is at best a quasi-federal arrangement, that is a halfway-house between true federalism and mere municipal home rule or local self-government.[86]

It was not for the first time in this period that both the Canadian and South African legislative experiences were alluded to as possible models for the United Kingdom, but federalism remained under the shadow of 'home rule all round'.

Notes

1. Bulpitt, J. (1983), *Territory and Power in the United Kingdom*, Manchester, Manchester University Press, 124.
2. Keating, M. (1988), *State and Regional Nationalism: Territorial Politics in Western Europe*, Brighton, Harvester Press, 80.
3. See Kendle, J. (1989), *Ireland and the Federal Solution: The Debate over the United Kingdom Constitution, 1870–1921*, Kingston and Montreal, McGill-Queen's University Press.
4. Boyce, G. (1991), 'Federalism and the Irish Question', in A. Bosco (ed.), *The Federal Idea: The History of Federalism from the Enlightenment to 1945*, Vol. I, London, Lothian Foundation Press, chapter IX, 119.
5. Kendle, J. (1989), *Ireland and the Federal Solution*, 8.
6. Keating, M. (1988), *State and Regional Nationalism*, 82–3.
7. Bulpitt, J. (1983), *Territory and Power in the United Kingdom*, 104.
8. Colley, L. (1992), *Britons: Forging the Nation, 1707–1837*, New Haven and London, Yale University Press, 367.
9. Boyce, G. (1991), 'Federalism and the Irish Question', 121.
10. Keating, M. (1988), *State and Regional Nationalism*, 83.
11. Bowen, G.F., (1886), 'Federation of the British Empire', *Proceedings of the Royal Colonial Institute (PRCI)*, 17, 282–316.
12. Galt, Sir A. (1883), 'The Relations of the Colonies to the Empire: Present and Past', *PRCI*, 14, 391–408; and (1886), 'The Means by which Imperial Federation may be Carried Out', *Imperial Federation*, I, 207.
13. *Hansard*, House of Commons (HC), 12 April 1886, 304, 1368.
14. *Hansard*, HC, 10 May 1886, 305, 637.
15. Forster to Bowen, August 1885, in Lane-Poole, S. (ed.) (1889), *Thirty Years of Colonial Government: A Selection from the Despatches and Letters of Sir George Ferguson Bowen*, 2 vols, London, Longmans & Co., II, 359–60.
16. Freeman, E.A. (1874), 'Federalism and Home Rule', *Fortnightly Review*, 22, 204–15.
17. Freeman, E.A. (1886), 'Prospects of Home Rule', *Fortnightly Review*, 46, 317–33.
18. Freeman to Bryce, 4 July 1886, *Bryce Papers*, Bodleian Library, Oxford, Mss. 7, 236–9.
19. See Hamer, D.A. (ed.) (1971), *The Radical Programme: Joseph Chamberlain and others*, Brighton, The Harvester Press, and Thornley, D. (1964), *Isaac Butt and Home Rule*, London, Magibbon & Kee.
20. Jay, R., (1981), *Joseph Chamberlain: A Political Study*, Oxford, Clarendon Press, 348.
21. Ibid., 123.
22. Jay, R. (1989), 'Nationalism, Federalism and Ireland', in M. Forsyth (ed.), *Federalism and Nationalism*, Leicester and London, Leicester University Press, chapter 8, 220–1.
23. Jay, R. (1981), *Joseph Chamberlain*, 351.
24. Kendle, J. (1989), *Ireland and the Federal Solution*, 25.

25. See his 'Local Government and Ireland', *Fortnightly Review* (July 1885), 1–16; and his 'A Radical View of the Irish Crisis', *Fortnightly Review* (February 1886), 273–84.
26. Chamberlain to Harcourt, December 1886, quoted in Balfour, M. (1985), *Britain and Joseph Chamberlain*, London, George Allen & Unwin, 168.
27. Hamer, D.A. (ed.) (1971), *The Radical Programme*, 239.
28. Ibid., 241–7.
29. Ibid., 252–9.
30. Ibid., 261–2.
31. Kendle, J. (1989), *Ireland and the Federal Solution*, 29. On Parnell's motives and activities, see O'Day, A. (1977), *The English Face of Irish Nationalism: Parnellite Involvement in British Politics, 1880–86*, Dublin, Gill & Macmillan, and O'Day, A. (1986), *Parnell and the First Home Rule Episode, 1884–87*, Dublin, Gill & Macmillan.
32. *The Times*, 9 and 16 September 1885, and Boyd, C.W. (ed.) (1914), *Mr. Chamberlain's Speeches*, 2 vols, London, Constable, I, 241–3, quoted in Kendle, J. (1989), *Ireland and the Federal Solution*, 29–30.
33. Chamberlain to Labouchere, 26 December 1885, in Thorold, A. (1913), *The Life of Henry Labouchere*, London, Constable, 272.
34. Chamberlain to Dilke, 26 December 1885, in Gwynn, S. and Tuckwell, G. (1917), *The Life of the Rt. Hon. Sir Charles Dilke*, 2 vols, London, John Murray, II, 199–201.
35. Dilke to Chamberlain, 1 May 1886, and Chamberlain to Dilke, 3 May 1886, in ibid., II, 216–17.
36. Kendle, J. (1989), *Ireland and the Federal Solution*, 31.
37. Jay, R. (1981), *Joseph Chamberlain*, 125.
38. Balfour, M. (1985), *Britain and Joseph Chamberlain*, 183.
39. *Hansard*, HC, 9 April 1886, 304, 1206.
40. Jay, R. (1981), *Joseph Chamberlain*, 123.
41. Ibid., 124.
42. Ibid., 123.
43. Strauss, W.L. (1942), *Joseph Chamberlain and the Theory of Imperialism*, Washington, DC, American Council on Public Affairs, 54–6.
44. Rawtenstall, 8 July 1886, in Boyd, C.W. (ed.) (1914), *Mr. Chamberlain's Speeches*, I, 279.
45. Chamberlain to Sir A. Galt, 20 July 1886, *Chamberlain Papers*, Birmingham University, JC/15/138. Galt was the first Canadian High Commissioner in London.
46. Jay, R. (1981), *Joseph Chamberlain*, 327–8.
47. Rosebery to Gladstone, 11 August 1889, *Gladstone Papers*, British Library, London, Add. Mss. 44289, 97. For Rosebery's views, see Burgess, M. (October 1979), 'Lord Rosebery and the Imperial Federation League, 1884–1893', *New Zealand Journal of History*, 13, No. 2, 165–81.
48. Munro-Ferguson to Rosebery, 30 August 1889, *Rosebery Papers*, National Library of Scotland, Edinburgh, Ms. 10017, 148–9.
49. Childers to Gladstone, 10 October 1889, *Gladstone Papers*, Add. Mss. 44132, 295–6.
50. T.E. Ellis to Herbert Lewis, 21 June 1889, *T.E. Ellis Mss.*, National Library of Wales, Aberystwyth, quoted in Hamer, D.A. (1972), *Liberal Politics in the Age of Gladstone and Rosebery*, Oxford, Clarendon Press, 156, fn. 3.
51. Childers to Gladstone, 18 October 1889, *Gladstone Papers*, Add. Mss. 44132, 299.
52. Bulpitt, J. (1983), *Territory and Power in the United Kingdom*, 129–30.

53. Ibid., 128.
54. Ibid., 129.
55. Ibid.
56. See Kendle, J. (1975), *The Round Table Movement and Imperial Union*, Toronto, University of Toronto Press.
57. Grey to Curtis, 14 December 1909, quoted in ibid., 132–3.
58. Kerr to Curtis, 29 July 1910, quoted in ibid., 135.
59. Kendle, J. (1975), *The Round Table Movement*, 337.
60. Kerr to Curtis, 10 August 1910, quoted in ibid., 136.
61. Boyce, D.G. and Stubbs, J.O. (October 1976), 'F.S. Oliver, Lord Selbourne and Federalism', *Journal of Imperial and Commonwealth History*, 5, No. 1., 54.
62. Kendle, J. (1975), *The Round Table Movement*, 136.
63. See Murphy, R. (1986), 'Faction in the Conservative Party and the Home Rule Crisis, 1912–1914', *History*, 71, 222–34.
64. Jalland, P. (October 1979), 'United Kingdom Devolution 1910–14: Political Panacea or Tactical Diversion?', *English Historical Review*, 94, No. 373, 760–2.
65. Jalland, P. (October 1979), 'United Kingdom Devolution', 763. For further information, see Hanham, H. (1969), *Scottish Nationalism*, London, Faber and Faber, 91–118.
66. Kendle, J. (1975), *The Round Table Movement*, 349.
67. Jalland, P. (1980), *The Liberals and Ireland: The Ulster Question in British Politics to 1914*, Brighton, Harvester Press, 37. See also Loughlin, J. (1986), *Gladstone, Home Rule and the Ulster Question*, Dublin, Gill & Macmillan.
68. Jalland, P. (1980), *The Liberals and Ireland*, 38–9.
69. Asquith's speech, *Hansard*, HC, 11 April 1912, 36, 1399–1426.
70. Jalland, P. (1980), *The Liberals and Ireland*, 40.
71. See Gibbon, P. (1975), *The Origins of Ulster Unionism: The Formation of Popular Protestant Politics and Ideology in Nineteenth Century Ireland*, Manchester, Manchester University Press, 9. See also Savage, D. (1960–61), 'The Origins of the Ulster Unionist Party, 1885–6', *Irish Historical Studies*, XII, 185–208, and Buckland, P. (1973), *Ulster Unionism and the Origins of Northern Ireland, 1886–1922*, Dublin, Gill & Macmillan.
72. Jalland, P. (1980), *The Liberals and Ireland*, 52.
73. Jalland, P. (October 1979), 'United Kingdom Devolution', 784.
74. Jalland, P. (1980), *The Liberals and Ireland*, 260.
75. Kendle, J. (1971), 'Federalism and the Irish Problem in 1918', *History*, 56, 213.
76. Ibid., 214.
77. Ibid., 217.
78. Ibid., 216 and Kendle, J. (1989), *Ireland and the Federal Solution*, 197. For further details about how Irish home rule was finally resolved, see McDowell, R.B. (1970), *The Irish Convention, 1917–18*, London, Routledge & Kegan Paul, and Boyce, D.G. (1970–71), 'British Conservative Opinion, the Ulster Question and the Partition of Ireland, 1919–21', *Irish Historical Studies*, XVII, 89–112.
79. Kendle, J. (1989), *Ireland and the Federal Solution*, 205.
80. Ibid., 205–6.
81. 'Ireland and a Federal Solution', *The Times*, 19 June 1918.
82. Kendle, J. (1971), 'Federalism and the Irish Problem in 1918', 207.
83. See Boyce, D.G. and Stubbs, J.O. (October 1976), 'F.S. Oliver, Lord Selbourne and Federalism', 53–81 and Kendle, J. (1989), *Ireland and the Federal Solution*,

192–3 and 208.

84. Kendle, J. (1971), 'Federalism and the Irish Problem in 1918', 230.

85. The classic work on this subject is Chiao, W.-H. (1926), *Devolution in Great Britain*, New York, Columbia University Press (reprinted and republished in 1969 by AMS Press), but Coupland, Sir R. (1954), *Welsh and Scottish Nationalism: A Study*, London, Collins, 321–5 is also informative.

86. Chiao, W.-H. (1926), *Devolution in Great Britain*, 33–4.

CHAPTER 5

The enigma of Ireland: federal ideas in a truncated state, 1921–95

Northern Ireland: the politics of partition, 1921–25

The partition of Ireland came into effect on 7 June 1921 when the Stormont Parliament was formally opened in Belfast. Having swept the polls on 24 May 1921 at the first general election in the British Isles to be held under a proportional representation system (PR), the single transferable vote (STV), James Craig, the leader of the Unionists, became the first prime minister of Northern Ireland. For the following fifty years, up until 1972, Northern Ireland was the only part of the United Kingdom to gain practical experience of devolution. But what did partition mean and what was its significance for the British federal tradition? Historical interpretations of Anglo-Irish relations and the imaginative constitutional reform agenda that these relations have intermittently inspired, especially during the period 1910–20, remain understandably contentious. Indeed, history itself has become part of the problem. It, too, is a prisoner of the past. Both the interpretation and the teaching of Irish history have become weapons of competing partisan loyalties. They legitimise communal identities and rival views of partition. It is still impossible today to liberate Irish history from this particularly sterile and suffocating form of imprisonment.

The constitution of Northern Ireland has been described and analysed in a number of authoritative studies and only a broad outline is necessary in order to answer the two questions posed above.[1] In retrospect, the complex circumstances surrounding its slow emergence were as important as the act itself. In a short survey of these circumstances, Nicholas Mansergh observed that the constitutional settlement which was finally agreed as a result of the 1918–19 discussions 'was the only outcome consistent with semblance of Coalition Cabinet consensus and parliamentary viability'. The Act of 1920 was 'fashioned in cabinet committee and carried the unmistakable marks of successful committee searching for compromise'. It was the product of 'the continually narrowing range of choice, which had confronted each successive British government since the outbreak of War'.[2]

The 1920 Act provided for separate parliaments in Northern and Southern Ireland as a solution to the home rule controversy. Patrick Buckland has argued that the Act was 'basically a device adopted by the British government and parliament anxious to get rid of the Irish question and yet obliged to redeem pledges to Ulster unionists'.[3] In the event only the Northern Ireland Parliament was established. And the proposed Council of Ireland, a body of representatives elected by each parliament whose main purpose was to encourage the two parliaments to work together in a 'bond of union' with a further devolution of authority anticipated at a later date, never functioned at all.[4] The Northern Ireland Parliament was a bicameral legislature and in addition there was reduced, but continuing, representation (13 members) at Westminster. The Parliament to which authority was devolved consisted of a Governor, acting on behalf of the Crown, and two Houses. The House of Commons comprised 52 members elected, as we have already noted, by PR. The Senate, however, consisted of 26 members – 24 elected by the Commons in direct proportion to the party strength in that House, plus two *ex-officio* members, the Lord Mayor of Belfast and the Mayor of Londonderry. It is important to note that the Ulster Unionists did not see the necessity for a second chamber of the Northern parliament. It was pressure from the Southern Unionists, concerned to secure protection for themselves as a minority in the South, that persuaded the House of Lords to amend the original bill. The Northern Unionists, according to Buckland, did not give much, if any, thought to the question of the protection of minorities in the North. Indeed, so concerned were they with safeguarding their position as the majority that 'they made no attempt to associate the nationalist minority with the new state'.[5] This explains why the powers of the Northern Ireland Senate were modest. It was only ever intended to reflect the unionist majority in the northern House of Commons.

The Northern Ireland government operated with a written constitution comprising the Government of Ireland Act, 1920 and subsequent amendments. The Act of 1920 was, as Mansergh has observed, 'Northern Ireland's constituent Act'.[6] It laid down the basic lines along which the devolved system was to operate, specified the financial arrangements that were to apply, and defined precisely the roles and powers of the governments at Stormont and Westminster. Of equal though neglected importance was the administrative history of British disengagement from Ireland and the establishment by the British government of 'central administrative apparatus working in the interests of the prospective Northern Ireland government'. This effectively gave the Ulster Unionists their official blessing and active assistance in the process of 'building the wall of administrative partition'.[7] Although Northern Ireland remained part of the United Kingdom, therefore, it was equipped with 'all the panoply of a modern parliamentary state on the Westminster model'.[8] In these peculiar circumstances Northern Ireland's system of government sustained two foci: an internal focus which encompassed the working of the parliamentary and cabinet system, together with an inherited administrative structure, and an external focus which referred to its special relationship with the Westminster government. Given the unyielding unitary, majoritarian nature of Unionist thought and practice in Northern Ireland, we will concentrate upon the external relationship with Westminster.

What was the precise constitutional status of Northern Ireland under the Act of 1920 and how far did it contribute to the British federal tradition? The politics of partition during these years remains the subject of much debate and controversy. Let us look first at this contentious issue before we address the questions posed above. Recent research into the subterranean administrative manoeuvrings of the British government suggests that it played a much more significant role in partition than has hitherto been acknowledged.[9] But the conventional scholarly view that the partition of Ireland was achieved by default has endured. George Boyce provides an example of this dominant interpretation:

> There is no reason to believe that the British public was insincere in its conviction that north and south would unite at some future date, that Irishmen had no irreconcilable conflict but a community of interests that both sides obstinately refused to recognise.[10]

Mansergh, too, claimed that the 1920 Act was 'drafted for application in Southern as well as in Northern Ireland'. 'That', he argued, 'was of the essence'. Indeed, this was why the institutions of devolution in the six counties were 'on so elaborate a scale'.[11] They were intended to be put to the service of Irish unity. We are left, then, with a remarkable irony. Among the many paradoxes evident in any historical survey of Anglo-Irish relations, one in particular is outstanding: that after such a long period of active resistance to Irish home rule Northern Ireland should be the one part of the United Kingdom to be given it.

The historical evidence that the Ulster Unionists did not want home rule is overwhelming. Their overriding preference was for straightforward exclusion together with direct rule from Westminster. Buckland's conclusion is representative of the conventional historical verdict:

> ... the creation of Northern Ireland was not the product of the demand of a local Ulster nationalism à la Basque. Ulster unionists had not asked for their own state. Originally they had wanted to block home rule completely and to remain part of the United Kingdom, just like Yorkshire or Scotland. ... Yet it would not be strictly accurate to say that Ireland was arbitrarily partitioned by Britain.[12]

Political scientists and lawyers have concurred with this verdict. The famous statement made by Sir James Craig to Lloyd George that in accepting the 1920 Act Ulster had made the 'supreme sacrifice' is often used to reinforce the point. In consenting to the establishment of a separate parliament much against their wishes, Craig claimed that the Ulster Unionists had acted in the interests of peace and as 'a final settlement of the long outstanding difficulty with which Great Britain had been confronted'.[13] The Ulster Unionists realised very quickly the real advantage of having their own local parliament. The creation of Northern Ireland with its built-in Protestant and Unionist majority would be their best guarantee against being forced into a united Ireland at some future date. Indeed, with a parliament of their own – giving them a real legitimacy – they would be more secure than if they were governed directly from Westminster. In the Westminster Parliament, where they would have at most thirty elected members, they could easily be out-voted and Northern Ireland constitutionally handed over to Dublin against their wishes. It was no accident that Craig called for the 'dignity' of the new parliament 'so that no opponents at any time dare come forward and say of that great structure ... that it is only a small affair, and we can easily sweep it to one side'.[14]

It is only in the light of these circumstances that devolution to Northern Ireland can be accurately portrayed as having arisen out of 'a historical fluke'.[15] But history is littered with such examples of human promise unfulfilled. In politics the temporary often becomes permanent. We are left with strange legacies: the politics of unintended consequences. This was the position and status of Northern Ireland and therefore of the Irish Free State – the truncated state – after 1922. The constitutional status of Northern Ireland can now be summarised. Section 75 of the Act of 1920 was explicit: the Parliament of the United Kingdom remained the supreme authority and retained 'unaffected and undiminished' authority over 'all persons, matters and things' in Northern Ireland. Crucially, the power of constitutional amendment resided with Westminster. But Stormont was empowered to pass legislation (using the terms of the preamble to Canada's constitution, the British North America Act) for the 'peace, order and good government' of Northern Ireland in matters relating exclusively to it. The Act set out the subjects which were excluded from its purview, classified as 'excepted' and 'reserved' services. 'Excepted' services were matters which concerned the United Kingdom as a whole and included the Crown, armed forces, foreign relations, external trade, naturalisation, coinage, aerial navigation, wireless telegraph, weights and measures, and patent rights. The 'reserved' matters were fewer and included the Post Office, reserved taxation, savings banks, designs for stamps, registration of deeds, land purchase, and the Supreme Court of Northern Ireland. It was originally intended that the subjects which were reserved by Westminster would be transferred eventually to the transitional Council of Ireland, pending an agreement by the two parliaments to establish an all-Ireland parliament.

Responsibility for all services other than those excepted and reserved was transferred to Northern Ireland. But there were important limitations placed upon the Northern Ireland Parliament. Section 5(1), for example, attempted to entrench religious freedom by prohibiting laws interfering with religious equality; Section 6(2) provided that in the case of a conflict of laws passed after 1921, the Westminster Act would prevail; and Section 12(2) required the Lord Lieutenant, and later his successor the Governor, to withhold assent to legislation of the Northern Ireland Parliament when so instructed by the King. There were, then, several constitutional restrictions imposed upon Northern Ireland which rendered both the government and the parliament subordinate to Westminster. In summary, it can best be described as a system of legislative devolution in which a range of responsibilities was devolved from Westminster to Stormont. But this short survey of the constitutional status of Northern Ireland does not tell the whole story. We must look in a little more detail at what lies behind this formal constitutional picture.

It is well known that despite the formal division of powers between Westminster and Stormont, and the formidable array of legislative, financial, economic, political and judicial controls both explicit and implicit in the 1920 Act, there was in practice considerable room for local autonomy.[16] This was due in part to what Richard Rose has described as keeping Northern Ireland problems 'at a distance'.[17] The process began very early in the life of the devolution experiment. Successive British governments have reinforced a constitutional convention that they would not legislate for Northern Ireland without its own consent. As early as 1923 the Speaker of the Westminster House of Commons ruled that no question could be asked there on matters transferred to the Northern Ireland Parliament. Furthermore, Section 6(2) was largely evaded by the insertion into the Westminster Act of a provision deeming that Act to have come into force 'before' 1921. In a case of conflict therefore the Northern Ireland Act would prevail.[18] Section 12 also became a dead letter after 1922 when the Governor reserved the Bill abolishing PR in local government elections. Faced with the threat of resignation by the Unionist government of Sir James Craig, the British government was forced to give way. Section 12 was never invoked again.

Both the constitutional facts and the conventional realities confirm that Northern Ireland, even in this early period, was 'indubitably different'.[19] As Brigid Hadfield has recently remarked, it was a part of the United Kingdom, but it was also 'a place apart'. Northern Ireland was 'possessed of all the trappings of a "mini-state" and, whatever the strict legal form, the appearances gave rise to suggestions that Northern Ireland was akin to a province or a state in a federal system'.[20] In his classic *Federal Government*, Kenneth Wheare denied that Northern Ireland was an example of a federal relationship.[21] From the strict standpoint of law, this view is clearly correct. But, as Vernon Bogdanor has remarked, in practice Northern Ireland 'gained a degree of autonomy more appropriate to that of a provincial unit in a federal system'. Whatever the constitutional and legal provisions, 'the system of government in Northern Ireland ... can be classified as quasi-federal, in that it displayed many of the characteristics of a federal division of powers'.[22]

This interpretation of Northern Ireland's constitutional status in the United Kingdom further enhances the British federal tradition. It demonstrates, once again, how far the structure of the United Kingdom has been able to accommodate, when necessary, a wide diversity of political relationships. The

1920 Act underlined the constitutional subordination of Northern Ireland to Westminster, but this was never the whole story. As Richard Jay has observed, the real basis of this new relationship was 'neither constitutional nor judicial, but political'. In practice, relations between London and Belfast 'assumed a quasi-federal nature'.[23] And it is also important to look a little more closely at the division of powers between Westminster and Stormont. The 1920 Act gave the Northern Ireland Parliament and government a wide range of powers which could be used to pursue policies separate and different from the rest of the United Kingdom. Initially Northern Ireland secured a large measure of financial freedom, 'comparable to that which might be enjoyed by a province in a federal system' and it did develop 'many of the characteristics of an independent state' with its own parliament, civil service and security forces. Indeed, given the distancing of Westminster from Northern Ireland, 'it is arguable that in practice the status of the Stormont government was closer to the federal model than the devolution model'.[24]

The responsibilities left to the Northern Ireland Parliament were significant and included the following: preservation of law and order; public health; hospitals; social security and other social benefits; education; roads, railways and internal transport services; agriculture, industry, and trade; housing; planning; and local government. This quite remarkable battery of powers and responsibilities was the result of a particular approach to devolution: the powers of the Northern Ireland Parliament were never specified. What were specified, it will be recalled, were the powers it could not exercise. This is an interesting set of conditions and circumstances for the student of contemporary federal systems. In such systems the question of where the 'residuary' powers are located is of critical importance both for the character of the federation and for its subsequent development. In the case of Northern Ireland, the enumerated powers were retained by the originating authority, namely, Westminster, while the residuary powers were handed over to Stormont. In comparative perspective, this example was in keeping with the federal model of the United States of America. William Livingston was correct therefore to underline at the outset 'not the limitations imposed upon the Northern Ireland Parliament, but the extensive powers of self-government that are conferred upon it'.[25] His interpretation of the United Kingdom of Great Britain and Northern Ireland was categorical:

> Here within the most unitary of unitary states is a local parliament elected by and responsible to a local area, which enjoys the right to legislate on an impressive list of subjects, and indeed on any subject at all not excluded by the limitations of the Act itself.[26]

And Livingston further emphasised the continued, if reduced, representation of the six counties at Westminster as yet another 'federal element' in the Act of 1920. In his view this firmly established a 'federal relation' between the people of Northern Ireland and 'the United Kingdom as a whole'.[27]

Before we bring this section to a close, it is necessary to pay some limited attention to the chronological sequence of events which enables us to depict 1925 as a watershed in Anglo-Irish relations. Without wishing to enter into a detailed debate about the creation of the Irish Free State in 1922, it is none the less important to note that the Articles of Agreement for a Treaty, commonly known as 'the Treaty', of December 1921 had significant implications for the British federal tradition. The creation of the Irish Free State gave Dominion status to the twenty-six counties in the South and this was also offered to the six counties of the North-East. Northern Ireland, however, was given the alternative option of retaining its status under the Government of Ireland Act, 1920, and within a month this option was exercised. In this event it was provided that Northern Ireland should be allowed to do so subject to a subsequent revision of its frontiers by a Boundary Commission. The terminology used to describe the role of the Commission was fraught with ambiguity. Its purpose was to 'determine in accordance with the wishes of the inhabitants, so far as may be compatible with economic and geographical considerations', the boundary between Northern Ireland and the rest of Ireland.[28] Needless to say, the Northern Ireland government refused to appoint its Commissioner in accordance with the terms of the Treaty and the British government was forced to intercede by appointing a Commissioner on its behalf. However, no agreement was reached and no report was published, the Free State nominee having resigned. Consensus of a kind between the three governments was finally reached in December 1925 when the existing boundary as defined in the 1920 Act was confirmed. The schedule to the Ireland (Confirmation of Agreement) Act, 1925 recorded the formal agreement between the British government and the Irish Free State that the extent of Northern Ireland should be fixed by Section 1(2) of the 1920 Act, namely, the six counties of Antrim, Armagh, Down, Fermanagh, Londonderry and Tyrone.

The overriding significance of the 1925 Agreement was that it secured at least the formal recognition of partition by the government of the Irish Free State. This, however, was not to last for very long and it was in such difficult circumstances that the Northern Ireland state made what can only be described as an unpromising beginning. But it had survived. The politics of partition during these years had presented the United Kingdom with its greatest constitutional challenge. The Treaty of 1921 altered the constitutional landscape both for the United Kingdom and for Ireland in a way that none of the interested parties had originally desired. Under the 1920 Act Ireland had been divided into two political and administrative units of equal authority, but after 1921 one of these units became virtually an independent state while the other remained as a semi-autonomous province – constituting a significant federal element – within the reconstructed United Kingdom.

Many commentators on the practical experience of devolution in Northern Ireland emphasise the uniqueness of the experiment. Devolution was a last resort – an official response to a set of circumstances that were peculiar to that province. In short, it was both contingent and circumstantial. Consequently, it has no necessary implications for the rest of the United Kingdom. There is much to be said for this view. The obvious example is the way that Stormont was given the unusual constitutional responsibility for maintaining an effective monopoly of force and for defending its borders as an integral part of the United Kingdom. Richard Rose underlined this unique predicament: Westminster handled the problem of Northern Ireland by denying the integrity of the United Kingdom.[29] Such a novel predicament could scarcely be imagined for either Scotland or Wales.

The creation of Northern Ireland, then, symbolised both the partial disintegration and the residual reconstruction of the United Kingdom. But the partition of Ireland also created a new and wholly unprecedented pattern of formal constitutional relationships both within the United Kingdom and between it and the Irish Free State. The peculiar constitutional and territorial outcome was an extensive form of devolution, one that contained strong federal elements. We will look now at how far the consolidation and subsequent development of Northern Ireland contributed to the British federal tradition. But we must not view it in complete isolation from the truncated state in the South. On the contrary, it is vital to our investigation that we use an all-Ireland framework because it has been one of the main vehicles of federal ideas up until today. Consequently, Irish federalism has continued to be an integral part of the British federal tradition.

Federalism in an all-Ireland framework, 1926–95

Bulpitt claimed that the tripartite agreement of December 1925 was 'the best indication that the period of challenge and crisis' in the United Kingdom 'had come to an end'. His thesis suggests that 1926 can be taken as 'the beginning of a new territorial era, one which was to last for nearly forty years'. He has labelled the period from 1926 until the mid-1960s as the United Kingdom's *ancien régime* during which time it operated as a 'Dual Polity'. This meant in practice that 'the degree of interpenetration between Centre and periphery was low'. Neither Westminster nor Whitehall had much to do with the concerns of Scotland, Wales and Northern Ireland.[30] Indeed, in the case of Northern Ireland political stability and collaboration between the Ulster Unionists and the Centre was such that there was no major public conflict between London and Belfast for almost fifty years.[31] London accepted variations in the degree of duality between different territorial sections and different policy arenas. Distinct policy patterns were followed in both Northern Ireland and Scotland, but in the former the model of quiescence was sustained only by 'the Centre's indifference, not by peripheral strength'. In short, the Ulster Unionists did not wish to provoke conflict with London because they could not afford to lose the disputes which might follow, while the Centre was either 'unable or unwilling to impose policy uniformity' from above.[32]

In the period of the so-called 'Dual Polity', the United Kingdom may be characterised as a system of mutual tolerance and tacit understandings. It illustrated once again the capacity of the central elites in London to accommodate difference and diversity. Given the relative harmony between London and Belfast, it is not surprising to learn that the Ulster Unionists were never receptive to the British federal tradition. Indeed, they were suspicious of any constitutional reform ideas which questioned the existing *status quo*. From their own particular standpoint they had very few realistic constitutional options. Federal ideas were, at best, irrelevant and, at worst, downright dangerous. They might be used as a smokescreen for a united Ireland. These fears and anxieties were entirely justified because that is precisely the context in which they were later to reappear.

To discover how and why federal ideas surfaced in the contemporary Irish polity, we must return to the very foundation of the state and underline the subsequent changes in Anglo-Irish relations. Richard Jay has traced the idea of a federated Ireland back to its creation in 1921. At that time sections of the Sinn Fein leadership became acutely aware that the immediate prospects of a unitary republic were slim, but were reluctant to concede continued British tutelage over the North. Accordingly, a think-tank led by Professor O'Rahilly of Cork University offered Switzerland as a possible federal model. Recent research has shown that Eamonn de Valera, the Sinn Fein leader who led political opposition to the Treaty of 1921, founded Fianna Fail and later became Prime Minister and President of the Irish Republic, was briefly a convert to federal principles. His commitment to a united Ireland, however, remained unswerving. Federation, in consequence, was purely expedient and amounted in practice to 'a proposal for repartition'.[33] De Valera never contemplated anything more than an advanced form of devolution for Ulster within a reunited Irish state. One possible solution, which received a good deal of attention from Dublin in 1921, was constitutional entrenchment: to convert the former majority Protestant position in North-East Ulster into a minority community with guaranteed safeguards within a reunited Ireland. This idea had surfaced in November 1921 shortly before the signing of the Treaty. Lloyd George proposed to Sir James Craig that the powers retained by Westminster under the Government of Ireland Act should be transferred to an all-Ireland parliament. Northern Ireland would send its elected representatives to that parliament instead of Westminster and within the six counties the provincial legislature would continue to exercise the powers already conferred upon it. There would be a permanent guarantee that these powers could not be changed nor its existence threatened except with the consent of a majority of its members. The proposal, however, was immediately rejected by Craig.[34] Subsequent changes in Anglo-Irish relations pushed the federal idea to the very margins of practical politics. De Valera's principal concern after 1925 was to defend the interests of the Irish Free State and to promote its own distinct identity. His efforts culminated in 1937 in the new constitution which, in Articles 2 and 3, claimed sovereignty over the whole island of Ireland. And when, in 1949, the Irish Free State became the Republic of Ireland and officially left the British Commonwealth, Section 1(2) of the Ireland Act of that year (an act of the Westminster Parliament) declared that Northern Ireland remained both a part of the United Kingdom and of the Dominions. It also affirmed that 'in no event will Northern Ireland or any part thereof cease to be' such a part 'without the consent of the Parliament of Northern Ireland'. In response to this the Dail Eireann unanimously passed the following declaration in May 1949:

> Solemnly re-asserting the indefeasible right of the Irish nation to the unity and integrity of the national territory. Re-affirming the sovereign right of the people of Ireland to choose its own form of Government and, through its democratic institutions, to decide all questions of national policy, free from outside interference. ... [Calling] upon the British Government and people to end the present occupation of our six north-eastern counties, and thereby enable the unity of Ireland to be restored and the age-long differences between the two nations brought to an end.[35]

These developments are interesting in the light of another event which, albeit briefly, brought the federal idea back within the boundaries of practical politics. At a critical phase of the Second World War in the Atlantic, with the fall of France and the German seizure of the Channel ports in May 1940, the British War Cabinet drafted proposals for an Irish bargain. They were prepared to offer Irish unity after the war in return for immediate Irish entry into the war. London clearly thought that Irish neutrality was negotiable and tentatively explored the possibility that de Valera might be tempted to trade it in for Irish unity based upon a 'post-war federal constitution'.[36] In retrospect, this proposal may seem incredible. But it has to be seen in a wider historical perspective than just Ireland. Churchill, we must remember, had also offered at this time an extraordinary federal proposal to France – involving a combined Anglo-French parliament – to prop up the collapsing Reynaud government of the Third Republic in the face of the Nazi juggernaut. De Valera, however, refused to compromise Irish neutrality in this way. He regarded it as a question of the sovereignty of the Irish Free State which would not be infringed by British promises of federal reunification. Dedicated to Irish unity, de Valera none the less repudiated this cynical deal; Irish reunification would be achieved by proper, carefully considered, constitutional negotiations with no strings attached.

It is noteworthy just how far British governments have been willing to give serious consideration to far-reaching constitutional proposals for a reconstruction of the United Kingdom state in such times of crisis. They have been unusually flexible and innovative when the circumstances have demanded it, that is, when the very survival of the state has been in question.

The most serious threat to the integrity of the United Kingdom state since the end of the Second World War has been located in Northern Ireland and it has been twofold: first, the peaceful political and (some would say) constitutional challenge of the civil rights movement; and, secondly, the growth of sectarian, terrorist violence. The status quo of devolution, effectively established in 1921, was first seriously challenged in 1968 by the Northern Ireland Civil Rights Association, representing mainly Roman Catholic minority interests. Between 1968 and 1972 a series of dramatic and turbulent events led to the prorogation of the Northern Ireland Parliament, the suspension of the government and the transference of all legislative and executive powers to Westminster. The experiment of devolution which had survived intact for fifty years – and in which Northern Ireland's position had been very much 'akin to that of a unit in a federal state' – gave way to direct rule from Westminster.[37] The political history of Northern Ireland since 1972 has been the search for a new constitutional settlement.

Since then, there have been countless attempts to bring the competing political parties and vested interests to the negotiating table and a variety of constitutional power-sharing ideas have been discussed and discarded. The most famous of these initiatives was the Sunningdale Agreement of 1973 and the abortive Executive in which both Unionists and Nationalists shared power in Northern Ireland. Federal ideas have jostled for attention in these discussions, demonstrating once again both their resilience and their continuing relevance to the problems of the United Kingdom. Perhaps surprisingly, federal principles were propounded by the Provisional IRA during 1971–72. At this time they revived the scheme for a federal Ireland based upon the four historical provinces of Ulster, Leinster, Munster and Connaught. But, according to Jay, the IRA's real intentions were obvious: the burden of the scheme 'rested upon repartition within a basically majoritarian conception of popular sovereignty, rather than upon federation'.[38] The Eire Nua federal proposal was couched in terms of traditional republican values, but it was in any case dropped in 1981 in favour of a unitary republic. Small wonder, then, that the Ulster Unionists have viewed such political ideas with a great deal of consistent scepticism.

The most recent example of federal ideas in contemporary Ireland emerged from the New Ireland Forum. Preparations for this fresh initiative were made in April 1983 when the leaders of the four participating political parties met to discuss arrangements for the Forum. Those present were the Irish Taoiseach, Dr Garret FitzGerald TD, leader of the Fine Gael party; Mr Charles Haughey TD, leader of the Fianna Fail party; the Tanaiste, Mr Dick Spring TD, leader of the Labour party; and Mr John Hume, MP, MEP, leader of the Social Democratic and Labour party (SDLP) in Northern Ireland. The original purpose of the Forum was to have organised political discussions about the future of the island within an all-Ireland framework. The Ulster Unionists, however, refused to participate. Consequently, the ensuing report of the Forum included the views and opinions of only the SDLP from Northern Ireland.

Meeting on 30 May 1983 in Dublin Castle, the first session was chaired by Dr Colm Ó hEocha and addressed by the leaders of the four participating parties. The goal of the Forum was carefully worded:

> The New Ireland Forum was established for consultations on the manner in which lasting peace and stability could be achieved in a new Ireland through the democratic process and to report on possible new structures and processes through which this objective might be achieved.[39]

Among the reasons given for the new initiative was 'the inherent instability of the 1920 constitutional arrangements' which had resulted in the 'arbitrary division of Ireland'. It was these arrangements which were responsible for the violence, discrimination and repression that each generation since then had suffered. Accordingly, Northern Ireland was characterised by 'the fact that neither section of the community' was 'happy with the status quo' or had 'confidence in or a sense of direction about the future'. It was deemed essential for any new proposals to 'assure the identity and security of both unionists and nationalists'. The underlying quest therefore was to find 'common ground' between both sections of the community in Northern Ireland and among all the people of the island.[40]

The Forum Report was published on 2 May 1984. Before we look at its conclusions, and in particular at the federal option, it is important to make two preliminary observations. First, there was a realistic acknowledgement of the nature of the Unionist majority in Northern Ireland. The Report recognised that Section 1 of the Northern Ireland Constitution Act, 1973 would allow a change in the constitutional status of Northern Ireland in the United Kingdom only if supported by a majority of the people (as opposed to the former parliament) of Northern Ireland. But it also noted that in practice this had been tantamount to a Unionist veto on any political change affecting the exercise of Nationalist minority rights and on the form of government for Northern Ireland. The overall result had been a particularly stultifying political deadlock in which decisions had been based on sectarian loyalties. These loyalties had thus been reinforced and the dialogue necessary for political progress had been prevented. In these sterile circumstances the Report called for the British government to reassess its own policy position on Northern Ireland. It warned that the risks of doing nothing were greater than attempting to tackle the fundamental issues. Constitutional politics were on trial and there would have to be action soon to 'create a framework' in which constitutional politics could operate.

Secondly, there was a clear determination not to be imprisoned by history. The Report recognised the origin of the contemporary problem, namely, the 'imposed division of Ireland' which had created 'an artificial majority in the North'. Once again the British government's responsibility was underlined. But the real obstacle to significant political progress in Northern Ireland lay in one simple fact: the problem itself transcended the context of Northern Ireland. Consequently, the only way to remove the obstacle was to change the context in which the socio-political conflict had been frozen. Rival values, attitudes and perceptions derived from particular contexts. If the context was changed, the problem itself would be transformed.[41] What in practice did this mean? The solution was baldly stated and lay in 'new structures' that would accommodate together two sets of legitimate rights:

1. the right of nationalists to effective political, symbolic and administrative expression of their identity; and
2. the right of unionists to effective political, symbolic and administrative expression of their identity, their ethos and their way of life.[42]

The Forum Report urged the British government to help create the conditions which would allow the process of genuine dialogue to develop. Among the 'elements of a framework' within which a new Ireland could emerge, there was an unequivocal recognition that any political arrangements for a 'new and sovereign Ireland' would have to be 'freely negotiated and agreed by the people of the North and by the people of the South'. Moreover, the validity of 'both the nationalist and the unionist identities' would have to be accepted and have 'equally satisfactory, secure and durable, political, administrative and symbolic expression and protection'. Lasting stability would be found 'only in the context of new structures' in which no tradition would be allowed to dominate the other. In summary, the new political structures would have to preserve and protect individual human rights together with the communal and cultural rights of both Unionists and Nationalists. This would result in a 'broader and more comprehensive Irish identity' because it would 'necessarily accommodate all the fundamental elements in both traditions'.[43]

In the variety of written submissions and oral presentations made to the Forum, the federal idea was particularly conspicuous. We will look at just a few of these suggestions. In October 1983 Sean MacBride, the veteran republican and civil liberties campaigner, put his proposal to the Forum for a federal Ireland based upon the Swiss model. But, as Jay has observed, it was in reality a revival of the O'Rahilly proposal of the early 1920s and deservedly suffered the same fate. It aroused considerable interest because of MacBride's own prestige but in the end 'the Swiss analogy was not convincing'. Jay's conclusion was that the scheme was 'largely abstracted from the kind of context in which a "federal bargain" could be struck between unionists and other parties on the island'.[44] None the less, the recurring appeal of the Swiss federal model as a potential solution to the Irish problem is interesting in itself. It adds to the richness of the British federal tradition.

Another federal scheme was promoted by Michael O'Flanagan in January 1984. As a former public relations officer for Sinn Fein who had left that party because of its abandonment of a federal policy, O'Flanagan resurrected the idea of a nine-county Ulster. According to this scheme, Ireland would be reconstituted as a federation of four constituent units with a weak central government. The old historic Ulster would be reformed and the Protestant majority thereby reduced. Given its historical resonance, this proposal had obvious attractions for many of the Forum members. But it was a proposal which was not conceptually much different from the regional idea propounded by the journalist, Desmond Fennell:

> I am not saying a regional planning authority or industrial development authority, or some gimmick like the once mooted Western Development Board. I am saying a regional government such as, in various forms, there are 20 of in Italy, 11 in West Germany, 26 in Switzerland and a number which I cannot give exactly in Spain. I mean, in other words, an institution with much the same powers as the Northern Ireland regional parliament and government which existed until 1972. ... This is not ... merely a matter of giving the regions, including Dublin, a sound self-controlled basis for improving their economies and their quality of life. It is also about introducing a significant degree of real democracy. Very decisively, it is about showing the Ulster British that we have some serious intention of accommodating them in Ireland.[45]

When Fennell elaborated the key theme of democracy, he arrived at a federal destination. He reasoned that any all-Ireland scheme would have to include significant powers of self-government for those parts of Ireland where the 'Ulster British' formed either a majority or at least a substantial section of the population. In his view only two approaches were available: either devolution in a unitary state or a fully-fledged federation. In rejecting the former as unacceptable to the Unionists, he none the less acknowledged the enormous difficulties inherent in the latter:

> Two-unit federations have seldom been attempted and have never succeeded. ... Political science and common experience teach that a federation, to be successful, must be composed of at least four or five and preferably more units. However, the Forum might well decide for reasons of tact and simplicity ... to propose a two-unit federation and to leave further examination of the federal structure until later.[46]

Fennell's federal submission to the Forum is interesting for the study of comparative federal political systems. His remarks underline two important considerations for the theory and practice of federation. First, they demonstrate a keen awareness of the existence of other regional and federal political systems which might have a practical bearing upon constitutional reform in Ireland. His comments about Italy, Spain, West Germany and Switzerland remind us how far established political traditions can, as it were, imbibe the values, beliefs and principles of other traditions. Since political traditions are not impervious to exogenous influences, they are all ultimately dynamic and derivative. Secondly, his remarks bring into sharp focus the thorny question of the number of constituent units in federations. This remains a matter of considerable debate and disagreement among theorists of federation. In a volume of essays which was devoted to the discussion of constitutional and political solutions to the conflict in Northern Ireland, Maurice Vile was sceptical about the two-unit federal proposal:

> Two units, each dominated by a different communal majority, would seem almost inevitably to come into head-on conflict sooner or later, with none of the mechanisms available to mediate such conflict in federations with a larger and more varied collection of units. The problem of creating a federal government which would not be either totally dominated by one unit or totally deadlocked by the other seems to be insuperable. The Catholic population in the North would gain a great deal of confidence because of the association with the South, but the Protestant majority of the North would have no allies to turn to in the game of coalition-building and would therefore tend to maintain its present attitude of a total unwillingness to compromise.[47]

This scepticism is certainly well-founded in political practice and experience. Two-unit federal experiments are inherently difficult to operate. But the recent example of Belgium, which established such a federation in July 1993, shows that these difficulties are not insurmountable.[48] Moreover, there are many different mechanisms and procedures which can be constitutionally entrenched to protect cultural identities and simultaneously furnish the basis for political cooperation in divided societies. The special position of Quebec in Canada is another example of a successful federal experiment where one culturally distinct province has survived intact for nearly one hundred and thirty years. Although Canada has ten rather than two constituent units, the socio-cultural character of Quebec has meant that in practice it has construed many federal government policies in terms of two basic political units, namely, Quebec versus the 'rest of Canada' (widely referred to as ROC). In many cases policy-making and implementation in Canada have been conducted in terms of two distinct units.[49]

In practical terms the Forum's Report identified three possible structures to facilitate a united Ireland: first, a unitary Irish state embodying the North; secondly, a federation or confederation; and, thirdly, a joint British–Irish authority for the government of Northern Ireland. We will concentrate upon the federal/confederal option. The Forum members were presented with a variety of federal, confederal, regional and constitutional hybrid proposals. One feature common to all of them was the overriding attention paid to federation as essentially a legal bargain. As Neil Collins has remarked, federation in Ireland was never viewed as 'an organic product and preserver of differences in society'. Most of the federal solutions submitted to the Forum 'laid great stress on institutional formulae rather than on social processes'.[50] What, then, was the Forum Report's own federal option? How did it seek to reconcile two quite distinct conceptions of Ireland?

Taking account of the variety of federal and federal-type suggestions made to the Forum, the Report veered uneasily between a federation and a confederation of two states. Let us look at the specifically federal option. The Report recognised that a federal Ireland would have to reflect 'the political and administrative realities of the past 60 years' and that it would also 'entrench a measure of autonomy for both parts of Ireland within an all-Ireland framework'.[51] It then outlined the contents of a federal constitution for Ireland:

> A federal constitution would be non-denominational and capable of alteration only by special procedures. There would be safeguards within each state and in the country as a whole for the protection of individual and minority rights. There would be a federal Supreme Court to interpret the constitution and to adjudicate on any conflicts of jurisdiction between federal and state governments, which could be made up of an uneven number of judges, one of whom could be from another country – possibly a Member State of the European Community – with the remaining judges coming in equal numbers from North and South. There would either be a special Bill of Rights or, alternatively, all the rights already defined and accepted in international conventions to which Ireland and the UK are signatories would be incorporated in the new federal constitution. The constitution could only be formulated at an all-round constitutional conference convened by the British and Irish governments.[52]

With regard to the distribution of powers, the Report stated that 'certain powers would be vested in the two individual states' while the residual powers 'would rest with the central government'. This decision would have to be negotiated, but it was claimed that agriculture, industry, energy, transport, industrial promotion and marketing would be 'more efficiently administered on an island basis at federal level'. Other services such as education, health, housing and social welfare would be entrusted to the individual states. Mechanisms for ensuring full Northern participation in the federal civil service would have to be devised. Each state would have its own parliament and executive, but security matters would be vested in the federal government 'in order to gain widespread acceptability'. The federal parliament could have one or two chambers – a House of Representatives and/or a Senate. Laws relating to previously agreed 'fundamental issues' could be passed only according to a weighted majority of the Senate in a two-chamber system or of the House of Representatives in a single-chamber system. Special attention was paid to the sensitive question of safeguarding Unionist identity and the Unionist way of life. The Northern Parliament would have powers which could not be removed by an act of another parliament. Existing civil and religious rights in the North would be unaffected. Unionists could maintain parallel British citizenship and special links with Great Britain. All the cultural traditions in Ireland, both North and South, would be guaranteed full expression and encouragement.[53]

In summary, the Report adopted the classic federal position: the central authority would promote the common interests of all the citizens while the constituent state authorities would protect their local individual interests. It must be acknowledged that the particular structure of political unity which the Forum favoured was a unitary state, achieved by agreement and consent, but it is also worth noting that the Taoiseach, Garret FitzGerald, called for careful consideration of the federal/confederal options. These had been fore-shadowed in the Fine Gael policy document of 1979 entitled 'Ireland – Our Future Together'. Moreover, FitzGerald himself had been influenced in his early intellectual development by the Catholic social philosophy of Jacques Maritain which sensitised him to the virtues of federal ideas as a means of social and political organisation. Finally, it is of considerable significance for the British federal tradition that we note the public support for the federal option reflected in opinion polls taken after the publication of the Forum Report. Collins has pointed to the edition of the *Irish Times* for 22 May 1984 which published the results of a survey of 1,000 electors in the Irish Republic. The survey evidence confirmed that the federal option was favoured by 55 per cent and opposed by 32 per cent of respondents. A similar survey conducted in Northern Ireland found 29 per cent in favour of the federal option and 56 per cent opposed to it, making the federal/confederal idea the least objection-able Forum option to Ulster Unionists. It was also supported by more Northern Ireland Catholics and SDLP sympathisers than the unitary state option.[54]

This survey of federal ideas in an all-Ireland framework has merely scratched the surface of the subject. Today the 'Irish Question' is even more complex and multi-dimensional than it was during the late nineteenth and early twentieth centuries. The long experience of living in a truncated state which is now an integral member of the expanding European Union has left its mark, as has the fifty-year experience of devolved government in Northern Ireland. In both cases the sense of difference has been strengthened, despite the undoubted socio-economic realities of cross-border linkage between the two parts of the island. Any attempt to analyse this labyrinthine relationship must accommodate at least four distinct, if overlapping, dimensions: London–Dublin relations; Belfast–London relations; Dublin–Belfast relations; and bi-communal relations in Northern Ireland. In 1981 there was an attempt formally to establish a new North–South Irish dimension when the British and Irish prime ministers instituted the Anglo-Irish Intergovernmental Council which was designed to facilitate at the institutional level contacts between the two governments on matters of common concern, including cross-border cooperation. The signing of the Anglo-Irish Agreement in November 1985, which established the Anglo-Irish Intergovernmental Conference, further re-inforced the Dublin dimension to these complex relations. Since 1985 it now has three formal aspects: the East–West dimension (that is the Council, dealing with matters of common concern to the United Kingdom and the Irish Republic); the North–South dimension (the Conference, handling matters of common concern north and south of the Irish border); and the internal Northern Ireland dimension (the Conference, to which the Irish government can put its views and proposals, especially concerning the interests of the minority Catholic community).[55]

Alongside these piecemeal, cumulative intergovernmental developments, there remains, in the absence of devolution, a political vacuum in Northern Ireland. Direct rule from Westminster has resulted in a lack of accountability and a lack of public participation. Both representative and participatory democracy in Northern Ireland are minimal. It seems reasonable to claim that the problem of the democratic deficit is peculiar to Northern Ireland and that it is unlikely to be resolved by any particular form of relationship with either Great Britain or the Irish Republic. One step forward, then, has to be the restoration of democracy – in its many different forms – in Northern Ireland. But it was not the intention of this chapter to suggest what constitutional and/or political reforms might be appropriate in Northern Ireland. Rather our purpose was to demonstrate the resilience and continuing relevance of federal ideas to the issue of Irish unity in order ultimately to underline the continuity of the British federal tradition.

Federalism has retained its vitality in the constitutional discourse about Irish unity precisely because the 'Irish Question' remains a problem of the United Kingdom. The Northern Ireland conundrum is one which transcends its own context. It is a living legacy of British political failure. Since 1921 the federal idea has waxed and waned in Anglo-Irish relations, but to have any practical relevance today it must be seen to offer substantial benefits to the Unionist community in Northern Ireland. This chapter has shown that since 1921 the 'Irish Question' has continued to generate federal ideas which have become part and parcel of the British federal tradition. During the last century, both the British empire and Ireland have been the vehicles for these political ideas. Now it is time to turn our attention to the third vehicle for British federal ideas, namely, Europe.

Notes

1. I have relied principally upon Mansergh, N. (1936), *The Government of Northern Ireland*, London, George Allen & Unwin, and Bogdanor, V. (1979), *Devolution*, Oxford, Oxford University Press, chapter 3.
2. Mansergh, N. (1974), 'The Government of Ireland Act, 1920: Its Origins and Purposes. The Working of the "Official Mind"', *Historical Studies*, IX, Belfast, Blackstaff Press, 46–8.
3. Buckland, P. (1973), *Ulster Unionism and the Origins of Northern Ireland, 1886–1922*, Dublin, Gill & Macmillan, 125.
4. Mansergh, N. (1936), *The Government of Northern Ireland*, 110.
5. Ibid., 124.
6. Mansergh, N. (1991), *The Unresolved Question: The Anglo-Irish Settlement and its Undoing, 1912–72*, New Haven and London, Yale University Press, 244.
7. McColgan, J. (1983), *British Policy and the Irish Administration, 1920–22*, London, George Allen & Unwin, 132.
8. Buckland, P. (1973), *Ulster Unionism*, 127.
9. See, for example, McColgan, J. (1983), *British Policy and the Irish Administration*.

10. Boyce, D.G. (1972), *Englishmen and the Irish Troubles*, London, Jonathan Cape, 113.
11. Mansergh, N. (1991), *The Unresolved Question*, 244.
12. Buckland, P. (1973), *Ulster Unionism*, 125–6.
13. Northern Ireland (NI) House of Commons Debates, 20 September 1921, Vol. 1, 48–9 quoted in Bogdanor, V. (1979), *Devolution*, 47 and in Mansergh, N. (1991), *The Unresolved Question*, 248.
14. Mansergh, N. (1991), *The Unresolved Question*, 249.
15. Maguire, P.R. (1992), 'Why Devolution?', in B. Hadfield, (ed.), *Northern Ireland: Politics and the Constitution*, Buckingham, Open University Press, chapter 2, 13.
16. For a detailed survey of these controls, see Birrell, D. and Murie, A. (1980), *Policy and Government in Northern Ireland: Lessons of Devolution*, Dublin, Gill & Macmillan, chapter 1.
17. Rose, R. (1982), 'Is the United Kingdom a State? Northern Ireland as a Test Case', in R. Rose and P. Madgwick, *The Territorial Dimension in United Kingdom Politics*, London, Macmillan, chapter 4, 129.
18. Hadfield, B. (ed.) (1992), *Northern Ireland: Politics and the Constitution*, chapter 1, 3.
19. Rose, R. (1982), 'Is the United Kingdom a State?', 129.
20. Hadfield, B. (ed.) (1992), *Northern Ireland: Politics and the Constitution*, 3.
21. Wheare, K.C. (1963), *Federal Government* (fourth edn), Oxford, Oxford University Press, 31–2.
22. Bogdanor, V. (1979), *Devolution*, 50.
23. Jay, R. (1989), 'Nationalism, Federalism and Ireland', in M. Forsyth (ed.), *Federalism and Nationalism*, Leicester, Leicester University Press, chapter 8, 223.
24. Birrell, D. and Murie, A. (1980), *Policy and Government in Northern Ireland*, 28.
25. Livingston, W.S. (1956), *Federalism and Constitutional Change*, Oxford, Clarendon Press, 274.
26. Ibid.
27. Ibid., 274–5.
28. A detailed survey of the Boundary Commission is in Mansergh, N. (1936), *The Government of Northern Ireland*, 116–22.
29. Rose, R. (1982), 'Is the United Kingdom a State?', 129.
30. Bulpitt, J. (1983), *Territory and Power in the United Kingdom*, Manchester, Manchester University Press, 134–5.
31. Ibid., 145.
32. Ibid., 141–2 and 146.
33. Jay, R. (1989), 'Nationalism, Federalism and Ireland', 227–8. The research referred to is Bowman, J. (1982), *De Valera and the Ulster Question, 1917–1973*, Oxford, Oxford University Press, 186–7.
34. For the details of this proposal, see Wilson, T. (1989), *Ulster: Conflict and Consensus*, Oxford, Basil Blackwell, 54–5.
35. Quoted in Hadfield, B. (ed.) (1992), *Northern Ireland: Politics and the Constitution*, 4.
36. Mansergh, N. (1991), *The Unresolved Question*, 312–13.
37. Bogdanor, V. (1979), *Devolution*, 71.
38. Jay, R. (1989), 'Nationalism, Federalism and Ireland', 229,
39. *New Ireland Forum Report* (1984), Dublin, Stationery Office, chapter 1, preface, 1.
40. Ibid., 5–7.
41. Ibid., 17–22.
42. Ibid., 23.

43. Ibid., 26–7.
44. Jay, R. (1989), 'Nationalism, Federalism and Ireland', 229.
45. Collins, N. (1986), 'Federal Ideas in Contemporary Ireland', in M. Burgess (ed.), *Federalism and Federation in Western Europe*, London, Croom Helm, 114.
46. Ibid.
47. Vile, M. (1982), 'Federation and Confederation: The Experience of the United States and the British Commonwealth', in D. Rea (ed.), *Political Cooperation in Divided Societies*, Dublin, Gill & Macmillan, 225.
48. See Alen, A. (ed.) (1992), *Treatise on Belgian Constitutional Law*, Deventer, The Netherlands, Kluwer, and Witte, E. (October 1992), 'Belgian Federalism: Towards Complexity and Asymmetry', *West European Politics*, 10, No. 4, 95–117.
49. For further details on the Quebec–Canada relationship, see Watts, R.L. and Brown, D.M. (eds) (1991), *Options for a New Canada*, Toronto, University of Toronto Press, and Gagnon, A.-G. (ed.) (1993), *Quebec: State and Society*, Scarborough, Ontario, Nelson Canada.
50. Collins, N. (1986), 'Federal Ideas in Contemporary Ireland', 117–18.
51. *New Ireland Forum Report*, 34.
52. Ibid.
53. Ibid., 34–6.
54. Collins, N. (1986), 'Federal Ideas in Contemporary Ireland', 122.
55. See Connolly, M. and Loughlin, J. (1986), 'Reflections on the Anglo-Irish Agreement', *Government and Opposition*, 21, No. 2, 146–60; Cox, W.H. (January 1987), 'The Anglo-Irish Agreement', *Parliamentary Affairs*, 40, No. 1, 80–97; and O'Leary, B. (January 1987), 'The Anglo-Irish Agreement: Folly or Statecraft?', *West European Politics*, 10, No. 1, 5–32.

PART THREE

Europe

CHAPTER 6

British federal ideas and the future of Europe, 1870–1945

British federalism: intellectual and philosophical origins

The nations of Europe must constitute themselves into some form of federation. ...
[W]e shall never abolish war in Europe unless we ... take up a completely new
citizenship. We must cease to be mere Englishmen, Frenchmen, Germans and must
begin to take as much pride in calling ourselves Europeans. ... [A]ll schemes will fail
which propose to unite Europe merely by adding together the states that compose
it. The individual, and not merely the state, must enter into a distinct relation to the
Federation. ... [T]he federation wanted ... is a real union of peoples.[1]

These words were neither written nor spoken by one of the continental
founding fathers of postwar West European unity. They have been culled
from the speech of a prominent Englishman who addressed the Peace Society
on the 'United States of Europe' in 1871. Sir John Seeley, Regius Professor of
Modern History at Cambridge between 1869 and 1895 and the chairman of
the Cambridge branch of the Imperial Federation League during 1886–93,
conveyed an idea and urged a political strategy which grew slowly but surely
in the minds of many public men and women in the following century.[2] It
was no accident that his work – an uneasy combination of inductive political
science and earnest patriotic commitment – reflected the contemporary trends
of his day. Seeley, echoing James Froude in his imperial themes and his anxiety
about the new era of large states which both German and Italian unification
seemed to presage, sought salvation in the British empire. But his own understanding of the relationship between history and politics compelled him in
The Expansion of England, first published in 1883, to see in the federal idea the
consolidation of the British state.[3]

Federation, then, would be the only way to guarantee peace and liberty in
an age of large-scale political units. Seeley had fastened on to an important
theme in his conception of international relations. The emphasis of his work
lay not just in the evolution of political forms; he was also specifically interested in the historical role of what he called 'the English state'. It was the
nation-state 'whose emergence to self-realisation in foreign policy in the seventeenth and eighteenth centuries he traced' and whose future 'he tried

anxiously to make out in the crystal-ball of inductive political science'.[4] Unlike Freeman, Seeley's conception of history gave precedence to the present over the past. Understanding the past was important for the present: it could teach policy-makers how to avoid repeating the mistakes of their forebears. The federal idea emerged from this particular juxtaposition of history and politics. Seeley fits into the British federal tradition therefore in an obvious way but at two discrete levels: first, his practical political concern for the future of the United Kingdom at the dawn of a new era of large states (he viewed Russia and the United States with particular anxiety); and, secondly, his more general academic interest in the historical evolution of the international states system. The answer to the former question was imperial federation while the solution to the latter problem, if his speech to the Peace Society in 1871 meant anything, was a genuine federation of European states and citizens. It would be a new peace order. The distinguishing hallmark of an international federal union of states and citizens was crucial. It was to feature prominently in the intellectual debate about a federal Europe throughout the next century.

Seeley's intellectual contribution to the British federal tradition, however, is interesting in another sense. So far in this book we have been concerned with the internal structure and the changing domestic problems of the United Kingdom. Both empire and Ireland furnished challenges and potential solutions to Rose's United Kingdom as an 'intellectual puzzle'.[5] Now, however, we must incorporate the European dimension into our analysis of the British federal tradition. It, too, has become both a challenge and a potential solution to the outstanding problems of the United Kingdom in the late twentieth century. Seeley's speech to the Peace Society in 1871 can be understood in these terms. His macrocosmic conception of history and international relations revealed the primary cause of war to be inherent in the nation-state itself. This fundamental assumption compelled him to situate the United Kingdom in the larger context of a European federation. It was not something which he believed could be translated into practical politics in the 1870s, but it was none the less the logical theoretical outcome of his own beliefs about history and politics.

Relatively little attention has been paid to this aspect of the British federal tradition in the years before the First World War. The focus has been on intrastate rather than interstate relations. There are, however, some interesting developments. William T. Stead, for example, was representative of the early federal tradition which linked empire, Ireland and Europe. As Editor of *The Pall Mall Gazette* and an imperial federationist during the 1880s, Stead had used his position as a leading British journalist to publicise the federal cause and attack Gladstone's naval policies for the empire.[6] As Editor of the *Review of Reviews* in the 1890s, Stead toured Europe and published his book, *The United States of Europe on the Eve of the Parliament of Peace*, in 1899. The 'Parliament of Peace' referred to the Peace Conference which was held at The Hague during May to July 1899. Stead wrote that 'this far-off, unseen event (A United

States of Europe), towards which the whole continent has been moving with a slow but relentless march, has come within the pale of practical politics'.[7] Sir Max Waechter, a British industrialist of German origin, also typified this tradition. Convinced that Europe's national rivalries were nurturing a dangerous and costly armament struggle which would seriously weaken Europe's economic and moral position in the world, he urged the peoples and governments of Europe to move towards a federal system built around the United Kingdom and Germany. Waechter had many European contacts and was actively involved in the first Congress for European Federation held in Rome in May 1909. He also established the European Unity League in London in 1914 to work for a 'Federation of the States of Europe on an economic basis'.[8]

British federal ideas regarding Europe, then, were still largely academic before 1914. There was certainly nothing resembling an organised political movement on their behalf. Even among continental Europeans 'the movement to unite Europe politically did not really get under way before the First World War'.[9] In the United Kingdom, however, the threat of war did usher in a period of intellectual and political introspection sufficient to sustain an intense debate about federalism within the British political elite. Carl Pegg has claimed, for example, that 'some of the most impressive and optimistic assertions of the European idea' in 1914 'were in England'.[10] The Union for Democratic Control, founded in London by Ramsay MacDonald, Charles Trevelyan and Norman Angell, declared in its first manifesto that: 'Policy should no longer be aimed at a balance of power but should be directed to establishing a European federation of states'.[11] The widely read *Review of Reviews* and the working-man's *Daily Citizen* both told their readers that future peace and stability in Europe depended upon the federal solution. In its first issue after the outbreak of war, *Review of Reviews* carried an article entitled 'The United States of Europe: The Only Way Out' and 'every issue of the journal for many months carried at least one article arguing the political organisation of Europe'.[12]

It is clear that at this time British federal ideas were propounded not only because of the Irish problem and the question of the future of the British empire, but also due to the existence of conflict which was widely perceived as inherent in the international states system. Sovereign nation-states, in the absence of some kind of effective overarching international machinery to arbitrate peacefully between them, equated security simply with military strength. They were in a condition of perpetual rivalry and permanent conflict which would intermittently, but inevitably, lead to war. War and the imminent threat of war have always had a catalytic effect upon intellectual thought and practice. The years immediately preceding 1914 and the experience of the First World War itself are further testament to this assertion. Looking back, we can see how the British federal tradition was enhanced and enriched by intellectuals whose response to the great cataclysm of 1914 was a critique of the nation-state itself. John Pinder has written in detail about federalism and the British Liberal tradition and he has underlined the emergence of a new school of federal ideas rooted in these particular concerns.[13] The intellectual source of these ideas can be traced back to the German jurist and legal historian, Otto von Gierke, who in the late nineteenth century resurrected the federal political ideas of Johannes Althusius.[14] It was the great Cambridge legal historian, Frederick William Maitland, who was responsible for the English reception of Gierke's theory of associations and his defence of corporate personality. This school of thought, led first by Ernest Barker, who in 1928 became Professor of Political Science at Cambridge, is generally known as English political pluralism. It is most closely associated with the writings of John Neville Figgis, G.D.H. Cole and Harold J. Laski, but it derived its inspiration at least in part from federalism. One writer on the subject of English pluralism, David Nicholls, has acknowledged that 'the pluralist movement can be regarded as an aspect of federalism' and 'pluralist writers are the inheritors of a long tradition'.[15] Indeed, in his magisterial work entitled *The Problem of Federalism*, Sobei Mogi claimed that 'the greatest contribution to the federal idea in Great Britain is, without doubt, the rise of the pluralist theory of the state'.[16] And Paul Hirst has argued recently that 'it would not be exaggerating to say that English political pluralism set the agenda for political theory in the first two decades of this century in Britain'.[17]

Barker's *Political Thought in England* was first published in 1915 and in it he wrote that there was 'much talk of federalism these days'.[18] Reflecting the strong current of anti-statist opinion in English intellectual circles at this time, he confidently declared that 'the state has generally been discredited in England'.[19] Behind these statements, as Pinder has emphasised, there lay the feeling that the much-vaunted 'single unitary state' with its 'single sovereignty' was a 'dubious conception' which simply failed to correspond with the realities of life. On the contrary, Barker, echoing the influence of Gierke, claimed that every state was 'something of a federal society'.[20] Barker himself wrote no major work on pluralism, but he had been Laski's tutor and it is clear that his sympathy for federalism and pluralism left its mark on his prodigious student. According to Nicholls, 'Barker tells us that it was Figgis, and through Figgis, Maitland and Gierke, who were the chief influences on Laski in his New College days'.[21]

These various intellectual influences upon Laski were evident in his most famous works which were tantamount to a critique of the state and the conventional principle of sovereignty. They were: *Studies in the Problem of Sovereignty* (1917); *Authority in the Modern State* (1919); *The Foundations of Sovereignty and Other Essays* (1921); and, perhaps his most influential contribution, *A Grammar of Politics* (1925).[22] We can now see clearly how the intellectual and philosophical origins of the British federal tradition were reinforced by concern for both international power politics in general and the European power balance in particular. The First World War demonstrated the futility of the traditional nineteenth-century assumptions upon which British foreign policy had been based. The British could no longer maintain a healthy distance from what were perceived as purely continental European affairs. The idea that they would intervene directly and decisively in these affairs only when their interests were at stake was redundant after 1919.

The inter-war years between 1919 and 1939 can be seen as something of an intellectual watershed in terms of their increasing receptivity to federal ideas. At both elite and mass levels in British society, federalism gradually gained widespread support as the means whereby war could be averted. We must be careful not to exaggerate its significance during these years when the sovereign nation-state was still 'very much of a reality both as an institution and in the mind of the public at large'.[23] But it is also true that after 1923 'whole staffs of periodicals, associated pressure groups in many countries, and at least two dozen books published every year' pursued the aim of 'an effective league of European states' against the renewed threat of nationalism.[24] In 1923 the Pan-Europa Union was founded in Vienna by Count Richard Coudenhove-Kalergi as an all-party mass political movement. It had very little impact in the United Kingdom but quickly became the best organised association advocating federation to emerge in Europe in the 1920s. As a result of the success of the First Pan-European Congress in Vienna in October 1926, in which over 2,000 European politicians, educationalists, businessmen, lawyers and journalists took part, the Pan-Europa Union established national committees in all the major European capitals.[25]

How, then, did British federal ideas reappear in the 1930s? What was it that propelled them to the forefront of the public policy debate among political elites in the United Kingdom? In order to explain the emergence of federal ideas which were specifically directed towards a new international peace order it is necessary to return to the influence of the Round Table movement in British politics. We are reminded of the important role played by the Round Table movement in attempting to mould and shape British intellectual thinking about the problems of Ireland and the empire both immediately before and during the First World War.[26] One of the early leaders of this movement was Philip Kerr, who in 1930 became the eleventh Marquis of Lothian. Recent revisionist historical accounts have successfully reinstated Lothian as one of the most original British thinkers concerning international federation.[27] Accordingly, his significance to the British federal tradition has at last been firmly underlined.

Kerr began his long journey towards international federation as the solution to war in 1905 when he formally joined Sir Alfred Milner's famous 'Kindergarten' in South Africa. There, as Pinder has shown, he was 'immediately exposed to the theory of federalism and the practice of unification'. In a letter concerning the future of South Africa which he wrote in 1907 he judged that 'Federation is what will ultimately come. It is really only a matter of time'.[28] In this judgement he was eventually proved wrong, but the federal idea stayed with him and when he returned to the United Kingdom in 1909 he became a leading figure in the Round Table movement dedicated to the 'organic union' of the British empire. There is no doubt that the genesis of the Round Table movement in 1909–10 was heavily influenced by the South African experiences of the 'Kindergarten' and their overriding concern for the problems of imperial defence and foreign policy must have helped Kerr in his intellectual voyage towards the notion of a federal peace order. According to Kendle, 'religion was the mainspring of his being' and his conversion to the religious beliefs of Christian Science in 1914 undoubtedly spurred him to reflect upon the nature and causes of war.[29] His spiritualism and idealism combined with his practical, first-hand administrative experiences in South Africa and the important part which he played as Lloyd George's Private Secretary both during the war and at the Versailles Peace Conference, enabled him to develop 'the most powerful analysis of the federal principle and its relevance to the international system to appear from any writer in any country during the interwar period'.[30]

When he left his post as Lloyd George's Private Secretary in 1921, Kerr developed the conceptual basis to his evolving idea of a universal federal peace order during two periods of study and lecturing at the Institute of Political Studies in Williamstown, Massachusetts during 1922 and 1923. These lectures, which were informed by Kerr's consistent admiration for the *Federalist Papers* and the practical success of American federalism, revealed a clarity of thought and practice and were published in *The Prevention of War* in 1923.[31] It is clear that by the early 1920s, then, Kerr had already begun to formulate a set of assumptions and beliefs about the causes of war which led him inexorably towards a federal goal. By the time he made what became his definitive statement on the subject in the Burge Memorial Lecture at Lincoln's Inn on 28 May 1935 – a lecture which was subsequently published as *Pacifism is not Enough (nor Patriotism Either)* – the League of Nations was already crippled. Europe was about to repeat the mistakes of 1914.

The intellectual and philosophical origins of British federal ideas during the inter-war years lie essentially in the critique of national sovereignty furnished by the experience of the First World War and the subsequent failure of the League of Nations. Both Laski and Kerr shared a basic set of assumptions about the role of the state in international relations. And while Laski diverted his scholarly attentions to Marxism and socialism in the 1930s, Kerr continued to develop his own original ideas about the nature of war and peace in international society. According to Andrea Bosco, Lothian's political doctrine could never be completely divorced from utopianism; it lacked a concrete political programme and it ultimately failed to create the political conditions in which a federal union of states was possible. But Lothian's lasting legacy lies less in his own political activities than in his penetrating analysis of international relations. Pacifism was not enough because justice without force to support it was idealistic; patriotism was equally inadequate because self-centred force was simply self-destructive. The genius of these words lay in their simplicity. Bosco's research into Lothian's life and work aptly summarises his contribution to the British federal tradition:

> The climax of the political career of Lothian, a man of thought and action, was embodied in federalism. In fact, the guiding principles of his conception of international relations had their roots in federalism itself. ... That conception was able to give a 'positive' interpretation of international relations, taking them out of the domain of the irrational, and placing them in that of political science. It is in this domain that Lothian's contribution to the tradition of federalist thought is significant.[32]

In this field of enquiry, of course, Laski and Lothian (as he was after 1930) are both part of a long tradition of Enlightenment thinking which dates back at least to Kant. And in the British federal tradition it is important to emphasise the intellectual and philosophical links between Seeley, Laski and Lothian, despite the differences which undoubtedly existed between them.

This brief outline of Lothian's federal ideas explains both how and why British federalism reappeared with such vigour in the 1930s. It sprang from rigorous historical and theoretical analyses of the causes of war and the practical experience of international relations during the inter-war years. But Lord Lothian's contribution to the British federal tradition achieved its full significance only after Federal Union was formed in 1938 and it is to this organisation that we must now turn our attention.

Federal Union: Europe, the Atlantic and the world

Prior to the formation of Federal Union in 1938, the only political organisation which championed the federal idea in the United Kingdom in the 1930s was the New Commonwealth Society (NCS). Created in 1932, its founding figure and main driving-force was Lord David Davies. Strictly speaking, the NCS advocated not federation but a fundamental reorganisation of the international states system. None the less, Davies did promote a conception of world order which owed much to federalist influences. His book, entitled *A Federated Europe*, was published in 1940 and depicted a United States of Europe as a regional bloc in the League of Nations. His was really a confederal scheme which preserved the decision-making integrity of the member-states, but it did challenge the traditional notion of national sovereignty. According to Lipgens, the NCS, with Winston Churchill installed as the President of the British group, had branches by the end of the 1930s in all English-speaking and West European countries. Its many publications between 1933 and 1939 urged a reinforcement of the League of Nations by the creation of a compulsory court of arbitration and a strong international body of troops under the League to enforce its decisions.[33] These prescient pleas foreshadowed the eventual creation of the United Nations at the end of the Second World War.

The NCS was the precursor of easily the most important British political organisation which championed the federal cause during the inter-war and the war years, namely, Federal Union. Up until recently, there was no definitive study of Federal Union. Those students who were interested in the organisation and its political ideas were forced to rely upon sources which were useful but none the less fragmentary. These circumstances changed in 1990 with the publication of *Federal Union: The Pioneers*, written largely by John Pinder and Richard Mayne.[34] As a result we are now in a much better position to understand precisely how and why the movement was formed in the years immediately preceding the outbreak of the Second World War. In this section, then, we will not provide a detailed examination of the formation of the new movement. This is now well documented. Instead we will look at a general profile of the organisation: its dominant political activists and its main intellectual influences and output.

The genesis of Federal Union can be dated as the autumn of 1938. On the 14 September 1938 Derek Rawnsley and Charles Kimber, two Oxford graduates, organised a meeting for friends and acquaintances whom they thought might be interested in launching a new political movement to prevent war. They were joined in October by another Oxford contemporary, Patrick Ransome, and together they quickly gained the support of several distinguished public figures: Lionel Curtis, Lord Lothian, Barbara Wootton, Wickham Steed, and Sir William Beveridge. The movement which was formally founded in November 1938 produced a provisional 'statement of aims' in the spring of 1939 which is worth quoting at length:

> National sovereignty leads to competition in armaments, economic self-sufficiency and internal regimentation, and thus inevitably to war, imperialism, poverty and loss of individual liberty, because where sovereign States fail to agree there is no remedy save resort to violence in the form of power politics or war. No international order based on co-operation between sovereign States will prove either efficient or durable, since all sovereign States in the last resort seek their own national self-interest. Nothing less than a union of the peoples can end this anarchy and give peace, justice and freedom to all.
>
> Accordingly we advocate:
>
> I. A Federal Union of those nations which hold that the State exists for the freedom and responsibility of man, and that government must be conducted with the consent of the governed.
> II. That this constitutional Union will assure national self-government to all units within the Union in those affairs which are solely of national interest, and will establish legislative, executive and judicial organs representative of and responsible to all the citizens of the Union for such common affairs as defence and order, currency, trade, communications and migration, and will possess the taxation and borrowing powers necessary to finance its own activities.
> III. As a first step a Federal Union of the established democracies to form a nucleus of the future world federation; such a nucleus to be open to accession by other nations which accept its basic principles, and to act as a loyal member of any larger organizations designed to promote international co-operation.[35]

This general declaration in favour of a union of democracies concealed what later came to be a highly contentious and deeply divisive issue, namely, the scope of the future federation. But in its initial formulation we can easily detect how far the intellectual ideas of Seeley, Laski and Lothian resonated in the movement's early goals. Indeed, it should come as little surprise to learn that the 'statement of aims' outlined above was printed in Lord Lothian's pamphlet entitled 'The Ending of Armageddon' which appeared in June 1939. According to Lipgens, Federal Union 'received strong backing and real momentum' from Clarence K. Streit's book entitled *Union Now*, which was first published in New York in March 1939.[36] In the United Kingdom the organisers of Federal Union first heard of Streit's book from Harold Butler, former head of the International Labour Office. Although they were sceptical about his idea of a nucleus of fifteen democratic countries, including the United States and the United Kingdom, linked to a federal union, there was a genuine convergence of informed elite opinion about the need for some new form of international government. The British publishers of *Union Now*, Jonathan Cape, allowed Federal Union to insert postcards in the UK edition, giving the organisation's London address and inviting enquiries.[37]

Union Now was an important and influential book which underlined the beliefs of those in Federal Union who wanted to see some sort of Atlantic union. But it certainly did not inspire the movement's creation. Nigel Forman claimed that 'the seminal publication which served to crystallise much of federalist thinking at the beginning of the War' was *The Case For Federal Union*, written by W.B. Curry, the headmaster of Dartington Hall School in Totnes, Devon.[38] Curry's book, which was published as a Penguin Special in the autumn of 1939, just as war loomed, had Federal Union's blessing and contained an epilogue urging readers to join it. Curry acknowledged his debt to Streit's book but stated that he had been inspired to make the attempt by the writings of H.G. Wells and Bertrand Russell. The war had merely emphasised the urgent necessity for putting these ideas into practice. Within six months *The Case For Federal Union* had sold 100,000 copies.

Barbara Wootton addressed the first public meeting of Federal Union on 18 May 1939 and its active local organisations numbered just over twenty in February 1940. But during 1940–41 it reached the height of its effectiveness and popularity 'having grown with astonishing speed and produced an equally astonishing output of books and pamphlets'.[39] The movement claimed an average of 200 press mentions each week during the early months of the Second World War and by June 1940 it had 225 branches with 12,000 members. Organised along regional lines, Federal Union activities included conferences, study groups, weekend schools and public meetings. Membership was set at one shilling for a year, but ten shillings and sixpence entitled a member to receive regular copies of *Federal Union News* for three months. These activities and procedures bore a remarkable resemblance to the organisation of the Imperial Federation League some sixty years earlier. However, poor financial husbandry almost ruined the organisation in its euphoric days so that in March 1941 fully paid-up membership amounted only to 1,351, with large company debts. These difficulties were largely resolved by the end of 1942 and in September 1944 the official membership figure had recovered to a healthy 4,727.[40] Like its predecessor, the Imperial Federation League, the success of Federal Union depended as much on sound financial organisation as it did on the enthusiasm and energies of dedicated political activists.

Let us look now at the intellectual basis of support for Federal Union. Like its two forerunners, the Imperial Federation League and the Round Table movement, Federal Union had an impressive array of support from among the established British intellectual and political elite. A brief profile of this august group of academics, novelists, lawyers, journalists, economists, trade unionists and politicians which, in one way or another, championed the federal idea in international relations, reveals once again the strength of the British federal tradition. The platform which facilitated a genuine intellectual debate about federation during the war was the Federal Union Research Institute (FURI) established in March 1940. Its energetic chairman was the Master of University College, Oxford, Sir William Beveridge, a former distinguished civil servant and Director of the London School of Economics during 1919–37. With Patrick Ransome as its secretary, FURI served as a veritable hive of intellectual activity, organising academic conferences and publishing federalist literature of the highest analytical quality. Apart from the ubiquitous influences of Lionel Curtis and Lord Lothian, the following abbreviated list of prominent public men and women who were actively associated with FURI gives a good idea of the strength of the movement: K.C. Wheare, Sir W. Ivor Jennings, Professor C.E.M. Joad, Professor A.L. Goodhart, Ramsay Muir, Arnold Toynbee, J.B. Priestley, H.N. Brailsford, James Meade, Lionel Robbins, Frederick von Hayek, Barbara Wootton, Lord Lugard, Ronald W.G. Mackay MP and the young economist and future Labour prime minister, Harold Wilson.

Between them this glittering intellectual group produced a wealth of detailed federal studies which continues today to repay further reading. Some of this literature was as bold as it was lucid. In his book entitled *A Federation for Western Europe* published in 1940, for example, Sir Ivor Jennings even included a draft treaty in his analysis of federation.[41] Lionel (later Lord) Robbins, the distinguished economist, had arrived at the same federal destination as Lothian, Curtis and others via a different route. His book, entitled *The Economic Causes of War*, was published in 1939 and it was to occupy a pivotal place in the evolving federalist thinking of the continental European Resistance movement in Italy.[42] Robbins approached the subject from the economic standpoint of free trade, migration and a common currency, and this led him naturally to reject narrow-minded national economic practices as detrimental to international peace and union among states. Kenneth Cecil Wheare (later Sir K.C. Wheare and Vice-Chancellor of Oxford University) was an Australian by birth and a Fellow of University College, Oxford, where he had already become something of an authority on constitutional law. Today Wheare is probably best remembered among academics for his classic study on *Federal Government*, first published in 1946, but his short essay entitled 'What Federal Government is' appeared much earlier, in 1941, as *Federal Tract No. 4* and it contained the same clarity of exposition as his later, more substantive, work. In 'What Federal Government is' Wheare conceded that the tone of his pamphlet was 'dogmatic' and that his own view of what constituted federal government was uncompromising. He believed that it was 'not an end in itself' but was merely 'a means to providing a system of government in circumstances where people are prepared to give up only certain limited powers and wish to retain other limited powers, both sets of powers to be exercised by co-ordinate authorities'. He concluded, with typical intellectual dispassion, that federal government was at least 'government' and that it signified 'order, not anarchy' and 'peace, not war'.[43]

Like the Imperial Federation League and the Round Table movement before it, Federal Union owed no special allegiance to any political party or ideology. However, it is clear that it managed to maintain this position only with great diligence. In the early years the representation of socialist views was manifestly strong. Barbara Wootton, for example, wrote a cogent essay entitled 'Socialism and Federation' while Professor Joad, the Head of the Department of Philosophy and Psychology at Birkbeck College, London University, and later a celebrity on the BBC's 'Brains Trust' radio programme, sketched his own left-wing views in 'The Philosophy of Federal Union'. H.N. Brailsford, a prominent member of the Independent Labour Party and a frequent contributor to the *New Statesman*, also wrote a forceful pamphlet entitled 'The Federal Idea' while other notable left-wing sympathisers, like Harold Wilson and Konni Zilliacus, ensured that socialist views were well ventilated. Indeed, such was the strength and visibility of socialist beliefs and ideas that Federal Union's Executive Committee, chaired after August 1941 by Miss F.L. Josephy, made a conscious effort to 'seek contributions of a more conservative complexion'.[44] Given the fundamentally humanist bases to international socialism – its optimistic view of human nature, its strong pacifist strain and its firm devotion to the comity of nations and the cause of world peace – it is not surprising that socialists and socialism should appear at the forefront of a public organisation like Federal Union.

The Labour party was also well represented. Probably its most prominent activist was Ronald W. Mackay, Australian by birth and a former lecturer in Philosophy, Economics and History at Sydney University. He had settled in the United Kingdom as a solicitor in the 1930s and in 1940 wrote *Federal Europe* which was later revised and reissued in 1941 as *Peace Aims and the New Order*. Mackay became Chairman of Federal Union's Executive Committee and took the lead in 1941 in rescuing the organisation from bankruptcy. He became Labour MP for Hull North-West during 1945–50 and for Reading

North during 1950–51. His last book, published posthumously in 1961 and unequivocally entitled *Towards a United States of Europe*, can still be located on the shelves of most established university libraries.[45] Mackay was accompanied by Henry Usborne, John Parker, Victor Collins and Rev. Gordon Lang, all Labour MPs, and the support of both Ernest Bevin and Clement Attlee was noteworthy in the early years.[46]

Federal Union was adept at collecting and collating the essays and pamphlets of its own contributors. In 1940 it published an impressive collection of essays, edited by M. Chaning-Pearce, entitled *Federal Union: A Symposium*. And in 1943 the series of Federal Tracts referred to above were republished as a book entitled *Studies in Federal Planning*, edited by Patrick Ransome. Together, these two books provide the student of British federal ideas with a wealth of historical material which furnishes an invaluable glimpse into the past. It also serves to buttress the British federal tradition as a perfectly legitimate, if neglected, part of the larger British constitutional and political tradition.

We have provided a general profile of Federal Union and we have looked briefly at its political activists and their activities. In addition we have commented upon its intellectual influences and output. But it is also important for us to look a little more closely at the key issue which served more than any other to divide the movement in its early years, namely, the scope of the federation to be achieved. As with both the Imperial Federation League and the Round Table movement, those who joined Federal Union did so from a mixture of motives. The single factor which served to unite the membership was a basic belief in the need to prevent a recurrence of world war in the future. With the failure of the League of Nations a recent and bitter memory, they sought a new postwar international order. They advocated federal union in order, once and for all, to curb the excesses of rampant nationalism. Only federal union would bring about that qualitative change in conventional international relations which was deemed essential to genuine world peace.

The original goal had been to prevent war in Europe but when this failed it was superseded by the grander aim of a world federation. There were, however, many differences of opinion about this more grandiose aim just as there were many gradations of thought about the strategy required to achieve it. Once federation had been rejected as a peace aim, it came to be regarded by many as both the building-block and the terminus of a future world order. Forman claimed that once the Second World War had begun, the earlier bold attempt to carry the country and convert British public opinion to the federal cause was quietly and necessarily abandoned. In its place a new political strategy, most closely associated with Ronald Mackay, was devised which had as its chief criterion 'political effectiveness'. This meant in practice the concerted attempt to persuade politicians and government officials alike to include at least a commitment to future federation in any peace settlement. The leaders of Federal Union therefore decided to construct a realistic statement of immediate proposals. They were committed to the elaboration of a

set of war aims, directed at the peoples of Europe, which would transcend
the war itself.[47] They looked therefore not merely towards the defeat of Hitler,
but also at what would replace Nazism. They opposed Hitler not in the name
of the nation-state, but in order to replace it. In this they shared an aim
which was common to all the Resistance movements in continental Europe,
namely, the desire to nurture a new European society.

The shift in political strategy from doctrinaire purity about federalism to
the pursuit of political influence clearly reflected the failure of Federal Union
to galvanise British public opinion on any significant scale. But the strategic
change also harboured difficulties for the movement. It brought to the surface
the deep-seated differences of opinion about the scope of the proposed federation. The first Annual Delegates' Conference of Federal Union, held in February 1940, presented a draft programme entitled 'Aims and Policy' and was
finally adopted by the Federal Union Council on 31 March 1940. This focused
on a federation of 'the Allies' with the nucleus being the United Kingdom and
France, but with Germany's inclusion explicitly forseen. World federation
remained the ultimate aim but the specific policy was formulated thus:

1. To work for an Allied Statement of Peace Aims challenging the idea of race
   superiority with a declaration of the rights of man, and the method of aggression
   with a decalaration of readiness to federate with any people whose government
   is prepared to recognise these rights.
2. To welcome any steps towards such a federation of the Allies or any other groups
   of peoples, provided that at the time of its formation the federation is declared
   open to accession by other nations, including Germany.[48]

Federal Union's aims were couched in anodyne terms but they never succeeded in reconciling the two broad schools of thought about international
federation which gradually emerged during 1941–42. One school, led by Miss
F.L. (Jo) Josephy, put the achievement of a European federation before all
other more extensive projects, while the other tendency, most closely associated with the members of the 'Peace Aims Committee' and in particular with
Konni Zilliacus and Charles Kimber, insisted upon an overall confederal world
order into which regional federations could be fitted. Zilliacus, a radical
socialist in the Labour party, was understandably concerned about Anglo-
Soviet postwar cooperation. These differences of opinion developed into a
real rift with the submission of the 'Peace Aim – War Weapon' report to the
main Annual Conference during March–April 1942. The attempt to clarify
the movement's goals and strategies resulted in an uneasy compromise. The
new text clearly gave weight to the proposal for a new world order and it
emphasised that a federal initiative should not take place independently or
outside of the overall confederal design:

It will be seen that the world government envisaged after the war comprises two
essential features: (1) a Federal Union of Democracies; (2) the World Confederation

of States of which it would be the nucleus. Both must be established as parts of a single treaty.[49]

Forman claimed that in reality the division was 'really a disagreement about means and not ends, since both factions thought it essential to include Germany in the councils of a federal Europe'.[50] His claim makes sense if we remember that several regional federations were envisaged within the World Confederation. The possibilities included, for example, a European Union (including the UK); an American Union (possibly embracing Australia); a Far-Eastern Union; and a Eurasian Union (incorporating the USSR). The genius of this compromise, at least theoretically, was that it would facilitate 'all sorts of half-way houses and intermediate arrangements between Federation and Confederation'.[51] But Forman's assertion may none the less be judged an over-simplification. He himself has acknowledged that the entrance of the United States into the War in December 1941 prompted many supporters of the federal idea to consider the prospect of further Anglo-American cooperation in more institutional terms. Views like these had already been expressed by several members of Federal Union from its very inception. Prominent among them was Professor George Catlin, who believed in Atlantic union and had worked towards the conversion of Anglo-American cooperation into the nucleus of a future world federal government.[52] Here the influence of Clarence Streit's remarkable book, *Union Now*, was manifest. And in addition to the goal of Atlantic union, there were many other sources of division within Federal Union which reflected various cross-currents of opinion about the movement's goals and strategies. Indeed, given the nature of the organisation, it would have been astonishing if these had not existed.

The overriding goal of a federal Europe finally triumphed in the Federal Union in September 1944. A resolution to amend its basic guidelines was passed by a two-thirds majority at the Annual General Conference during 23–24 September and embodied the following statement of objectives: '(a) World Federation as the long-term aim; (b) educating the public in the meaning of and need for federation; (c) immediate aim the promotion of a democratic federation of Europe as part of the postwar settlement'.[53] The devastation wreaked by the dropping of the atom bomb on Hiroshima and Nagasaki in 1945 underlined the continuing relevance of world federation, but the reassertion of the European nation-state after the defeat of Hitler ruled out any immediate prospects of success. Moreover, the emergence during and after the Second World War of two Herculean military superpowers – the United States and the Soviet Union – further reduced the possibilities of a genuine world government. The subsequent military and ideological division of Europe between East and West after 1947 confirmed that the goal of Federal Union would have to be a federation of Western Europe, at least for the forseeable future.

It can be seen, then, that at the end of the Second World War the three broad objectives towards which Federal Union's activities were directed, namely, European federation, Atlantic union and world federation, remained unfulfilled. But it would be wrong to construe this as failure. In retrospect, Federal Union had exerted an enormous influence upon British public opinion as an avowedly propagandist pressure group. Moreover, its very composition indicates how far it was able to secure a privileged access to official government circles. Its direct impact upon British public policy, with one or two exceptions, is not easy to assess. However, there is no doubt at all that it helped to familiarise British elite opinion with the federal idea. And in helping to shape and mould British public attitudes towards West European integration after 1945, it also played a largely unsung role in the United Kingdom's efforts to join the European Community in the 1960s and early 1970s.

This chapter has looked at the intellectual and philosophical origins of British federal ideas regarding international relations. It has demonstrated a fundamental continuity of federalist thought stretching from Seeley through Laski and Lothian to the present day. The development of these ideas owed much to the changing role of Britain in world affairs – a role which came increasingly to be viewed in terms of relative international decline. The link between British domestic and foreign policy during this period is also important to emphasise. The internal challenges to the integrity of the United Kingdom state, which have been so well documented by Bulpitt, interacted in a complex way with British foreign policy. The combination of these intra-state and interstate challenges during the years between 1870 and 1945 helped to strengthen the British federal tradition. The shift from British empire to Commonwealth, the truncation of Ireland and the partial disintegration of the United Kingdom, and the new constellation of power relations in Europe each assisted towards a gradual reassessment and reappraisal of British interests at home and abroad. Looked at from this broad historical perspective, it is small wonder that British federal ideas should have surfaced with such vigour and resilience. In summary, they both underlined and encapsulated these momentous historical changes.

We have now reached the point where it is appropriate to examine the nature of the British federal tradition after the Second World War. Since there are many standard commentaries upon British foreign policy towards Europe after 1945, we will not adopt the conventional, often largely descriptive, approach to this subject. It tends inevitably to focus upon the 'official mind' and understandably emphasises relations between states. Consequently, we never probe further than official British foreign policy and its outcomes. The approach is predominantly intergovernmental. Its principal focus is upon ministers and senior civil servants at the expense of other actors in the policy process. For a study of the British federal tradition, this singular approach is unhelpful. It is much more useful for us to investigate the British federal tradition from a different developmental angle. We will therefore look at the evolution of federal ideas about Europe through the prism of British parliamentary debates from 1960 to 1973. The arguments and anxieties refracted through this prism furnish an interesting route into how these ideas were perceived and debated by successive British governments and parliamentarians.

Notes

1. Seeley, J.R. (1871), 'The United States of Europe', *MacMillan's Magazine*, XXIII, 441–4.
2. For Seeley's political ideas, see Wormell, D. (1980), *Sir John Seeley and the Uses of History*, Cambridge, Cambridge University Press, chapter 6.
3. On Seeley's conception of history and political science, see his *Introduction to Political Science* (1896), London, Macmillan and Co., and Collini, S. et al. (1983), *That Noble Science of Politics: A Study in Nineteenth Century Intellectual History*, Cambridge, Cambridge University Press, 225–34.
4. Collini, S., et al. (1983), *That Noble Science of Politics*, 233–4.
5. Rose, R. (1977), 'The United Kingdom as an Intellectual Puzzle', in D. Jaensch (ed.), *The Politics of 'New Federalism'*, Adelaide, Australian Political Studies Association, chapter 3, 21–34.
6. Whyte, F. (1925), *The Life of W.T. Stead*, 2 vols, London, Jonathan Cape, I, 145–55.
7. Stead, W.T. (1899), *The United States of Europe on the Eve of the Parliament of Peace*, London, The Review of Reviews, 30.
8. See *The Times*, 31 January 1914. The whole of page 6 is devoted to the projected Unity League which had its headquarters at 39, James Street, London.
9. Lipgens, W. (1982), *A History of European Integration*, Vol. 1, 1945–1947, Oxford, Clarendon Press, 35.
10. Ibid., 36.
11. Ibid.
12. Pegg, C.H. (1983), *Evolution of the European Idea, 1914–1932*, North Carolina, University of North Carolina Press, 9.
13. Pinder, J. (1991), 'The Federal Idea and the British Liberal Tradition', in A. Bosco (ed.), *The Federal Idea: The History of Federalism from the Enlightenment to 1945*, Vol. I, London, Lothian Foundation Press, chapter VIII, 99–118.
14. See Burgess, M. (ed.) (1986), 'Federalism and Federation in Western Europe', in M. Burgess (ed.), *Federalism and Federation in Western Europe*, London, Croom Helm, chapter 2, 24–5; Carney, F.S. (1964), *The Politics of Johannes Althusius*, London, Eyre and Spottiswoode; and Ehrlich, S. (1982), *Pluralism On and Off Course*, London, Pergamon Press, chapter 3.
15. Nicholls, D. (1975), *The Pluralist State*, London, Macmillan, 32. See also Hirst, P.Q. (ed.) (1989), *The Pluralist Theory of the State*, London, Routledge.
16. Mogi, S. (1931), *The Problem of Federalism*, 2 vols, London, Allen and Unwin, I, 312.
17. Hirst, P.Q. (ed.) (1989), *The Pluralist Theory of the State*, 8.
18. Barker, E. (1915), *Political Thought in England from Herbert Spencer to the Present Day*, London, Williams and Norgate, Home University Library, 181.
19. Barker, E. (February 1915), 'The Discredited State', *Political Quarterly*, 5, 101. This is not the same journal as the later and better-known *Political Quarterly*.
20. Pinder, J. (1991), 'The Federal Idea and the British Liberal Tradition', 112.

21. Nicholls, D. (1975), *The Pluralist State*, 45.
22. See the following books written by Harold Laski: (1917), *Studies in the Problem of Sovereignty*, New Haven, CT, Yale University Press; (1919), *Authority in the Modern State*, New Haven, CT, Yale University Press; (1921), *The Foundation of Sovereignty and Other Essays*, London, Allen and Unwin; and (1925), *A Grammar of Politics*, London, Allen and Unwin.
23. Lipgens, W. (1982), *European Integration*, 41.
24. Ibid., 38.
25. For a detailed analysis of Coudenhove-Kalergi's activities, see Zurcher, A. (1958), *The Struggle to Unite Europe, 1940–1958*, New York, New York University Press.
26. Kendle, J. (1975), *The Round Table Movement and Imperial Union*, Toronto, University of Toronto Press.
27. For the recent revisionist literature, see Pinder, J. (1983), 'Prophet Not Without Honour: Lothian and the Federal Idea', *The Round Table*, 286, 207–20; Bosco, A. (July 1988), 'Lothian, Curtis, Kimber and the Federal Union Movement, 1938–1940', *Journal of Contemporary History*, 23, No. 3, 465–502; Turner, J. (ed.) (1988), *The Larger Idea: Lord Lothian and the Problem of National Sovereignty*, London, The Historians' Press.
28. Pinder, J. (1983), 'Prophet Not Without Honour', 208.
29. Kendle, J. (1975), *The Round Table Movement*, 16.
30. Pinder, J. (1983), 'Prophet Not Without Honour', 209.
31. Kerr, P. and Curtis, L. (1923), *The Prevention of War*, New Haven, CT, Yale University Press.
32. Bosco, A. (July 1988), 'Lothian, Curtis, Kimber and the Federal Union Movement, 1938–1940', 471–2.
33. Lipgens, W. (1982), *European Integration*, 43, 63 and 159.
34. Mayne, R. and Pinder, J. (1990), *Federal Union: The Pioneers*, London, Macmillan.
35. Lipgens, W. (1982), *European Integration*, 143.
36. Ibid., 64.
37. Mayne, R. and Pinder, J. (1990), *Federal Union*, 13.
38. Forman, N. (1973), 'The European Movement in Great Britain, 1945–1954', unpublished MPhil. thesis, University of Sussex, chapter 3, Part 1, 62–90. See also Wilford, R.A. (1980) 'The Federal Union Campaign', *European Studies Review*, 10, 101–14.
39. Lipgens, W. (1982), *European Integration*, 142.
40. Mayne, R. and Pinder, J. (1990), *Federal Union*, 31–2.
41. Jennings, W.I. (1940), *A Federation for Western Europe*, Cambridge, Cambridge University Press.
42. Robbins, L. (1939), *The Economic Causes of War*, London, Jonathan Cape.
43. Wheare, K.C. (1941), 'What Federal Government is', *Federal Tract No. 4*, London, Macmillan, reprinted in Ransome, P. (ed.) (1943), *Studies in Federal Planning*, London, Macmillan, 17–38.
44. Mayne, R. and Pinder, J. (1990), *Federal Union*, 45–6.
45. Mackay, R.W.G. (1941), *Peace Aims and the New Order*, London, Michael Joseph, and (1961), *Towards a United States of Europe*, London, Hutchinson.
46. On the general question of British socialists and Europe, see Newman, M. (1980), 'British Socialists and the Question of European Unity, 1939–45', *European Studies Review*, 10, 75–100.

47. Forman, N. (1973), 'The European Movement in Great Britain', 76–7.
48. Lipgens, W. (1982), *European Integration*, 144.
49. Ibid., 146.
50. Forman, N. (1973), 'The European Movement in Great Britain', 79.
51. Lipgens, W. (1982), *European Integration*, 146, fn. 115.
52. Mayne, R. and Pinder, J. (1990), *Federal Union*, 13.
53. Lipgens, W. (1982), *European Integration*, 148.

CHAPTER 7

From the European Community to European Union: British federal ideas and the building of Europe

Federalism and sovereignty in British parliamentary politics, 1960–63

In the early postwar years the idea of a federal Europe opened up a glaring gap in British politics between rhetoric and reality. The years between 1946 and 1949 were the heyday of European federal ideas and new federalist organisations sprang up across the whole continent. Churchill's call in Zürich in September 1946 for a 'United States of Europe' and his subsequent creation and leadership of the British United Europe movement in January 1947 was matched by Ronald Mackay's less ostentatious activities in the Labour 'Europe Group' which was created in December 1947 in the House of Commons for those Labour MPs interested in promoting the economic and political integration of Europe. In March 1948 cross-party collaboration between Mackay and Robert Boothby, the chief European federalist in the Conservative party, produced an All-Party Group for European federation numbering 133 MPs which reached agreement on the text of a motion advocating a new constituent assembly for Europe. By April 1948 the signatures had grown to 190.[1] The prospects for a federal Europe therefore seemed bright and the federal idea flourished once again in British parliamentary politics and public life.

In continental Europe there were exciting new developments. The Montreux Congress of federalists in August 1947 and the Hague Congress of May 1948, from which the Council of Europe emerged in 1949, suggested a genuine spiritual reawakening of Europe and a resurgence of political will and energy for new forms of international association. In the United Kingdom, however, the rhetoric of European federation quickly succumbed to the reality of British foreign policy. Neither the Labour government nor the Foreign Office 'official mind' favoured federal ideas. The British Foreign Secretary, Ernest Bevin, who had been a federalist sympathiser before the Second World War, supported new forms of international cooperation but not economic and political integration. His famous 'Western Union speech', delivered in the House of Commons in January 1948, referred to a 'consolidation' of Europe, but it was vague and non-committal. Party politics was also a significant factor in the fortunes of the federal idea; large sections of the Labour party were opposed to any organisation led by Churchill and others were ideologically hostile to what they regarded as the isolation of the Soviet Union. Furthermore, the Foreign Office raised two objections: first, the fear that Germany would in the long-term come to dominate any continental federation if Britain was not a member; and, secondly, that Britain's overseas commitments and her special relationship with the United States prevented the merging of 'her own in some European sovereignty'.[2]

By 1950 Bevin's vision of a 'Western Union' had faded and he was far more attracted to the Atlantic community. While he still wanted West European cooperation, and something more than just a military arrangement, his faith in the British Commonwealth and the partnership with the United States grew stronger. When the Schuman Plan was first mooted in early 1950 therefore, it became a real litmus test of British attitudes towards European economic and political integration. The new French proposals for a supranational European coal and steel community provoked an official response which, in its strong scepticism, has since become the indelible hallmark of Britain's relations with the European Union (EU). The obvious potential of the Schuman Plan had 'led certain ministers and officials to consider accepting a limited loss of sovereignty' but the British government was not prepared to countenance 'an open-ended commitment to the principle of supranationality'. John Young's historical analysis of the period reminds us just how far the definitions and assumptions of the 1950s have endured:

> Behind this definition lay Britain's faith in national independence (strengthened by Labour's belief in a planned, national economy), her contempt for continental weakness and 'impracticality', and the idea that Britain could remain a world power, aided by America and the Commonwealth. In 1950 such thinking was inevitable: Britain, the victor of 1945, was psychologically incapable of surrendering her independence.[3]

Jean Monnet, the architect and builder of the European Community (EC), was correct when he predicted that Britain would eventually find its destiny in Europe. But it was not until the European idea – first with the European Coal and Steel Community (1951) and then with the European Atomic Energy Community and the European Economic Community (1957) – had been translated into practical politics in the late 1950s that the United Kingdom formally acknowledged this destiny. By then of course the EC had firmly established itself and the British had missed the opportunity to give shape and direction to the EC at its inception. When the Conservative government, led by Harold Macmillan, made the first formal application to join the EC in July 1961, it was with the view that the Paris–Bonn axis, rather than Washington, DC or the Commonwealth, would be the future pivot of British national interests.

It is generally accepted that the decision to cross the Rubicon by requesting membership of the EC in 1961 was taken by Macmillan. It was a prime ministerial decision. But his determination to join the EC should not surprise us. He had long been favourable towards a European unity in which the United Kingdom would play an active role. Macmillan himself has since recalled that he had written to Churchill as early as 1951 to protest when the new Conservative government, elected in that year, failed to nudge Britain towards the European Coal and Steel Community.[4] He had already construed West European integration in terms of British national interests. It is the timing of his momentous decision, then, which has been the real source of debate among historians and political scientists.

The timing of Macmillan's decision is important because it also helps to explain his motives. There has been no shortage of interpretations suggesting reasons for Macmillan's decision which, according to the chronology of public statements made on the subject, appears to have been taken during late December 1960.[5] It is now conventional wisdom to claim that a combination of various factors influenced the Prime Minister to arrive at a decision at the end of 1960 which represented a dramatic rupture with the past: his own ability to sense which way the economic wind was blowing in the late 1950s; his unflinching belief that the constitutional and political aspects of membership could be confined to modest proportions which would enable Britain to preserve her other important links with the Commonwealth and the United States; the impact of the Suez débâcle; the conclusions of an early report by an interdepartmental group of senior civil servants assembled to study possible association with the Six; the visible short-term benefits which entry would offer the Conservative government and party by enabling them publicly to differentiate themselves on a clear policy issue from the Labour party (after a brief spell in which the two major parties had drifted closer towards the political centre in the public mind); and, not least, Macmillan's belief that membership would be a lasting achievement with which to cap his own political career.[6]

In summary, a conjunction of circumstances during 1960–61 persuaded Macmillan to make what was a remarkable policy change. But what is the significance of this issue for the British federal tradition? How did it affect the nature of the parliamentary debate about the EC during the early 1960s? The standard commentaries on the role of interest groups in the formation of British foreign policy towards Western European integration between 1956 and 1967 show quite conclusively that considerations of a broad national interest, interpreted in terms of Britain's overall international position, took precedence over basic cost–benefit calculations about the likely impact of membership.[7] In short, the official announcement of the start of negotiations concerning EC entry was the outcome of a political rather than an economic judgement. And, significantly, the question of European integration rapidly became a highly politicised policy issue. Unlike earlier public attitudes towards the Treaty of Rome between 1958 and 1960, the 1961 episode bore all the hallmarks of a major constitutional question. The negotiations were handled by the Foreign Office, the public at large was drawn into the debate and the major political parties became embroiled in the issue to the extent of clear partisanship. But it was precisely at this juncture – when public opinion was receiving information about the Conservative government's intentions – that a curious twist in events occurred. Despite the increasing politicisation of the European issue (which Macmillan himself had helped to create), the Prime Minister chose to present it to Parliament and the public largely as an economic issue. Macmillan had operated 'by disguising his strategic choice as a commercial deal' and this approach was to have enormous consequences for the ensuing parliamentary debate.[8] It had a decisive impact upon parliamentary perceptions of the EC. Not only did it serve to confuse MPs engaged in debating what was in reality a major constitutional issue, but it also created the mistaken impression that the Conservative government was embarking upon a new and radical policy whose real political consequences were being deliberately concealed from both the public and Parliament. Macmillan's approach therefore unintentionally determined the curious and fragmentary nature of the great debate which persisted in the House of Commons between 1961 and 1963. It also explains why both federalism and sovereignty emerged in the contorted way that they did.

The earliest public indication of what was on Macmillan's mind appears to have occurred in May 1961. During a general debate on foreign affairs on 17 May, Edward Heath, Lord Privy Seal charged with the responsibility for British negotiations, made an unexpected intervention which, according to Douglas Houghton, 'was the signal for perturbation to be publicly expressed throughout the Commonwealth'.[9] Pressure on the government for information about its intentions had already begun to build up early in May in the customary form of parliamentary questions. But it was not until Heath's speech in the House of Commons foreign affairs debate that parliamentary suspicions were confirmed. Thereafter, as Macmillan noted in his diary, the question of EC membership 'held the attention of Parliament, the Press and to some extent the public', although no formal policy statement was made.[10]

In the House of Commons, Edward Du Cann badgered the Prime Minister to make a further statement of government intentions and insisted that public opinion continued to be 'anxious' about the subject. He claimed that the economic implications of entry were 'largely understood' but the likely political consequences were not. And when John Biggs-Davison candidly asked if the sovereignty of Parliament might be surrendered, merged or limited by EC membership of any 'supranational or international body', Macmillan's reply was equally frank. He agreed that 'some limitations' on British sovereignty were inevitable, but refused to be drawn into a detailed discussion about what they would be. Macmillan's casual candour prompted Biggs-Davison to pursue the Prime Minister over the idea that Britain might join or 'be merged in a federal union'.[11] This time Macmillan's reply was typically short and evasive. He believed that this possibility would depend upon how far the 'purely commercial and economic aspects' involved 'a derogation of sovereignty' and how far the British people would be prepared to accept it.[12] These tentative exchanges were among the first examples of an early concern in the summer of 1961 about the real constitutional and political implications of EC membership. Since Macmillan had decided to focus parliamentary attention almost exclusively upon the economic aspects of entry, it was hardly surprising to find him both secretive and evasive in his verbal exchanges with MPs on both sides of the House.

On the Conservative side, John Biggs-Davison, Nigel Birch and the in-defatigable Sir Derek Walker-Smith never tired in their relentless pursuit of the likely political scenario which EC membership would occasion. But it was from among the official Labour Opposition ranks that the loudest noises were to be anticipated. The clutch of Labour backbenchers which gave the government the most trouble over the EC question included Sydney Silver-man, John Stonehouse, Maurice Edelman and Emanuel Shinwell. Together, this parliamentary coterie of extremely unlikely bedfellows were able convin-cingly to portray Macmillan's decision as at once dishonest, reprehensible and hurriedly ill-conceived. He appeared not to know the full political con-sequences of his own actions. It was reminiscent of Ernest Bevin's famous phrase about opening Pandora's Box only to find it full of Trojan horses.

The real beginning of the 'Great Debate' (as Macmillan described it in his memoirs) must be recorded as the three-hour debate which occurred on 28 June 1961 on a private member's motion. From this date the question of British entry was hotly contested and the controversy about the nature of the EC as a political union assumed a growing importance. Trojan horses abounded. Sydney Silverman described the EC as 'a phoney gerrymandering of bits of Europe in the name of a United States of Europe or a common European Community', while Gilbert Longden noted that 'although the Treaty of Rome says nothing about Federation, we all know that much closer ties are the main aim of its signatories'. He wanted to know precisely how much further Macmillan expected the EC to develop.[13] Roy Jenkins, an ardent Labour advocate of a British voice inside the EC, repudiated the popular analogy between the EC and the British Commonwealth as a 'false choice': the latter was entirely unsuitable to be a 'tight economic and political union'. Jenkins also represented that school of thought which claimed that British sovereignty in the new age of global competitiveness had already been ir-retrievably eroded and that British membership of NATO, EFTA and WEU underlined this fact.[14] Emanuel Shinwell, however, remained unconvinced:

The fundamental object of the Treaty of Rome has always been the progressive creation of a minimum of political unity ... the Common Market of the Six is inconceivable in any other perspective ... there is a real distinction between handing over some part of our authority to some international organisation and going lock, stock and barrel into the Common Market.[15]

The main focus of the early debate, then, had been about the government's intentions, but it is clear from the above examples that the phobia of federalism and the loss of British sovereignty had begun to characterise the parliamentary debate.

A flow of parliamentary questions followed. Walker-Smith, who seemed to regard his own party leader as the villain of the piece, pressed Macmillan on the political implications of the Treaty of Rome. The Prime Minister acknowledged that 'some merging of sovereignty in the commercial, economic and social fields covered by the Treaty' was inherent in the very idea of the EC, but he denied that it also applied to defence, foreign policy and public order.[16] Walker-Smith disagreed, declaring that political sovereignty was 'at the heart of the matter'.[17] When, on 31 July 1961, Macmillan's conversion to the EC was made official in a public announcement to Parliament, the Prime Minister could no longer deal with federalism and sovereignty, as he put it, 'by the recognised Parliamentary evasions'.[18] One scholar referred to Macmillan's historic announcement as having been 'brief' and 'delivered in a surprisingly uninspired way'.[19] None the less, the focus of the debate now shifted from economic to political matters. In the main parliamentary debate on 2 August 1961, Macmillan was forced to confront the thorny question of sovereignty.

The word 'sovereignty' did not worry him. He did not think that it contained any particular mystique. However, he equally did not underestimate its significance. On the contrary, he attached 'the highest importance' to the problem. In simple terms he defined it as 'a nation's freedom of action' which, in the end, was 'perhaps a matter of degree'.[20] Moreover, he believed that the actual amount of sovereignty which might be lost or forfeited in accepting the Treaty of Rome did not seem to him to be very great. Turning to the related anxiety about the possibility of Britain entering a reorganised West European federation, Macmillan was adamant. Reported parallels with the United States of America were, in his opinion, based upon 'a completely false analogy'. He rejected the views of the federalist movement supported by some Europeans. Instead, he believed that the alternative concept of 'confederation' was much more in tune with European traditions and chimed with General De Gaulle's conception of a Europe of nation-states. He concluded that there was nothing in the Treaty of Rome which committed members of the EC to any kind of federal goal. Nor could such a system ever be imposed upon member countries. There was, then, nothing on the constitutional side of which anybody need fear.[21]

Hugh Gaitskell, the Labour leader, replied for the Opposition and challenged Macmillan on the subjects of federalism and sovereignty. He reminded him about what the President of the Board of Trade in the Conservative government in 1951 had warned concerning the implications of the Treaty of Rome:

The whole idea of the Six, the Coal and Steel Community and Euratom is a movement towards political integration. That is a fine aspiration, but we must recognise that for us to sign the Treaty of Rome would be to accept as the ultimate goal political federation in Europe, including ourselves.[22]

Gaitskell certainly had a point. And he observed that there was no question whatsoever of Britain entering a federal Europe in the early 1960s because British public opinion was simply not ready for it. The EC's central institutions were also problematic. The Commission, for example, was 'foreign' to the British conception of a civil service and the European Assembly, once it was directly elected, would have strong federalist overtones.

The attack on the government's policy did not end there. The repeated interventions of Sir Derek Walker-Smith, the irrepressible Conservative Member for Hertfordshire East, ensured that serious analytical discussion of the constitutional and political implications of EC membership would not go by default. He emphasised that the debate involved nothing less than Britain's future as a separate sovereign state. Indeed, the loss of sovereignty would be immediate. He pinpointed the exact areas where the derogation of sovereignty would occur. Articles 48 and 49 of the Treaty of Rome, for example, were singled out for special attention because they demonstrated the loss of national control of the freedom of movement for workers. But he was particularly concerned that the House of Commons should not look at the question in a narrow context. The immediate consequences of membership were important but there were wider implications to be considered. Economic union, after all, was merely 'a prelude to political union'.[23] Walker-Smith warned the House that if it was content to overlook the long-term political implications of membership, these implications would eventually catch up with them. British entry to the EC represented a real challenge to the constitution and to parliamentary supremacy in certain aspects of law-making; it also suggested a radically new role for British law courts.

This cogently argued case against entry was based upon what Walker-Smith believed were the real political implications of EC membership and it certainly harmed the government. There seemed to be few defenders of the new policy until Edward Heath entered the parliamentary fray in order to clarify what he called 'the politico-economic interactions'. In his view the problem involved three different aspects of the EC and its work: first, the institutional level which involved sovereignty and dealt with the economic policy of the Community; secondly, the effect of participating in the consultations of the Fouchet-Cattani Committee on political union already operating among the Six; and, thirdly, the long-term future of these economic and political consultations which might lead to federation or confederation, and could involve sovereignty. On the first point, Heath described the EC as 'a partnership in action with common policies' which involved not a surrender of sovereignty but a pooling of sovereignty with other states engaged in a joint enterprise. This, he was at pains to emphasise, did not mean an abandonment of sovereignty. It meant a sharing of sovereignty over a strictly defined field as stipulated in the Treaty of Rome. On the second aspect, concerning the consultations on political union, Heath reminded the House that they were purely exploratory and did not involve any loss of sovereignty. Finally, on the future of political cooperation, he stood firm on the Rome Treaty. It included nothing about any particular form of constitutional evolution and, in any case, unanimous agreement was required for any specific political commitment.[24]

Despite the evident unease with Macmillan's new departure in policy, the first major debate resulted in an overwhelming government victory in the House, giving it formal parliamentary approval to begin negotiations on 10 October 1961. Between then and June 1962 the parliamentary debate on the constitutional and political implications of EC membership remained fragmentary. Questions concerning federalism and sovereignty reappeared with almost monotonous regularity, itself a damning indictment of the government's mishandling of the case. In two short debates on 6 and 7 June 1962 they were again conspicuous. Peter Walker, the Conservative Member for Worcester, posed the key question in stark terms:

> First, are the government genuinely enthusiastic about going into a system of political federation in Europe? ... [T]he government have avoided facing the reality that much of Europe wants political federation and a European Parliament. If that is so, it would be a tragedy from the point of view of Europe for this government, if they do not wish to see such a federation, to join the Common Market and sabotage the movement towards federation. On the other hand, if the government are enthusiastic for the cause of European federation (they should) state it perfectly clearly so that the country can understand what is being offered to it is, over a period of years, joining a federation of Europe – not becoming an offshore island, but becoming an offshore province of the European federation.[25]

On the Opposition benches, Maurice Edelman endorsed these sentiments. He warned the House that what European unity really meant was 'unspecified' and that even if the government did not intend it, its existing course was inexorably to 'set Britain on the rails to a federal Europe' as the ultimate destination. Edelman added the rider that once inside the EC all economic arrangements would produce political institutions which would be 'none other than federal institutions'.[26] Harold Wilson echoed these remarks. He took a much stronger line of attack than Gaitskell, arguing that the evolution of the EC along political lines meant 'federation', a United States of Europe or a common foreign policy.[27] And, predictably, Sir Derek Walker-Smith weighed in with his familiar defence of British parliamentary sovereignty which he described as:

> ... a difficult thing to discuss ... (but something which included) real things, deeply felt, instinctively understood and traditionally cherished by the British people ... little noticed in their presence but valued beyond price in the event of their deprivation.[28]

Sovereignty was evidently no less real for being hard to define.

Federalism also reappeared in this debate. Edward Heath was forced once again to run the gauntlet of parliamentary scrutiny. Turning to what he called 'constitutional' questions which were commonly described as 'federal or confederal', Heath baldly stated that the presentation of the future political structure of the EC as either federal or confederal was an over-simplification. There were no such simple stark alternatives. Instead, he reassured the government's critics that the British took a 'pragmatic approach' of letting the EC institutions develop as the circumstances in Europe changed. He did not wish to anticipate what might happen. In conclusion he alluded to the EC as 'a new form of organisation' without precedent in Europe, adding that those with objections should take a broad view and 'set them in the larger context'.[29]

Only two major debates in the House of Commons followed these assurances by Heath and neither of them succeeded in removing the doubts and suspicions voiced by the government's opponents. Indeed, in the four-hour debate on 1 August 1962, one government spokesman, R.A. Butler, felt constrained to reassure the House that Britain was not being asked to join a federal union and surrender her sovereignty. Butler himself confessed that the term 'union' had led to misunderstanding and these exchanges indicated an increasing awareness of the importance of terminological precision if the parliamentary debate was to arrive at any accurate conclusions. The use of the term 'federalism' in particular seemed to perplex some Members who were unsure about where it would lead Britain, while it incensed others who felt that they knew exactly where that path led. It all depended upon how the word was interpreted.

Anthony Marlowe, the Conservative Member for Hove and an avowed anti-Marketeer, refused to soft-pedal when it came to the meaning of words. He acknowledged that the government was very clear about the economic aspects of entry, but that when the political implications were involved 'all became vague and obscure'. Moreover, it was his belief that the ambiguity was deliberate. It was an attempt 'to conceal from the public exactly what was involved'. And that political involvement meant political federation. The British people, he argued, had never understood the real political issues involved simply because the government had chosen to use the neutral name 'Common Market' which suggested that only a harmless commercial linkage was contemplated. The overall effect of this approach was deliberately to conceal the real political consequences from the public. Marlowe concluded that the government was perfectly aware of 'the emotional content of this matter' and that they had been especially careful never to disclose it to the public.[30]

This was a searing indictment of government policy which should have received a swift and convincing rebuttal. But none followed. Peter Smithers, the new Joint Under-Secretary of State at the Foreign Office, merely echoed

Heath's earlier references to the 'politico-economic interactions' built into the Treaty of Rome. He replied that it was impossible to 'draw a hard and fast line between what is political and what is economic', but admitted that the real purpose of the EC was political and so was the government's initiative. In his view the question of sovereignty was often misunderstood. It was meaningful only within an interdependent context. In both economic and financial affairs, he argued, British sovereignty could be exercised effectively only in conjunction with others. He ended his remarks by announcing firmly to the House that the Treaty of Rome was therefore simply the bold and logical extension of a situation which already existed.[31]

In the last major two-day debate on Community membership on 7 and 8 November 1962 the large question-marks hanging over the political implications of entry had still not been removed. In a repetitive but patient statement to the House, Heath denied that anybody who did not admit that EC membership would lead inevitably to federation was dishonest. He repeated that EC institutions would develop in a pragmatic fashion. They would evolve to meet the demands of changing circumstances. There was no hidden blueprint for a federal Europe. The most that could be conceded to the sceptics of entry was that the texts discussed had been 'broadly speaking, confederal texts'.[32] This statement was more than Hugh Gaitskell could tolerate and he pursued Heath with an uncompromising clarity of purpose. Federation, he argued, might be a good thing or a bad thing, but he was adamant that the government should at least admit that this was what entry involved. The parallel (Fouchet-Cattani) negotiations concerning political cooperation obviously loomed large in Gaitskell's mind. These negotiations, he believed, revealed the true intentions of the Six: economic union would lead to political union, and then to either federation or a supranational majority-decision council.[33]

Even after news of the final breakdown of the Brussels negotiations reached the House of Commons, the strong sense of legerdemain expressed by the Labour Opposition about Macmillan's handling of the question of EC membership did not disappear immediately. The Liberal leader, Jo Grimmond, had also warned the government in December 1962 to make their views on the political implications of membership more clear. The Liberal party of course had never flinched at the prospect of a federal Europe and had consistently supported active British participation in West European integration since the end of the Second World War. Another Liberal MP and future leader of the party, Jeremy Thorpe, noted that if the Conservative government had really believed that it had been negotiating purely for economic purposes, it was no wonder that the negotiations had finally collapsed.[34] Neither Macmillan nor Heath could be expected to accept this interpretation of events, but it was a solemn verdict delivered in a solemn debate.

What, then, did the House of Commons debate reveal about the constitutional and political implications of British entry into the EC? And, more specifically, what conclusions can be drawn about the nature of federalism and sovereignty in the particular context of the EC? One fact was outstanding: the eighteen months of sporadic parliamentary debate had indicated a widespread public feeling that the Prime Minister had been less than honest about the political implications of membership. Repeated denials were a poor substitute for convincing rebuttals. It seemed as if the Conservative government was determined to lead Britain into the EC blindfold. To some MPs the impression conveyed was that it wanted Community membership at almost any price. Most of them realised that acceptance of the Treaty of Rome suggested a real challenge to the independence of Parliament in certain well-defined areas of law-making. They were also perfectly aware that the EC's basic constitutional texts would provide Britain for the first time with a written constitution establishing new institutional relationships, imposing new obligations and creating new rights, none of which Parliament acting on its own would, in the future, be able to alter. Walker-Smith was quite correct to identify the particular threat to Parliament's legislative supremacy enshrined in the Rome Treaty by the right of Community institutions to legislate for Britain (without the prior consent of Parliament) and by the right of the law courts to rule on the admissibility of future Acts of Parliament. In short, adherence to the Treaty of Rome struck at the very roots of Dicey's venerated – if already outmoded – principle of parliamentary sovereignty. It entailed the possibility of an independent role for the law courts in the interpretation of constitutional provisions. Their traditional position of formal subservience to the will of Parliament would be replaced by a new relationship in which they could interpret Community law independent of what Parliament desired – a startling constitutional change.

In a political sense, too, many Members were aware of the implied subordination of national parliaments to the EC in matters where it would have sole competence. Critics of government policy on both sides of the House deprecated what they envisaged as the eventual emasculation of national parliaments in a dynamic Community process of increasing economic and political integration. To many of them, the Fouchet-Cattani discussions seemed to confirm this belief. The significance of the constitutional and political effects was bound to intensify *pari passu* with the gradual extension of the scope of EC integration inherent in the Rome Treaty itself. Britain's national sovereignty therefore would be progressively eroded. This general perception and understanding of national sovereignty, however, was a dangerously narrow one. It was also an over-simplification which encouraged the mistaken view that EC membership would involve a once-and-for-all loss of national self-determination. Edward Heath was at pains to dispel precisely this, largely emotional, feeling. He preferred to speak in terms of a pooling or a sharing of sovereignty because it corresponded more closely with the political realities of the contemporary world. Membership of any international organisation would increase national influence, freedom and self-determination in one

sense and simultaneously restrict it in another sense. It was a matter of making strategic political choices. There would always be a trade-off between
perceived gains and losses. It was a question of political judgement. And
Macmillan had made precisely that judgement of where Britain's national
interest lay in the early 1960s.

Wedded to the thorny question of sovereignty was the equally controversial
issue of federalism. Like sovereignty, the common perception and understanding of federalism was based upon old assumptions which had already
been undermined by the early 1960s. Old ideas and assumptions, however,
are notoriously resilient and it was widely believed that federalism and sovereignty were related in a particular way: federation involved the transfer of
certain well-defined rights to a new sovereign body. The idea of a federal
Europe therefore meant the creation of a new central authority, beyond the
nation-state, with specific powers and competences which would operate independently of its constituent parts. The obvious temptation was to view this
transition from a narrow national perspective. But the national perspective
was purblind: it could see only one dimension. The implication for national
parliaments and governments therefore was an immediate loss of autonomy
and status. It did not take into account the other dimension to the federal
transition, namely, that the national governments would also gain in autonomy, influence and status from being an integral part of a much larger union
of states and citizens. The discursive and fragmentary nature of the debate
about federalism in the House of Commons during 1961–63 ensured that it
remained a phobia in British parliamentary politics. Those who used the term
invariably misunderstood and misrepresented it. Federalism rapidly became a
term of abuse. This was partly because it was identified in the public mind
with Britain's decline in world affairs.

When we remember just how popular the federal idea was in Britain
during the Second World War when Federal Union was in the ascendant, it is
remarkable how the same idea came to be the object of so much anxiety and
derision during the postwar years. Clearly, the reassertion of the nation-state
is one obvious explanation, as is the change in the configuration of postwar
European politics. But in English (rather than British) minds Europe was both
a remote and an alien cultural concept. It was perceived as predominantly
Roman Catholic and it contained a myriad of strange foreign languages. It
belonged, in Linda Colley's words, to the category of the 'Other'.[35] But the
particular development of the EC itself is also another reason for hostility to
the federal idea in the United Kingdom. Parliamentary discussion of federalism in the early 1960s was inevitably determined by a particular view of the
way that the EC would develop. Some Members conjured up nightmarish
visions of a gigantic European super-state which would swallow up and destroy
individual nation-states. The distinctive British identity would disappear and
the British way of life would be lost forever. Indeed, many Members assumed
that the EC was already a kind of quasi-federal state. This may have been

due largely to a misinterpretation of the Treaty of Rome – a document more often alluded to than actually read – but there was certainly some basis for this assumption. The commitment to a directly elected European Assembly, for example, was an explicit federal element because it incorporated and engaged directly the 'people' of the Community as distinct from the governments of the member 'states' which comprised the EC.

There can be no doubt, then, that by the 1960s the federal idea had come to be associated in the minds of many public men and women with the continental European federalists of Italy, France and West Germany. It came to be regarded as something which the British exported to others, especially in the Commonwealth; it was deemed singularly inappropriate for the British themselves. Indeed, there was something distinctly 'un-British' about the idea of a federal Europe. Christopher Tugendhat summarised this very British view of the continental Europeans in the following way:

> Too often the British, untouched by so many of the horrors and humiliations of war – 1914–18 as well as 1939–45 – that inspired the Community ideal, still find it hard to comprehend the sentiments that in some countries underlie and underpin it and to which politicians both appeal and respond. It is against this background that the 'Euro-rhetoric' in those countries must be judged.[36]

The historical and psychological legacies of the Second World War in particular have made the British resistant to an idea which is actually a legitimate and, indeed, integral part of the British political tradition. It is both ironic and unfortunate that successive postwar British generations have not known about the British federal tradition. It has been largely forgotten.

In many ways the first House of Commons debate on the political implications of British membership of the EC was disappointing. It was both confused and fragmentary. But if many Members were guilty of incurably narrow minds when it came to discussing the key issues of federalism and sovereignty, much of the blame for this confusion was attributable to Macmillan and the Conservative government. The suddenness of the Prime Minister's decision to apply for membership gave the impression that he had not carefully anticipated the arguments regarding its constitutional and political implications. His parliamentary evasions seemed to confirm this view. He certainly believed that the implications could be confined to modest proportions, but he was unprepared for serious analytical investigation. Indeed, had it not been for the spirited and indefatigable activities of a knot of MPs who persisted in probing government spokesmen for eighteen months, the awkward questions about federalism and sovereignty would have been quietly and conveniently shelved.

Clearly, discussion of these important questions was incomplete. The parliamentary debate had suggested very little understanding and appreciation of the impulses behind Jean Monnet's conception of Europe. But it was an important debate in at least one respect: it assisted towards a gradual and painful process of unlearning what British politicians and the public had hitherto accepted as unchallengeable truths. The early 1960s were a time of piecemeal reappraisal when old assumptions were beginning to be questioned. The House of Commons debate on the political implications of British membership of the EC signified a reluctant awareness of these new challenges. Having looked during 1960–63 at the way in which the federal idea gradually came to be associated with the relative decline in Britain's postwar international status, it is important for us to probe a little further into British parliamentary perceptions and perspectives of federalism in the context of the EC. Let us look now at the subsequent years prior to British membership of the EC.

Parliamentary perspectives of federalism in British attempts to join the EC, 1964–73

Our detailed case study of the first parliamentary debate about British membership of the EC during 1960–63 reveals no public awareness of the British federal tradition. Indeed, it suggests a phobia of federalism. Let us look at what British MPs understood by federalism *per se* and how they related it to the question of EC membership in the years between De Gaulle's veto in 1963 and formal British entry in 1973. We will see that the fear of a federal Europe so forcibly expressed by a tiny but vocal minority of MPs during 1960–63 was extended into later debates. The historical analysis of the debates as events in time, then, is less important than what they reveal about the key concepts involved.

Since the reasons for Harold Wilson's decision to apply for EC membership in May 1967 are already well documented, we will not outline them here.[37] What is immediately apparent is the absence of a 'great debate' in 1967. There were several serious attempts to persuade the Labour government to discuss the major constitutional and political implications of membership, but as with the Macmillan application, they met the customary official evasions. Wilson, like Macmillan before him, was not prepared for a detailed analytical debate. In the parliamentary debate of 1960–63 he had been more worried about supranationalism than federalism. Along with Gaitskell, he had been at the forefront of the attack upon Macmillan's reticence to discuss the possible political implications of entry. But perhaps because of his early acquaintance with the Federal Union during the war years, Wilson never seems to have taken the widespread fear of federalism very seriously. He even acknowledged in the first debate that the Treaty of Rome did not imply federation. It did, however, indicate 'a great deal of supranationalism'.[38] In his prime ministerial statement in the House of Commons on 2 May 1967, Wilson admitted that there were certain 'anxieties' but that the Treaty of Rome need not constitute an impediment provided that British problems could be 'dealt with satisfactorily'.[39] He believed that the EC had undergone significant changes both in its organisation and in its practice in the intervening years between the two applications for entry. He was able to point to the 'Luxembourg compromise' of 1966 which suggested that the drive towards supranationalism in the EC institutions had weakened. And there were no separate investigations concerning political union to unsettle MPs in the parliamentary discussions of 1967. These considerations helped Wilson to disarm his critics.

When he was probed on the question of federal elements in the EC, Wilson construed these in specific terms, namely, foreign and defence policy. He believed that the time was right for Europe to 'move forward in political unity', but he claimed that the object of greater political unity did not mean 'advancing towards a federal control of foreign policy or the creation of a European defence policy'. He respected the views and intentions of some federalists but he also believed that a common foreign policy lay 'a very long time ahead'.[40] The analysis of *Hansard* for this period reveals very little about parliamentary perspectives of federalism because there was no real debate about the political implications of entry. Familiar fears were voiced from the backbenches, but no sustained debate occurred.

The concluding chapter in the thirteen-year history of British attempts to join the EC remains the subject of considerable disagreement among both scholars and politicians in the United Kingdom. In one particular respect the controversy is still unresolved: did the Conservative government of Edward Heath have the legitimate right to apply for British membership of the EC in 1971? Some critics of Heath have claimed that the issue of membership was placed a long way down the list of Conservative party priorities in the June 1970 general election campaign. Indeed, they claim that it was so far down the list of policy items that the public were misled by the party's intentions. Others have laid emphasis upon the Conservative government's self-confessed commitment only to negotiate – no more, no less. But these disputes about the legitimacy of Heath's political initiative must be set against the record of earlier applications. Macmillan, despite loud calls even from his own backbenches, did not consider going to the country on the question in 1961 and Wilson did not give the EC issue paramount importance in the Labour party manifesto of 1966.[41]

The Conservative government's second attempt to join the EC in the early 1970s rekindled the interest in the constitutional and political implications of membership. By this time the international political environment had changed significantly. In particular, General De Gaulle was no longer an obstacle to British attempts to join the EC. Pompidou, De Gaulle's successor as French President, and Willy Brandt, the new West German Chancellor, were in favour of the first EC enlargement. These circumstances augured well for a fresh British initiative. MPs were therefore well prepared for a long and wide-ranging debate on a public policy issue which this time held every prospect of success.

In the debate upon the government's White Paper, introduced by Edward Heath on 21 July 1971, the Prime Minister seized the opportunity to claim, somewhat extravagantly, that ten years of debate on the question of EC entry had produced 'a broad measure of agreement ... about the kind of Europe that most of us want to see and about Britain's place in that Europe'.[42] This proved to be a golden opportunity for those who feared the political implications of membership. Heath's rider that the Conservative government of Macmillan had long ago given 'priority to political considerations' provoked immediate and penetrative criticisms.[43] What form did the debate take and how far were federalist assumptions woven into the analysis of the EC's political development?

Clearly, Heath's opening remarks served to set the tone of the debate. All of the time-honoured objections concerning sovereignty and federalism were paraded by the EC's veteran critics in the House of Commons. The vision of the EC as merely a 'confederation' collided with the rival idea of it as ultimately 'one country'.[44] Here, once again, was the classic 'Bundesstaat-Staatenbund' perspective. But the underlying terminological confusion and fear of the unknown were also conspicuous. Neil Marten, an unrepentant Conservative critic of the government's policy, furnished evidence of this:

> A Confederation. A United States of Europe. Whatever we call it, it has to have one government. ... [T]he logical development of the Community is a constitutional mechanism ... still imperfect and incomplete, but ... federal in form. ... We shall have a President of Europe to appoint the ministers in the government. We shall have a President and a directly-elected Parliament, and obviously a government which will carry out the decisions of that Parliament. Otherwise, why have a Parliament? This is the logic of it all. Why go into the Community if we are not to have something like a federation?[45]

In the light of constitutional developments in the EC as a direct result both of the Single European Act (1987) and the Maastricht Treaty (1993), some commentators today might claim that Marten's observations were prescient. In his concern for the future political development of the EC and Britain's role in it, these remarks certainly foreshadowed the arguments and concerns of the latter-day Conservative 'Euro-sceptics' in the so-called Bruges Group. But it was another senior Conservative critic, Edward Du Cann, who summarised parliamentary concern in the most lucid terms. According to the former chairman of the Conservative party, progress towards economic unity was certain progress towards political unity; he wanted political union to be defined:

> If it is to be political union for the future, we come at once to the practical questions. How is this to be managed? ... How far is the process to go? ... The next ten years of the Community's life will be very different from the first ten years. As this process gathers speed, is it to be a 'Europe des patries'? Is it to be a federal Europe, a confederation, or what? ... All the time the Community evolves, there is this inevitability about it. We cannot, and we must not, ignore it.[46]

Du Cann had put his finger on a key theme of the thirteen-year debate. This was the question of 'automaticity', the notion that the EC possessed an inherent dynamic – a ratchet effect – which would propel it inexorably forward towards greater political and economic integration. This concern had surfaced only intermittently in the parliamentary debate, but it expressed the underlying doubts and uncertainties about British membership of the EC. The speed and the strategy of EC development could still be influenced, and its ultimate destination remained unclear, but the general direction was unambiguous. Indeed, this was deemed irreversible. And its irreversibility was further emphasised by Tony Benn, an increasingly vocal Labour party opponent of membership, who depicted Britain as a future 'California, the westernmost province of a United States of Europe' since entry was meaningful only 'in terms of a federation' which was much more than 'a treaty'.[47] Britain, in Benn's thinking, would become merely a component unit of a larger federal union which was intended to rival both the United States and the Soviet Union in world affairs. Federalism was both process and goal; it was the means by which Western Europe would be progressively united and it was intended to be the final goal, namely, a new state.

In the major debate on the government's motion to approve its application for membership between 21–28 October 1971, the spectre of federalism continued to haunt British attitudes towards the EC. Clearly, in the public mind in the early 1970s, political integration had become synonymous with federalism. And federalism meant *ipso facto* the surrender of British sovereignty. As the EC evolved it would progressively erode British political and economic independence to the point where Parliament's status would effectively be reduced to that of, in Du Cann's alarmist language, 'a Bavarian *Landtag* or an English County Council'. Rather than be brutally subordinated to the dreaded 'Eurocrats' in Brussels, the British would demand a real Western European suffrage and, to complete the circular argument, they would enter (in Benn's view) 'a fully-fledged federal European state'. These comments were typically representative of the tiny minority of MPs on both sides of the House who campaigned vigorously for a major debate on the political impact of EC membership. The language was, and today remains, melodramatic. But there were serious issues of a far-reaching constitutional and political nature which informed the EC debate, and they, too, continue today to be a source of lively political controversy.

In October 1972 at the Paris conference of the heads of state and government, the EC (with British, Irish and Danish participation) agreed that its main objective was to transform, before the end of the decade, 'the whole complex of the relations of the Member States into a European Union'. And the communique issued after the Paris meeting of the heads of state and government on 10 December 1974 reaffirmed this commitment and urged the Community of Nine to 'agree as soon as possible on an overall concept of European Union'.[48] The British had at last joined a unique international organisation which was committed to 'an ever closer union among the European peoples', but which, in the Schuman Declaration of 1950, had originally been inspired by a federal goal. Since 1973 British membership of the EC has provoked a variety of domestic policy debates and controversies, but the most divisive and emotional question remains that of the future constitutional evolution of the EC and its impact upon the United Kingdom. Ever since Macmillan first broached the subject of membership in the House of Commons in 1961, the parliamentary debate on this question has been driven essentially by fear of the unknown. It was, in Andrew Shonfield's solicitous phrase, a 'journey to an unknown destination'.[49]

In retrospect, the intensity of commitment to the EC tended to be in inverse ratio to the willingness to admit that the political implications were crucial. Those who supported membership often tended to stress the purely economic and commercial character of the EC while those who opposed it were equally insistent in portraying entry as a major British political commitment for which there was no parallel in the twentieth century. The key to understanding the nature of the EC lay less in its historical origins – though they were important – and more in its inherent developmental capacity. In other words, nobody could foresee precisely what the future held for the European project, but member-state governments would retain the ultimate power to decide how far and how quickly it would move forward. Shonfield described the strategy of the continental European federalists as a 'headlong flight into an unknown future, in order to escape from a fearful present'. For the British, the political implications of EC membership represented something more akin to a calculated gamble: a journey into an unknown destination in order to escape from a bleak future. And, as Shonfield remarked in the early 1970s, 'we don't know what the final answer will look like – or even should look like'. It was the joint decision to embark on the enterprise and then the experiences along the route that really mattered.[50]

The years between 1945 and 1973 were exceptionally difficult for British foreign and domestic policy-makers. At home they represented a period of tumultuous economic, political and social change while abroad they reflected a painful readjustment of British foreign policy priorities. The famous intersecting circles of influence – the relationship with the United States, the Commonwealth, and Europe – finally gave way to a concerted, if reluctant, European policy. This chapter has shown that in the agonising journey towards Europe, the British developed a phobia of federalism. Despite the energetic efforts of the British Council of the European Movement, the fear of federalism haunted the debate about British membership of the EC.[51] Keith Kyle's polemical article published in *The Times* in August 1976 and entitled 'Britain's Fear of the Dreaded "Federalism"', aptly summarised the phobia: the British fear was irrational. Continental Europeans could read the word 'without throwing a fit' and could 'continue with the argument', while the British – as the greatest drafters and proscribers of federalism for others – were 'terrified of any suggestion of it for themselves'.[52] The British had lost touch with the British federal tradition.

Notes

1. See Lipgens, W. (1982), *A History of European Integration, 1945–1947*, Vol. 1, Oxford, Clarendon Press.
2. Young, J.W. (1984), *Britain, France and the Unity of Europe, 1945–51*, Leicester, Leicester University Press, 109. For a useful summary of Bevin's role, see chapters 9–12 and 16–18.
3. Ibid., 164–5.
4. *The Sunday Times*, 31 July 1966.
5. For a detailed analysis of the shift in British policy, see Camps, M. (1964), *Britain and the European Community, 1955–1963*, Oxford, Oxford University Press, 274–312. Short summaries can also be found in Kitzinger, U. (1973), *Diplomacy and Persuasion*, London, Thames and Hudson, 27–31 and Holt, S. (1972), 'British Attitudes to the Political Aspects of Membership of the European Communities', in G. Ionescu (ed.), *The New Politics of European Integration*, London, Macmillan, 64–9.
6. For a detailed survey of Macmillan's views and role in the first British application for EC membership, see Moon, J. (1985), *European Integration in British Politics, 1950–1963*, Aldershot, Gower, 36–40 and 161–71.
7. See Lieber, R.J. (1974), 'Interest Groups and Political Integration: British Entry into Europe', in R. Kimber and J.J. Richardson (eds), *Pressure Groups in Britain*, London, Dent, 27–56.
8. Lieber, R.J. (1974), 'Interest Groups', 42.
9. *Hansard*, House of Commons (HC) Debates, 643 (28 June 1961), 553.
10. Macmillan, H. (1973), *At the End of the Day, 1961–1963*, London, Macmillan, 8.
11. *Hansard*, HC Debates, 641 (1 June 1961), 416.
12. Ibid.
13. *Hansard*, HC Debates, 643 (28 June 1961), 526–34.
14. Ibid., 538–9. Jenkins became the first British President of the Commission of the EC during 1977–81.
15. Ibid., 567–8.
16. *Hansard*, HC Debates, 644 (11 July 1961), 206–7.
17. Ibid., 207.
18. Macmillan, H. (1973), *At the End of the Day*, 15.
19. Camps, M. (1964), *Britain and the European Community*, 357.
20. *Hansard*, HC Debates, 645 (2 August 1961), 1491. For Macmillan's remarks about federalism and sovereignty in this debate, see 1491–1506.
21. Ibid., 1491.
22. *Hansard*, HC Debates, 645 (2 August 1961), 1498.
23. Walker-Smith's observations, ibid., 1507–11.
24. *Hansard*, HC Debates, 645 (2 August 1961), 1670–4. For a detailed analysis of the Fouchet-Cattani Committee discussions, see Bodenheimer, S. (1967), *Political Union: A Microcosm of European Politics, 1960–1966*, The Netherlands, Sijthoff-Leyden.
25. *Hansard*, HC Debates, 661 (6 June 1962), 581.
26. Edelman's remarks, ibid., 584–6.
27. *Hansard*, HC Debates, 661 (7 June 1962), 695.
28. Ibid., 718–20.
29. Heath's statement on federalism, ibid., 796–8.
30. *Hansard*, HC Debates, 664 (1 August 1962), 696–7.

31. Smithers's remarks in recognising the significance of the political implications of membership amounted to something of a turning-point in the debate. See *Hansard*, HC Debates, 664 (1 August 1962), 713–16.

32. *Hansard*, HC Debates, 666 (7 November 1962), 999–1000.

33. Gaitskell's speech, ibid., 1001–19.

34. Grimond's remarks, *Hansard*, HC Debates, 668 (6 December 1962), 1493 and Thorpe's comments, *Hansard*, HC Debates, 671 (11 February 1963), 1032–4.

35. Colley, L. (1992), *Britons: Forging the Nation, 1707–1837*, New Haven and London, Yale University Press, 1–9.

36. Tugendhat, C. (1987), *Making Sense of Europe*, London, Harmondsworth, 21–2.

37. See, for example, Robins, L.J. (1979), *The Reluctant Party: Labour and the EEC, 1961–1975*, Ormskirk, G.W. and Hesketh, A.

38. *Hansard*, HC Debates, 645 (2 August 1962), 1667–70.

39. *Hansard*, HC Debates, 746 (2 May 1967), 311.

40. Ibid., 314–26.

41. Du Cann was the first to press Macmillan for either a general election or a referendum on British membership in 1961. See *Hansard*, HC Debates, 641 (1 June 1961), 414. On Wilson's low key approach to Europe in the Labour party manifesto, see Robins, L.J., *The Reluctant Party*, 67.

42. *Hansard*, HC Debates, 821 (21 July 1971), 1452–3.

43. Ibid., 1454.

44. See the terminological dispute between Jeremy Thorpe and Neil Marten concerning the future shape that Europe would take in *Hansard*, HC Debates, 821 (21 July 1971), 1506–7.

45. Marten's views, ibid., 1507–8.

46. *Hansard*, HC Debates, 821 (22 July 1971), 1765–8.

47. Ibid., 1820.

48. Communique of the Paris summit meeting of Heads of Government, 21 October 1972, *Bulletin of the European Communities*, part 11, 1972, 9–71, and Communique issued after the Paris meeting of Heads of State, 10 December 1974, *Bulletin of the European Communities*, 12, 1974, 7–12.

49. Shonfield, A. (1972), *Europe: Journey to an Unknown Destination*, Harmondsworth, Penguin. This was an expanded version of the BBC Reith Lectures.

50. Shonfield, A. (1972), *Europe: Journey to an Unknown Destination*, 19.

51. For the important role that the Federal Union, the British Campaign for Europe and the British Council of the European Movement played in British entry into the EC, see Mayne, R. and Pinder, J. (1990), *Federal Union: The Pioneers*, London, Macmillan, chapters 11 and 12.

52. *The Times*, 3 August 1976.

CHAPTER 8

British federal ideas and the intellectual contribution to a federal Europe

During the 1980s federal ideas were gradually reinstated as a major political force in the European Community (EC). The principal vehicle of this restoration was the European Parliament (EP) and the main driving-force behind it was Altiero Spinelli. In this chapter we will look at how British federal ideas furnished the major intellectual influence upon Spinelli and were, in consequence, woven into the fabric of the EP's proposals for the European Union Treaty (EUT) of 1984. It is, as we shall see, a long and quite remarkable progeniture.

We will begin our investigation into the lineage of the EUT by examining the origins and nature of Spinelli's federal ideas, but first let us look at a short political profile of Spinelli himself. Born in Rome in 1907, Spinelli joined the Communist party in 1924 as a law student, being attracted chiefly by the 'internationalism' of Lenin and Trotsky. Arrested during the series of political trials in Italy during 1927–28, he was sentenced to sixteen years in prison. He was imprisoned for ten years and in the spring of 1937 sent into internal exile on Ponza, being transferred to the island of Ventotene, off the Naples coast, in June 1939. Spinelli was confined along with 'most of the extradited Reds' on Ventotene which was dubbed the 'capital' of the PCI underground.[1] There he met two fellow democratic socialist captives: Eugenio Colorni, who was already interned there with his wife, and Ernesto Rossi, a Professor of Economics, who arrived on the island shortly after him. After his years of imprisonment and much soul-searching, Spinelli deserted the PCI, having become disillusioned with Stalinism, and 'shifted to Socialism'.[2]

The earliest evidence of Spinelli's conversion to the idea of a federal Europe during the anti-Fascist Resistance years is dated as 1940–41. Along with Colorni and Rossi, Spinelli helped to form what was 'the first unmistakably federalist group to organize itself on Italian soil'.[3] In the first half of 1941 a statement, 'based partly on a reading of the Marxist classics on the one hand and partly on the Federalist Papers of Hamilton, Madison and Jay on the other', was compiled and in July 1941 smuggled to Rome.[4] Written by Spinelli and Rossi, it was entitled the 'Manifesto for a Free and United

Europe' but quickly found fame as the 'Ventotene Manifesto'. As recent research has shown, this manifesto provoked considerable debate among the 'programme drafters of the re-emerging Italian parties' and became 'one of the basic documents of the European federalist movement'.[5]

The goals and assumptions of the Ventotene Manifesto were unambiguous. Federal union was to have top priority among postwar tasks. But, as Walter Lipgens, astutely observed, the true character of the Resistance movements was that of an 'intellectual' resistance: the members of the Resistance fought not only *against* totalitarian rule, but even more, in their view, *for* something. In their quest for a better and peaceful society they fought Hitler not for the old nation-states but rather for a new European society.[6] The consensus of opinion which emerged independently among Resistance groups throughout Europe at this time was that the defeat of totalitarianism and the creation of a 'United States of Europe' in its place went hand in hand. To allow the old nation-states to recover and regain their former positions in a world of international rivalry would be to recreate the conditions for war and totalitarian rule. The Manifesto therefore elaborated the idea of a federal Europe as the panacea for virtually all the outstanding problems which would confront postwar statesmen.

After the war Spinelli was active among the plethora of federal groups and associations which sprang up and eventually coalesced under the broad title of the European Movement. He was among the Resistance leaders who formed the European Union of Federalists (UEF) in December 1946 and, after the split of 1955–56, was Secretary General of the new European Federalist Movement (MFE) until 1963. In 1966 he founded the Institute for International Affairs in Rome, was personal adviser to the Italian Foreign Minister, Nenni, during 1968–70, joined the Commission of the European Community with responsibility for Industry, Research and Technology between 1970 and 1976, and became a Member of both the Italian and European Parliaments. When he died in May 1986, Spinelli had established himself as the 'grand old man' of Europe and the leading protagonist of the European federal cause.

This short political profile gives us a good idea of 'Spinelli's prominence in the building of European Union. It also suggests that the chief driving-force behind both his wartime and his postwar activities was his aversion to international conflict. Like many in the Resistance generation, he sought principally to remove what he considered to be the main condition for war, namely, the nation-state. The dramatic and complete collapse of European states in the face of the Nazi *Blitzkrieg* convinced him that traditional state structures were obsolete. They no longer satisfied the basic needs of their populations. This view of the nation-state as both archaic and obsolete underpinned his intellectual argument consistently throughout the remainder of his life. But war and the threat of war do not, by themselves, explain how and why Spinelli was driven to champion the federal cause. This occurred in a somewhat odd and haphazard manner. Let us turn, then, to the intellectual origins of his federal ideas.

The source of Spinelli's federal ideas can be traced back to his confinement on the island of Ventotene in 1939. But the role of Professor Luigi Einaudi is central to an explanation of these ideas. An Italian Liberal and distinguished economist at the University of Turin, Einaudi was an influential figure in the anti-Fascist Resistance and worked together with Spinelli and others to consolidate the Movimento Federalista Europeo (MFE) which was formed in Milan late in August 1943. Einaudi subsequently became Italy's first President in 1948, but his influence upon Spinelli stretched back to arguments which were first formulated in 1918. It was in that year, according to Charles Delzell, that 'the keynote for this European federalist movement was sounded'.[7] In two 'letters to the editor' published in the Milan *Corriere della Sera* in January and December 1918, Einaudi criticised the idea of a new League of Nations which left intact the sovereignty of the member states. He compared the plans for the League to the American Articles of Confederation and argued that what Europe really needed was a replica of the American Constitution. These letters appeared under the pseudonym 'Junius' and were republished, together with a number of other articles, in a book entitled *Lettere Politiche* in 1920.

Spinelli acknowledged that these views were published 'as a personal opinion' and that 'no political movement developed from them', but he recognised the clarity with which Einaudi defined the problem and admired Einaudi's contribution which he considered to be 'federalist thinking of the highest calibre'.[8] Spinelli did not examine Einaudi's work until the first half of 1939, but it seems to have been a source of great inspiration to the handful of anti-Fascist internees on Ventotene. Delzell has claimed that the failure of the League of Nations and Hitler's growing military power caused Spinelli and his fellow travellers on Ventotene to 'reflect upon the essays of Einaudi'.[9] It appears therefore that Einaudi's essays on the subject of a United States of Europe, written in 1918, prompted Spinelli to search for a lasting solution to the problem of nationalism in Europe on the eve of the Second World War.

Since Einaudi's work suggested a federal solution to Europe's difficulties and identified both the United States and Anglo-Scottish constitutional relations as illustrations of the success of the federal principle, it is hardly surprising to learn that Spinelli turned for guidance to American, Swiss and British constitutional history.[10] It is important to underline this point if we are not to underestimate the part which Einaudi played in the development of Spinelli's ideas. His influence upon Spinelli was an 'intellectual' influence. But John Pinder has also demonstrated that Einaudi's role was pivotal in a different sense. According to Pinder, it was Einaudi who sent 'those of the British federal texts which he had been able to obtain' to Spinelli and his comrades on Ventotene.[11] The timing of this event is significant. Spinelli first became acquainted with Einaudi's federalist writings at the same time as he began to receive a steady flow of British federalist literature during the first half of 1939 until the appearance of the Ventotene Manifesto in the autumn of 1941. This sequence of events, then, suggests that he was already familiar with Anglo-American federal ideas prior to receiving the British federalist literature of the Federal Union.

We have already examined the scholarly federal ideas and writings of Federal Union in the United Kingdom during the late 1930s and the war years. What British federalist literature did Spinelli receive and read on the island of Ventotene in 1939 and which books and essays influenced him most? This information is now well known. Spinelli acknowledged that the views and arguments of Lord Lothian, Lionel Robbins and Sir William Beveridge, in particular, made a strong impression upon him.[12] And the impact of these ideas was both decisive and durable. In his autobiographical work the attraction of British federal ideas is clearly explained:

> Since I was seeking clarity and precision of thought, my attention was not attracted by the nebulous, contorted and hardly coherent ideological federalism of the Proudhonian or Mazzinian type, which throve in France or in Italy, but by the polished, precise and anti-doctrinaire thought of the English federalists ... who proposed to transplant into Europe the great American political experience.[13]

Spinelli certainly received and read Lord Lothian's *Pacifism is not Enough (nor Patriotism Either)*, which was first published in 1935, and Lionel Robbins' *The Economic Causes of War*, which appeared in 1939. He also confirmed that after the liberation of Europe in 1945 he 'managed to read a considerable quantity of British Federalist literature in the thirties in the library of the League of Nations in Geneva'. While he did not know about Clarence Streit's *Union Now*, he translated Robbins' book on Ventotene and the Italian translation was subsequently published by Einaudi.[14] In the following extract from an essay which he wrote in 1957 the impact on him of British federal ideas is reaffirmed:

> We are used to thinking of the British as completely averse to any idea of federation, and they, themselves, seem to strengthen this impression by often repeating that this is ... very foreign to their method of thinking. ... This is not actually so, however. ... The idea that it is possible to bring about a supranational government by means other than conquest, i.e., through free consent of states, and that it is possible to divide sovereignty, assigning portions of it to different organs of the government, is a typically Anglo-Saxon conception. ... We must conclude that the federal experience is very close to the British political spirit, and also that the British can easily understand the federal concept and its logical and economic implications. Another proof of this understanding is seen in the federalist literature of the Federal Union, which is of first quality and even today superior to the average Continental literature on the subject, because of the coherence with which the problems are presented, obstacles examined and solutions proposed. It is interesting to note here that the most coherent federalist movement today is the Italian, which has absorbed a great deal from the study of this English federalist literature.[15]

In the light of these statements, it was small wonder that Spinelli should have confessed in 1983 that the intellectual origins of his federal ideas were 'rooted in English political culture'.[16]

It can be seen, then, that if we study the role and activities of Altiero Spinelli in the 1980s in the European Parliament, they will lead us straight back to the British federal tradition. This in itself is of considerable intellectual interest since it highlights the interaction of British federal ideas with the 'postwar renaissance of the European federalist idea on the continent of Europe'.[17] But it acquires even greater contemporary political significance when we remember that Spinelli's federal ideas were absorbed directly into the Parliament's EUT of 1984.[18] This confirmed the links between the intellectual influences of the 1930s and 1940s and those of the 1980s. In short, it meant that through Spinelli the British had made an intellectual contribution to the political integration of Europe in a curious and quite remarkable manner scarcely known outside of federalist circles.

How were these federal ideas translated into practical action in the 1980s? Did Spinelli manage to bring his thinking down from the level of theoretical analysis to that of political strategy? Given the intellectual influences upon him it is no surprise to discover that the answers to these two questions lie in the impact of Federal Union literature. If we remember that the intellectual and historical bases of Federal Union literature derive in the main from nineteenth-century English liberal political thought, this helps to explain the content of the EUT. There was a strong nineteenth-century English liberal tone about the importance of constitutional and judicial guarantees, parliamentary representation and institutional checks and balances. Spinelli was in many ways a 'neo-institutionalist' in the sense that he always believed in the capacity of political institutions to change human perceptions and behaviour. His view was that in order for European attitudes and interests to be successfully canalised, the EC had to have the basic institutions essential for popular participation. For Spinelli, 'institutional reform of the Community and progress towards political union' were 'one and the same thing'.[19] The direct election of the EP was therefore an important step in this direction but it was only the first step. European Union, or, as Spinelli put it, 'the common elaboration' could be achieved on a gradual step-by-step basis provided that the EC was given the institutional legs to take these steps. He always insisted that Europe had to have an instrument around which the common ideas could be elaborated, a structure where there was 'a certain priority given to the common elaboration'. This meant that the efficient implementation of European policies had to be both gradual and piecemeal. But 'the political setting of the institutions' had to be solid; this could not be made step-by-step.[20]

According to Spinelli, nothing less than major institutional reform could solve the deep-seated problems of the EC in the 1980s. Europe needed a strong institutional framework which would foster and encapsulate a common political will. He believed that Europe already had an incipient unity. All that was necessary to distil and crystallise it was sound political institutions. The right kind of institutional reform could activate an extant common interest by allowing it to grow gradually and naturally, removing the obstacles to its development and encouraging European peoples to recognise that contemporary problems were common problems necessitating common solutions. The main assumption in Spinelli's thinking, then, was an optimistic belief that the common people, if allowed to determine themselves, would inevitably gravitate towards unity in cooperation. It was obsolete state structures and the anachronistic values of states' elites and interests which obstructed the 'common elaboration'.

This explains why Spinelli wanted a parliamentary initiative in the early 1980s. Previous moves had come 'from the governmental side' and they had all 'suffered the same fate of being dealt with in secret negotiations between national diplomatic delegations without any participation of the parliaments – European and national'. The result had been predictable: the commitments had been 'watered down to insignificant compromises and finally dropped'. Only by setting in motion 'a political process with a broad backing from political parties of all member states and all tendencies' could the elusive common political will be successfully encapsulated, thus avoiding the 'paralysing national nearsightedness' of national negotiators.[21]

Despite the pressure from the EP, acting as the constituent power of the nascent European citizenry, the EUT was never implemented. It did not reach the table for practical negotiations at the intergovernmental conference of 1985. But it is clear that without the relentless pressure of Spinelli and the EP during the early 1980s, the EC would not even have achieved the Single European Act (SEA), ratified in 1987. How, then, do these events relate to the British federal tradition? To what extent did they perpetuate this tradition in the EC after the death of Spinelli in 1986? There are two particular ways in which the British federal tradition has continued to make a significant contribution to the political and constitutional evolution of the EC. First, it remains alive in the EP's political strategy in the 1990s to achieve European Union and, secondly, it has been strengthened by the activities of an increasing number of British MEPs in both the Labour and Conservative parties in the EP. Let us look at these two separate contributions in a little more detail.

We will begin with the EP's political strategy to achieve European Union after the death of Spinelli in 1986. The introduction of the SEA in 1987 represented the culmination of a concerted attempt by the EP to distil the concept of European Union into a set of practical proposals. But the SEA was a disappointment for those who supported the federal cause. It was a concrete achievement with significant political implications, but it could never remotely be construed as tantamount to European Union. It was the result of yet another intergovernmental compromise in which member-state governments inevitably favoured national answers against European solutions. The EP, however, never regarded the SEA as anything more than another step towards the goal of European Union. But what would European Union look like? The answer was simple: it remained the EP's own European Union Treaty (EUT) of 1984. The EUT was the 'benchmark, an inspiration and a model'.[22] And if we look at the Herman Report of 21 December 1988, drawn up by the Committee on Institutional Affairs of the EP, we can easily identify the continuity in political strategy.[23] In other words, Spinelli continued to cast a shadow over the basic aims and the political strategy of the EP in the late 1980s. In a series of reports of the Committee on Institutional Affairs adopted in 1988 and 1989 the EP set out its new strategy for achieving European Union based upon its self-styled constituent role as part of the EC's dual legitimacy. The strategy was new only in the context of the failure of the EUT and the success of the SEA. Its aim was to combine a gradualist policy with a quantum leap, the first within the framework of the Treaties and the SEA, and the second with a view to transforming them or replacing them by a new treaty. In practice this meant exploiting to the very limit the possibilities offered by the SEA while simultaneously pursuing the goal of the 1984 EUT.

It is important to note that the goal of the EUT is not regarded by the EP as the Gospel. It is open-minded about accepting amendments to it provided that the basic principles remain firm. The culmination of the EP's efforts was the resolution in February 1994 for the 'Draft Constitution of the European Union'.[24] This is the latest of the EP's ideas and proposals for institutional reform in the 1990s. But these initiatives would never see the light of day if it was not for the concerted pressure of a critical mass of MEPs in the EP. The contribution of British MEPs in the movement to achieve a more binding federal union is particularly interesting. It is also important for what it tells us about the British federal tradition in the Europe of today. In the drive to translate European Union into a set of practical proposals in the 1980s, the role of some British Conservatives in the EP is especially noteworthy. Many were enthusiastic in their advocacy of the EUT and the core body of Conservative 'pro-Europeans' who regularly voiced support for Spinelli's initiative totalled at least fifteen by 1984.[25] Some, like Bill Newton-Dunn and Christopher Jackson, were self-confessed federalists although they were naturally very careful about the company in which they accepted this label. And though not avowed federalists themselves, Sir Christopher Prout and Derek Prag were prominent representatives of the Conservative group in the EP who were extremely active and progressive in their support for a stronger political Europe.[26]

The Conservative party in the EP, then, was always more progressive and imaginative in the quest for European Union in the 1980s than their counterpart at Westminster. Conservatives in the EC were largely inoculated against the narrow-minded 'Little Englander' mentality of the British Prime Minister, Mrs Thatcher. But British support for a federal Europe in the EP has also come from another, entirely unexpected, source. The new intake of forty-five

Labour MEPs after the EP elections of 1989 also included a new breed of European democratic socialists with progressive views about European Union which were far removed from those of their more insular predecessors. The leader of the British Labour group, David Martin, a young Scottish MEP who represented the Lothians, quickly adopted an active role in the struggle to build 'political Europe' during the early 1990s. The ease with which he accepted the term 'federal' in the political discourse about the future of Europe in the 1990s aptly demonstrated just how far the British Labour group in the EP had shifted in its attitudes towards European Union. Indeed, David Martin, who later became a Vice-President in the EP, was linked very closely to federalism in the Martin Resolution of 14 March 1990 which claimed that it was 'increasingly necessary rapidly to transform the European Community into a European Union of federal type' which would go 'beyond the single market and economic and monetary union'.[27]

The commitment to a European Union 'of federal type' was what Spinelli had called 'constitutionalism'. Another leading Italian federalist, Mario Albertini, had referred to this as the need for 'a much higher degree of construction' in the European project.[28] The Martin II Report of July 1990 endorsed the 'essential elements' which would achieve this:

1. Economic and Monetary Union (EMU) with a single currency and an independent central bank.
2. A common foreign policy, including joint consideration of the issues of peace, security and arms control.
3. A completed single market with common policies in those areas which require common action, especially economic and social cohesion and a balanced environment.
4. Elements of a common citizenship and a common framework for protecting basic rights.
5. An institutional system efficient to manage these responsibilities effectively and democratically structured, notably by giving the EP a right of initiative, of co-decision with the Council on EC legislation, the right to ratify all constitutional decisions requiring the ratification of member state governments and of electing the President of the Commission.

The Martin II Report claimed that these five 'essential elements' would form the basis for a new European constitution transforming the EC into a 'genuine union of federal type'.[29]

During the last decade both the political strategy of the EP and the important contributions made by British Conservative and Labour MEPs in pursuit of European Union have significantly reinforced the British federal tradition. We can trace a clear unbroken line of British federal ideas, influences and strategies for Europe over a century from Seeley, Lothian, Curtis, Robbins, and Beveridge to Spinelli and his federalist sympathisers in the EP. It is an intellectual lineage which serves to underline both the continuity and the resilience of the British federal tradition. But it is also an intellectual tradition which, until recently, was quite unknown, even to the British. They have made an important intellectual contribution to the building of Europe in a manner which is ironical given the conventional opinion of a traditional British antipathy to federalism. We will return to this paradox in the conclusion to the book which follows in the final chapter. For the moment, however, let us close this chapter with some concluding remarks about British federal ideas and the building of a federal Europe.

John Pinder concluded his essay on Lord Lothian with the observation that because the British took so little part in the early postwar federalist movement, 'they have tended to underrate its significance'.[30] This led them to stand on the sidelines while continental Western Europe organised its own destiny. Schuman's declaration in 1950, we are reminded, was a firm commitment that the European Coal and Steel Community would be 'the first concrete foundation of a European federation'. The subsequent negotiations at Messina in the mid-1950s seemed to suggest that the federal goal had faded and that the primary motives for a deeper union of states were economic rather than political. Historians might conceivably draw this conclusion from the recently released archives of the period. The detailed bargains and debates among state elites, evident in these archives, will doubtless emphasise economic imperatives. It would be odd if it was otherwise. But on the basis of this evidence alone it would be misleading to suggest that the main driving-force behind the building of Europe in the mid-1950s was solely economic. The negotiations which led to the Treaty of Rome in 1957 must not be examined in complete isolation from the overall progress and evolution of the European idea since 1950. The European federalist movement, in furnishing both the spirit and the purpose of the project, clearly influenced both the creation and the form that the EC took.

The underlying impetus for the construction of postwar Europe was political. The British missed the critical opportunity to give a direct lead – and hence a distinctly British input – in the decisive negotiations which resulted in the Treaty of Rome. In hindsight, this was a major failure of postwar British foreign policy. There is, indeed, nothing in the Treaty of Rome which smacks formally of a federal Europe but the commitment to 'an ever closer union among European peoples' could be construed in terms which are far more integrative and centralised than the federal goal. In his determination to rid the Maastricht Treaty of any reference to federalism, the British Prime Minister, John Major, conveniently overlooked substantive elements in the Treaty, like the concept of citizenship, which have obvious federal implications. Today, then, we are left with a curious disjunction between the British obsession with a federal Europe – the phobia of federalism – and the reality of the British federal tradition. Let us finally explore the nature and significance of the British federal tradition in the conclusion to the book which follows this chapter.

Notes

1. Delzell, C.F. (1974), *Mussolini's Enemies: The Italian Anti-Fascist Resistance*, New York, New York University Press, 190.
2. Ibid., 191.
3. Delzell, C.F. (1960), 'The European Federalist Movement in Italy: First Phase, 1918–1947', Journal of Modern History, 32, 243.
4. Lipgens, W. (1982), *A History of European Integration, 1945–1947*, Vol. 1, Oxford, Clarendon Press, 109.
5. Delzell, C.F. (1974), *Mussolini's Enemies*, 192 and Lipgens, W. (1982), *European Integration*, 109.
6. This point has been underlined in Lipgens, W. (1968), 'European Federation in the Political Thought of Resistance Movements during World War II', *Central European History*, 1, 5–19.
7. Delzell, C.F. (1960), 'The European Federalist Movement in Italy', 241.
8. Spinelli, A. (1957), 'The Growth of the European Movement since World War II', in C. Grove Haines (ed.), *European Integration*, Baltimore, Md, The Johns Hopkins University Press, 37.
9. Delzell, C.F. (1960), 'The European Federalist Movement in Italy', 244.
10. Ibid.
11. Pinder, J. (1983), 'Prophet Not Without Honour: Lothian and the Federal Idea', *The Round Table*, 286, 217.
12. In an interview with Spinelli in September 1983 the ideas of these three Federal Union activists were cited as having been especially influential.
13. Spinelli, A. (nd), *Il Lungo Monologo*, Rome, Edizione dell' Ateneo, 135. Pinder's translation in Pinder, J. (1983), 'Prophet Not Without Honour', 217.
14. Spinelli, A. and Rossi, E. (1988), *The Ventotene Manifesto*, Ventotene, The Altiero Spinelli Institute for Federalist Studies, 52. The English version is distributed in the UK by Federal Trust for Education and Research, London.
15. Spinelli, A. (1957), 'The Growth of the European Movement since World War II', 38–40.
16. Interview with Spinelli in September 1983.
17. Pinder, J. (1983), 'Prophet Not Without Honour', 217.
18. For a detailed analysis of the EUT, see Lodge, J. (ed.) (1986), *European Union: Europe in Search of a Future*, London, Macmillan.
19. Spinelli, A. (1972), *The European Adventure: Tasks for the Enlarged Community*, London, Charles Knight, 16.
20. Interview with Spinelli in September 1983.
21. *EP Working Documents*, 15 July 1983, Doc. 1–575/83/B, 5.
22. *Explanatory Statement of the Interim Report of the EP's Committee on Institutional Affairs*, 14 March 1990, (Martin I. Report), Doc. trav/conference, PE 068.
23. *Herman Report*, 21 December 1988, on the strategy of the EP for achieving European Union, Doc. A.2–322/88, 19.
24. *Draft Constitution of the European Union*, 10 February 1994, European Parliament, PE 179.622, Luxembourg, 1–27.
25. Burgess, M. (1989), *Federalism and European Union: Political Ideas, Influences and Strategies in the European Community, 1972–1987*, London, Routledge, 160.
26. For the active role of Conservative MEPs during 1984–89, see, Burgess, M. and

Lee. A. (1990), 'The United Kingdom', in J. Lodge (ed.), *The European Parliament Elections of 1989*, London, Macmillan, chapter 11.

27. *Martin I. Resolution*, EP, 14 March 1990, Doc. A3–47/90.
28. Albertini, M. (1986), 'Europe on the Threshold of Union', *The Federalist*, Year XXVII, 1, 27.
29. *Martin II. Report*, 11 July 1990, PE 143.503, 60–1.
30. Pinder, J. (1983), 'Prophet Not Without Honour', 217.

CHAPTER 9

Conclusion: the discredited state and the drift towards federalism

This study has confirmed the existence of the British tradition of federalism. It has demonstrated that during the last century there has been a fundamental continuity of British federal ideas about the reform of the United Kingdom. These political and constitutional ideas arose as a direct response to real and perceived challenges to the integrity of the state. They are British federal ideas for the British: an indigenous tradition of federalism. In order to substantiate this argument we have looked at three 'issue arenas', namely, 'Empire, Ireland and Europe' which together have provided a rich source of federal ideas and proposals spanning the last century. We have seen that both the history and the structure of the United Kingdom have prompted a succession of public men to champion federalism in order principally to buttress the Union. This is why federal ideas were sparked into existence and catapulted to the forefront of British political debate. They are a perfectly legitimate, if neglected, part of the overall British political tradition.

Bulpitt's historical analysis of territorial politics in the United Kingdom was used in this study in order to support our thesis of a distinct British tradition of federalism.[1] His survey of the general relationship between national and local politics – a study of power relations – helps to explain the emergence of federal ideas and the practice of federal relations in the polity. His developmental model depicted an elite operational code of territorial management designed to secure the goals of the authorities in London by a tacit system of indirect rule offering considerable autonomy to local elites. The territorial code worked in conjunction with an operative separation of powers. The constant reliance on indirect rule, involving in practice the granting of considerable reciprocal autonomy to collaborative local elites, meant that 'the Centre sought not to govern the United Kingdom, but to manage it'.[2] Centre–periphery relations therefore served to accommodate at different times a wide range of practical policy outcomes and institutional relationships. In the United Kingdom political practice often outstripped constitutional theory.

Recent research on the United Kingdom suggests that it is a strange union, full of historical paradoxes, curious conventions and bizarre practices. But it is a union which has endured. It is an *ancien régime* with a glorious imperial past and a venerable constitutional order which has successfully sustained a myriad of both formal and informal institutional relationships. Today, however, there are good reasons to believe that the British constitutional system is showing disturbing signs of wear and tear. There is now an increasing and familiar litany of complaints about our constitutional order. James Cornford has summarised them in the following way:

> ... an electoral system which seriously distorts representation, excludes middle opinion, and threatens to perpetuate rule by the largest minority party; a Parliament which is dominated by the executive through control of its procedures and the disciplines of party, patronage and the Press, and which therefore fails to scrutinise effectively the conduct of government or to play any constructive role in legislation; a national administration which practises excessive secrecy and against whose actions there is inadequate redress; a local government which is at once the dependent of and the scapegoat for central government and which enjoys little support either in Parliament or among the electorate; of a police force which has been used increasingly in a political role, which has little accountability, which has absorbed more and more resources while crime rates rise, and whose reputation for probity has been sadly dented.[3]

To this catalogue of criticisms and complaints we must add the battery of challenges to the contemporary state which we identified in the introduction to the book. These are the following: recent changes in the structure of the British economy; the governmental hegemony of the Conservative party; the intensification of widespread political discontent in Scotland; and increasing economic and political integration in the European Union. Alongside these imperatives for change must be placed the unresolved problem of Northern Ireland and a host of competing difficulties which include, *inter alia*, immigration, race relations, citizens' rights, welfare issues, and the future of the monarchy. Each of these challenges, it should be noted, has important constitutional implications. However, we have already acknowledged the genius of the British constitutional system in successfully disguising constitutional questions as mere political issues. In the past this has been a formula for great success. It has both deflected and defused potentially dangerous and divisive constitutional problems. Today, however, it is questionable whether this practice can continue. The combination of strains, tensions and challenges to the state, outlined above, suggests that the British state has become a discredited state. In consequence, considerable pressures are mounting in the polity for genuine constitutional reform.

In September 1911 Lord Selbourne wrote a letter to Austen Chamberlain, which included two confidential memoranda, concerning the constitutional crisis surrounding the Parliament Bill and the Conservative party's response to it. In the second memorandum Selbourne made the following observation which serves to underline the gist of our conclusion:

The electors have been very apathetic all through this constitutional crisis. Why? Because they have not understood all that is involved, nor does the British elector understand in the least, as the American elector does, what the constitution of his country means to him. That this is so is not the fault of the elector; it is the natural result of our peculiar history.[4]

Selbourne was right. The British understood political power but they did not understand constitutional power. They had no written, codified constitution to enable them fully to appreciate the benefits and virtues of genuine citizenship. Theirs was an aristocratic constitution which emphasised the passive role of the subject rather than the active role of the citizen. To Selbourne's 'British elector' in the United Kingdom, then, constitutional power was barely visible. But for constitutional conservatives the traditional lack of public understanding and awareness of what the constitution meant – and what it should mean – had certain merits. It had, for example, effectively excluded any major reappraisal of the British constitution. This, in turn, had ruled out any wholesale root-and-branch reform of the constitution. In short, the British lacked a genuine constitutional culture. This made them blind to the defects and shortcomings of their own constitutional order and unable to appreciate the merits and virtues of alternative systems.

The British tradition of federalism has been the victim of an elaborate constitutional deception. It has inevitably suffered from the success of the old constitutional system. After all, if it works why change it? But it has also suffered from genuine public misunderstanding and deliberate elite misrepresentation. The result has been intermittently to push British federal ideas to the very margins of mainstream political activitiy. But today the British constitutional system does not work well. There are clear signs that this constitutional inertia and complacency will no longer be tolerated. Certain informed sections of British public opinion outside London have already begun to forge an effective and convincing critique of the state. This increasingly vocal and vigorous intellectual and political critique of the basic principles upon which the British are governed is especially prominent in the Labour and Liberal Democratic parties, the Scottish Constitutional Convention and Charter 88. And what is particularly striking about this movement of critical opinion is its convergence upon the idea of constitutional power. There appears to be a growing consensus of informed opinion in favour of genuine constitutional reform in the United Kingdom.

Where, then, does this lively contemporary debate about constitutional reform in the United Kingdom leave the British federal tradition? What are the implications of this tradition for British government and politics? There can be little doubt that the restoration of the British tradition of federalism could assist towards a greater public understanding of the need for constitutional reform in the United Kingdom. This would be predicated upon a critique of the overweening centralisation of power in London. The present constitutional order survives intact largely because of public ignorance, indifference and neglect. But we pay a heavy price for this inertia. To re-instate British federal ideas as an important part of the larger British political tradition, then, would be a useful first step towards public enlightenment. The British tradition of federalism would expose the defects and deficiencies in the existing constitutional system and underline the many alternative reform agendas. British federal ideas therefore could point the way to the modernisation of the British state and the renewal of civil society.

It is not within the scope of this book to produce a blueprint for a new constitution. The diagnosis of major constitutional ills is, in any case, much easier to arrive at than their remedy. However, it is certainly appropriate to point out that one of the major obstacles to constitutional reform in the United Kingdom is the continuing reluctance of British political leaders to shed certain long-standing assumptions about government that have now become out-dated. In 1977 Anthony Birch identified four such out-dated assumptions: the belief in parliamentary sovereignty; the conviction that the United Kingdom, alone among the world's democracies, did not need a written constitution; the mixture of complacency and scorn with which most British politicians regarded federal systems of government; and the smug conviction that the British party system guaranteed more effective government than the multi-party systems of most continental West European countries.[5] Birch wrote these remarks in the wake of the *Report of the Royal Commission on the Constitution*, known as the 'Kilbrandon Report' after the name of its second chairman, which was pub-lished in October 1973. He noted that the Report rejected the federal solution in rather sweeping terms. In just ten pages it dismissed a federal United Kingdom as 'a strange and artificial system' not suited to the 'present stage of constitutional development'.[6] Birch, however, was singularly unimpressed by this peremptory dismissal of the federal solution:

> To adopt a federal constitution would of course be a complicated undertaking and would be a more radical reform than the British have ever previously made. But changes of one kind or another are imminent and the merits of federalism ought to be carefully weighed against the alternatives.[7]

The 'Kilbrandon Report' was hamstrung by the overriding desire to main-tain 'the undivided sovereignty of Parliament'.[8] Its observations about the federal idea were conditioned by this imperative. This undoubtedly explains why its remarks about the federal solution bordered on contempt and de-liberate misrepresentation. Dicey's legacy had endured. However, there was also a certain irony in the Report's reference to the encouraging experience in Northern Ireland under the Government of Ireland Act, 1920, when recom-mending legislative devolution for Scotland and Wales. Our study of Northern Ireland between 1921 and 1972 suggests strong federal elements both in constitutional theory and practice in the United Kingdom. But in forecasting that the power of Westminster would be invoked only in exceptional circum-stances in the case of Welsh and Scottish devolution, and in predicting that a convention would arise whereby Parliament would legislate for Wales on a transferred matter only with the agreement of the Welsh government, the Report came perilously close to proposing what one commentator called 'federal government without the courage of its convictions'.[9]

Before we bring this study of the British tradition of federalism to a close, it is important finally to confront the most durable and damaging concept of contemporary British parliamentary government, namely, sovereignty. This concept has two main faces: the international dimension and the domestic context. In their recent analysis entitled *The End of Sovereignty?*, Joseph Camilleri and Jim Falk point to the main deficiencies of the sovereignty model and suggest an alternative theoretical direction.[10] Their analysis indicates the existence of three boundaries which are central to the discourse of sovereignty: physical, cultural and conceptual. It is precisely at this juncture that we can return to the paradox of British federal ideas in the European Union which we mentioned in the previous chapter. It will be recalled that the British have made an intellectual contribution to the development of a federal Europe without knowing it. Why, then, does there exist a well-known British phobia of federalism? How can this paradox be explained? Let us focus once again upon the British perception of sovereignty.

The answer lies in a combination of the three boundaries central to the sovereignty discourse which we have already identified above. Membership of the European Union – a union which is gradually and inexorably acquiring the characteristics of a federal union – violates each of these boundaries. The physical boundary which separates the United Kingdom from continental Europe has already been breached in so many different ways, from the all-encompassing pull of the single European market to the corrosive penetration of an as yet incipient European social policy. The English Channel – so effective an obstacle to Napoleon and Hitler – is no match for the incisive intrusions of European economic and political integration. The cultural boundary which separates the 'Same' from the 'Other' has also been breached.[11] The British have at last been compelled formally to engage a continental Europe which they perceive to be characterised above all by foreign languages and Roman Catholicism. Language and religion are particularly difficult cultural barriers for the English – rather than the British – to overcome. Finally, the conceptual boundary which distinguishes the domestic from the international context remains confusing to the British. Many British citizens still regard the European Union as part of British foreign policy. They cannot entertain the idea that it is now domestic policy. As members of the European Union, then, the age of precisely demarcated boundaries for the British is well and truly over. The international dimension of sovereignty suggests penetration rather than inviolability.

Let us look now at the domestic context of sovereignty. Here, once again, we confront the celebrated doctrine of British parliamentary sovereignty, elevated almost to a deity by the writings of A.V. Dicey. According to his view, the great source of strength and power in the British constitution lay in the absolute omnipotence of Parliament. The dominant institutional position of Parliament, combined with a largely unwritten constitution built mainly upon statutes of the realm, common law, customs, and conventions, was the fruit of many centuries of growth. It had an organic quality about it. But Dicey's assertion that Parliament was the supreme law-making body in the land – which was certainly correct – must be distinguished from his more exaggerated claims for the dominant role of Parliament in the British constitution. The latter assertion was always a moonshot away from reality. None the less, the delusion of parliamentary sovereignty has endured. And Dicey's legacy has been both resilient and damaging.

Today it is obvious that authority is fragmented even in unitary systems of government. Camilleri and Falk remind us that in the British Westminster model 'in practice, but also in theory, it is not entirely clear whether ultimate authority resides in the House of Commons, both Houses of Parliament, the Crown, public opinion or the common law'.[12] Even so robust a defender of the British constitution as Lord Hailsham felt compelled to acknowledge that the sovereignty of Parliament had in practice become the sovereignty of the Cabinet largely because of the British party system. In his famous Dimbleby lecture in October 1976 he railed against what he called 'an elective dictatorship'. Concerned that the Labour party might be the beneficiaries of this trend and with an eye on the growing electoral popularity of the Welsh and Scottish nationalist parties, he opined:

> If it were not for the fact that they aim at the destruction of the United Kingdom ... I might have had most sympathy with the nationalists. They alone wish to get rid of the whole incubus of absolute central authority, and manage their own affairs themselves on a more modest scale. So far, if they only wished to achieve their purpose within the ambit of a new federal constitution, I cannot see anything unreasonable about their aim. After all, nations as diverse and as free as the Swiss, the Americans, the Canadians, the Australians and the Germans have all managed to achieve stability, efficiency and prosperity on these very lines.[13]

Hailsham's answer was a fully-fledged federal constitution with devolved English regional assemblies together with assemblies for Scotland, Wales and Northern Ireland. A written constitution would define their powers in relation to Parliament and there would be added a Bill of Rights: 'Thus Scotland, Wales and Northern Ireland would all obtain self-government in certain fields, within the framework of a federal constitution'.[14]

The myth of parliamentary sovereignty has been largely responsible for the blinkered attitudes of British political leaders in their dealings with the European Union and in their deep reluctance to countenance genuine constitutional reform in the United Kingdom. The evidence of a common diagnosis of the constitutional problem of course does not necessarily suggest a broad consensus of opinion on the constitutional remedy. But it does seem to point to at least some new form of constitutional reorganisation by the end of the century. Without wishing to present a blueprint for a new constitution, it does seem likely that any future proposals for reform will have to incorporate the basic federal principle of 'constitutional entrenchment'. Here the different territorial units of the United Kingdom would be granted different types and levels of autonomy according to major differences in their administrative and political circumstances. But these new forms of autonomy would be entrenched by special procedures as new 'constitutional' statutes. This would prevent the 'parliamentary despotism' of future British governments from reneging on the constitutional agreement of previous political forces. To do otherwise would be merely to tinker with the system. It would not create a genuine constitutional state.

It is doubtful that we can expect any serious constitutional reform agenda from the present Conservative government of John Major. The Conservatives have been the main beneficiaries of a massive centralisation of power in the name of democracy in the United Kingdom. London continues to hold sway over the rest of the country. The structure of the English – rather than the British – economy, anchored mainly in the south-east, is detrimental to the whole country. The political economy of the United Kingdom sublocates and stifles economic imagination and development in Bulpitt's periphery. The creative economic forces in Scotland, Wales and the north of England remain shackled to the interests of the south-east – a predicament which the opening of the Channel Tunnel seems certain to reinforce. But significant changes in the British political culture have already taken place in the 1990s. The British state, along with its European Union partners, cannot avoid the incoming tide of legal, political, economic, social and cultural imperatives which herald changes of enormous, if largely unforeseen, constitutional significance for the United Kingdom. Indeed, constitutional reform is already happening. The concept of citizenship, for example, has just begun to make an impact here. However, the real frontiers remain mental barriers. It is what is in men's and women's minds which will continue to form either the greatest stimulus or the largest obstacle to change in the United Kingdom. To paraphrase the dedication in Frederick Scott Oliver's book entitled *Federalism and Home Rule*, which was published in 1910, what we need are 'young men and women who see visions'.[15]

Notes

1. Bulpitt, J. (1983), *Territory and Power in the United Kingdom*, Manchester, Manchester University Press.
2. Ibid., 238.
3. Cornford, J. (1991), 'Towards a Constitutional Equation', in B. Crick (ed.), *National Identities: The Constitution of the United Kingdom*, Oxford, Blackwells, 158.

4. Selbourne to Austen Chamberlain, 4 September 1911, in Boyce, G. (ed.) (1987), *The Crisis of British Unionism: Lord Selbourne's Domestic Political Papers, 1885–1922*, London, The Historians' Press, 69.
5. Birch, A. (1977), *Political Integration and Disintegration in the British Isles*, London, George Allen & Unwin, 167–70.
6. *Royal Commission on the Constitution, 1969–1973* (1973), Vol. 1, Report, London, HMSO, chapter 13, 152–61.
7. Birch, A. (1977), *Political Integration*, 169.
8. *Royal Commission on the Constitution* (1973), 160.
9. Williams, D.G.T., quoted in Osmond, J. (1978), *Creative Conflict: The Politics of Welsh Devolution*, London, Routledge, 166.
10. Camilleri, J. and Falk, J. (1992), *The End of Sovereignty? The Politics of a Shrinking and Fragmenting World*, Aldershot, Edward Elgar.
11. Ibid., 237.
12. Ibid., 32.
13. Hailsham, Lord (21 October 1976), 'Elective Dictatorship', *Listener*.
14. Ibid.
15. The paraphrased quote is taken from Kendle, J. *The Round Table Movement and Imperial Union*, Toronto, University of Toronto Press, 144, fn. 28.

Index